"*Conservative Democrat Michael McCray deconstructs ACORN shenanigans from the LEFT in this groundbreaking memoir. His provocative exposé reveals an intriguing story of hypocrisy and deceit within a Democratic organization which is strong on substance and passion.*"

—The Honorable J.C. Watts, Retired
United States House of Representatives

"*McCray uses an absorbing 'you are there' style so the reader feels like an eyewitness to the glorious climax of ACORN's fairy tale success at organizing communities...*"

—Tom Devine, Legal Director
Government Accountability Project

"*McCray's chilling, compelling and captivating exposé traces ACORN and SEIU roots from the civil rights and labor movements all the way to Occupy Wall Street.*" It's a "*must*" read!

—Maynard Eaton,
National Communications Director
Southern Christian Leadership Conference
Eight-time Emmy Award Winning Journalist

"Beginning with *Wall Street* greed and corruption and an unbelievable case of commercial mortgage fraud on a national historic landmark, McCray unmasks deceit and corruption within the City of Atlanta, Fulton County and ultimately ACORN itself."

—Matthew Fogg, Retired
United States Chief Deputy Marshal

"Marcel Reid is one of the bravest people I know...she is a modern day Rosa Parks."

—**Glenn Beck, Fox News**

"The real ACORN story is the ACORN 8."

—**John Fund, Wall Street Journal**

"McCray covers the rise and fall of a fascinating organization..."

—**Blue Ink Reviews**

"McCray offers a powerful thesis on the importance of education and individual empowerment to mobilizing at-risk communities for direct action, and passionately describes what happens when that process goes awry."

—Dr. Linda Williams Willis, Director
Harris County Extension Service, Texas A&M System
Former Dean of Agriculture Prairie View A&M University

R A C E
POWER &
POLITICS

Jack,
Thank you for
your inspiration &
Chicken Soup for
Writers, God Bless
you.

Gabriel
Guy LeCray

A C 8 R N

R A C E
POWER &
POLITICS

*Memoirs of an ACORN Whistleblower
As Told by Marcel Reid*

Michael McCray, Esq., CPA

American Banner Books

In conjunction with

*The International Association
of Whistleblowers*

AMERICAN BANNER BOOKS, January 2012

Cover photo by Jennie Girtman

John Dunson, Black & White Publishing Group, editor;

Dolores Bundy, DB Corporate Networks, copyeditor;

15 14 13 12 11 10 9 8 7 6 5 4 3 2 1

Manufactured in the United States of America

Library of Congress Cataloging-in-Publication Number: 2011919180

Publisher's Cataloging-In-Publication Data
(Prepared by The Donohue Group, Inc.)
McCray, Michael.
  Race, power & politics : memoirs of an ACORN whistleblower as told by Marcel Reid / by Michael McCray ; [foreword by Tom Devine]. -- 1st ed.
   p. ; cm. -- (ACORN 8)

  Other title: ACORN 8. Race, power & politics

  ISBN: 978-0-9-846906-8-8 (hardcover)
  ISBN: 978-0-9-846906-7-1 (pbk.)

  1. ACORN (Organization)--Corrupt practices. 2. Primaries--United States--History--2008. 3. Obama, Barack. 4. Clinton, Hillary Rodham. 5. Whistle blowing--United States. 6. Community organization--United States. 7. Reid, Marcel. I. Reid, Marcel. II. Devine, Tom, 1951- III. Title. IV. Title: ACORN 8.
HN65 .M37 2012
322.44/0973

This book is dedicated to the loving memories of Stephanie Cannady, Herman and Miriam Reid, and Neal Blakely. Gone to soon and sorely missed, they will live forever in our hearts, our minds and through our advocacy.

Stephanie Cannady a fighter, and fierce advocate for people needing encouragement and support. We will miss her passion, devotion and courage. But through our work and our deeds, cancer will not silence her voice for the people or her fighting spirit.

Herman and Miriam Reid; a man of strength, a woman of grace both were natural leaders. Their humor, quiet poise and determination were an inspiration to us all.

And finally, Neal Blakely a father, husband, teacher and friend. He was a grassroots philosopher and man of action, one who walked with Kings but never lost the common touch.

Contents

Foreword i

Preface v

Acknowledgements ix

Introduction 1

Free the Winecoff 5

Rules for Radicals 13

Freedom Riders 27

New Party 37

Poison Paint 55

Public Nuisance 65

Take Back America 75

Front Runner 83

New Delegate 97

Militant Action 109

SEIU is ACORN 123

Mortgage Fraud 139

Black Labor 155

People's Platform 163

Banana Republic 177

Private Equity 189

Field First 201

Buffalo Soldiers 217

POTUS MAGIC 231

Watch Night. 243

Emancipation Day. 253

Decapitation 267

OBAMA Power. 277

Rathke Embezzlement 287

Iron Ladies 293

Crossroads. 299

Epilogue. 303

Coda. 307

Index. 311

Foreword

Whistleblowing is when citizens use free speech rights to challenge abuses of power that betray the public trust. As a lawyer who has worked with over 5,000 whistleblowers since 1979 at the Government Accountability Project, I could not put down Mike McCray's book about the community whistleblowing organization ACORN and those who blew the whistle about ACORN's own abuses of power. McCray uses an absorbing "you are there" style so the reader feels like an eyewitness to the glorious climax of ACORN's fairy tale success at organizing communities to fearlessly confront and defeat banks, multi-national corporations and others abusing power. But the author also brings readers to the front lines of disillusionment, explaining how in his view management corruption, intolerance and arrogance caused ACORN to implode even before it was infiltrated by right wing, undercover film-makers.

Under the historical narrative, McCray presents a relentless case for the imperative of two basic truths -- 1) the golden rule of living the standards and values we demand from others; and 2) the principle that the end does not justify the means. The story is told primarily through two protagonists -- the author, and a kindred spirit activist, DC ACORN President Marcel Reid. Ms. Reid is now a Board member of the activist Pacifica Foundation of community radio networks. The person who proved that these truths are inescapable was the organization's brilliant, inspirational leader Wade Rathke, perhaps one of the most effective organizers in history. But McCray also portrays him as the central figure of an almost Shakespearean tragedy, whose ruthless secret agendas and purges mirrored the abuses ACORN was created to challenge, and who quickly self-destructed when nearly a million dollars in fraud by his brother was exposed.

The book takes place during the 2005-2008 time frame, and McCray also shares the insider's view of his work for Hillary Clinton in the presidential primary campaigns that eventually led to President Barack Obama's nomination. As an early community organizer, Obama conducted training sessions for ACORN. And ACORN leader McCray credits use of the same organizing tactics for Obama's victory over Clinton, who relied on traditional Democratic party campaign strategies.

The scope of ACORN's activism was dizzying, with 105 corporations, 1,200 associated chapters and some 400,000 members spread within 105 cities and 42 states. Rathke also was a leader in the Service Employees International Union (SEIU), America's most aggressive and effective labor union, and which operated like a sister organization. ACORN's tactics were unabashedly, in your face confrontational, starting with protests that were more like invasions of corporate offices, meetings or conferences. As a rule, ACORN protests focused on individual corporate leaders to create personal accountability of those who normally are insulated from the consequences of their actions or the people affected. The protesters role was to disrupt, not talk. They served as the shock troops softening corporate arrogance for negotiators who followed. The philosophical pioneer for their strategy was legendary troublemaker Saul Alinsky, and ACORN's leaders trained members carefully in his tactics. Rounding out the activist campaigns was traditional advocacy such as lobbying and lawsuits.

McCray traces the effective use of these tactics in campaigns that challenged predatory lending, mortgage fraud, lead paint, voter registration barriers, budget cuts of social services, and even global giants like the Carlyle Group in the "takeover" industry of companies buying each other out. Yes, ACORN was fearless.

But McCray makes a powerful case that it was run like an out-of-control, autocratic family business with a hidden agenda and cut throat tactics, as well as hypocrisy both crude and fundamental. He described how there was a caste system in ACORN, with paid organizers serving and accountable to the national office, compared to members from the communities who were the organization's face but disenfranchised in all but taking risks. Sometimes it appeared they were sent in to near certain physical attacks to be martyred for publicity, without their knowledge. Other times the organization spoke in their names, without their knowledge and consent. While ACORN fought for non-unionized workers to receive fair wages, McCray charges that it did not pay its own staff the minimum wage. While it fought to help unions like SEIU organize, it used classic union-busting techniques when its own staff tried to start a union. Although it regularly blew the whistle on the power structure, it ruthlessly purged individual leaders or even state chapters that questioned the national office's own authority. While it led the nation in effective voter registration drives, it went decades without elections for its own national officers, all hand-picked by Rathke. And while ACORN relentlessly exposed corruption, the book chronicles disillusioning exposures of corruption from local chapter staff to the Rathke family.

Once you start, this book will not let you go. Beyond just a political history, McCray humanizes all the challenges and conflicts by helping you get to know the activists who made a difference for better or worse. You will learn their appearances, including McCray's own, self-described "rugged good looks". You will learn how they cope with stress, such as Marcel Reid's solace from preparing drop biscuits. You are a witness to the internal debates and arguments within the movement. You feel the betrayal when activists on the front line are surprised to learn of sometimes outrageous hidden agendas in the middle of an action. You feel the exhilaration of citizens who realize they not only can force the powers that be to deal with them, but that the community Davids can and do win against corporate Goliaths. And you sadly learn the lesson of those who put themselves above their values, and give themselves blank checks to engage in the same abuses of power their lives are supposed to be about challenging.

In other words, there is a lot to learn from this book. If you are feeling cynical and discouraged that you can't fight the powerful, read it! If you want to learn the tactics of effective guerilla activism, read it! If you want to learn the intricacies of how corporate abuses of power can threaten our families' bodies and health, read this book! If you want to feel the price of hypocrisy, read it! Michael McCray's experience as an everyman is one from which we all can learn.

—Tom Devin, Legal Director
  Government Accountability Project and
  International Award Winning Author of
  The Whistleblower's Survival Guide and
  The Corporate Whistlebower's Survival Guide

Preface

For decades, the Crescent City played host to one of the most feared and revered political organizations in America, the Association of Community Organizations for Reform Now (ACORN). Interestingly, most people hadn't heard of ACORN prior to the historic election of President Barack Obama—–and many more don't understand what community organizers actually do, why they do it, or how they get things done.

In 2008, Barack Obama, a skilled politician and talented community organizer, challenged the Democratic Establishment and won his party's nomination to the highest office in the land. The question Obama faced first—–could he organize the disparate sets of constituencies, which tend to be apathetic to the political process and convince them to come out, on a cold Iowa night to gather for hours to talk and discuss politics. The answer from Senator Obama was an emphatic YES WE CAN.

The fundamental goal of community organizing is to build an army of the masses, and to create a mass power organization. From Iowa, Barack Obama built a mass movement to change America. Senator Obama, as a well-trained community organizer, understood the process and discipline well. Organizing individuals and local leaders for mass action was the bread and butter for community groups like ACORN and Project Vote.

Barack Obama understood these fundamental organizing paradigms, and employed them all in Iowa. With friends in labor, allies in congress, and a man in the White House, the election of Barrack Obama, along with a Democrat controlled House and Senate marked the apex of ACORN political power and influence.

Born in Arkansas and nurtured in New Orleans, ACORN had become synonymous with community organizing, and was the largest grassroots organization of low and moderate-income people in America.

Not everyone approved of ACORN's confrontational tactics, but many know some of the impressive results achieved for poor people over the years. Like living wage laws to fight poverty, partnerships with unions to assist workers, or housing programs to get Americans one-step closer to the American dream––real, tangible victories which improve people's lives.

But equally real, was the tarnish to the once venerable association. A multi-million dollar embezzlement of money which should have been used to support its members and their campaigns for social and economic justice. And the needless stain of accusations of voter fraud, voter registration fraud, unpaid taxes, mistreatment of employees and undercover videos of a pimp and prostitute seeking tax advice in ACORN offices.

The very prospect that a community organizer could become Commander in Chief, is a testament to the power and effectiveness of nearly 40 years of community organizing and activism. Inspired by Saul Alinsky, trained and supported by Dr. George Wiley––Wade Rathke achieved what these self-proclaimed radicals only dreamed of, but could not create without many, many organizers.

As co-founder and Chief Organizer of ACORN, Wade Rathke built the army of organizers that Alinsky dreamed of––since then, ACORN has become synonymous with community organizing, and is the largest grassroots organization of low and moderate-income people in America. While Saul Alinsky had no direct ties to ACORN, the organization's mismanagement of money, embezzlement and nepotism would have drawn his scorn.

Mocked, ridiculed and misunderstood––explore the inside world of community organizing from leaders and insiders in ACORN, the most effective grassroots community organization in the world––whether you believe it is a religious cult, a partisan operation, or a even a criminal enterprise, learn the inside truth from people who are brave enough to speak out.

This is a story that had to be told. Hate it or love it, ACORN is a part of American history. Active in 42 states, 110 cities, and half-dozen countries—ACORN had the power to influence national elections and social policy across the country. With nearly a 40-year history of direct action, voter engagement and community activism; this is the only work told from an inside the board room perspective—about the rise and fall of ACORN–– without the hype and hyperbole.

—Michael McCray, Esq., CPA

Acknowledgements

First, our sincere thanks go to the American people and the fans who supported the ACORN 8. We could not have achieved this plateau without your acceptance. Additional thanks go to the original eight courageous ACORN insiders and whistleblower who challenged the ACORN establishment and stood up against the wrongdoing within the Association of Community Organizations for Reform Now. They have left their mark on history.

Marcel Reid, Washington, DC

Karen Inman, Saint Paul, MN

Fannie Brown, Oakland, CA

Coya Mobley, Dayton OH

Adrianna Jones, Grand Rapids, MI

Yvonne Stafford, Charlotte, NC

Louise Davis, Washington, DC

Robert Smith, Fort Worth, TX

And to all the members of the ACORN 8, LLC and other low and moderate income members who believed in us when the whole world doubted our advocacy. Very special thanks to my friend and editor John Dunson, author and publisher, and Dolores Bundy for excellent editorial services. Finally, Dr. Donald Fields of the Millicom Group for guerilla P.R. services and Jennie Girtman for the outstanding photographs.

RACE
POWER &
POLITICS

"Without the learning process, without education, training and empowering the membership—the building of community organizations (community organizing) simply becomes the substitution of one power group for another."

—SAUL ALINSKY

Introduction

Anyone watching all the incessant media coverage about the Association of Community Organizations for Reform Now (ACORN) should wonder what community organizing actually is or why anyone would join such a dysfunctional organization. Through these pages, the reader is introduced to what attracted me to ACORN, and get an insider's perspective on ACORN to learn the *"Who, What, When and Where"* concerning the rise and fall of the once venerable association.

I am a Conservative Democrat and former federal whistleblower from Arkansas, the birthplace of Arkansas Community Organizations for Reform Now and its native son William Jefferson Clinton. I was an ardent supporter of both Bill and Hillary Clinton and was a veteran of Clinton campaigns. Consequently, I have close ties with and a historical perspective on ACORN and the Clintons.

My chief collaborator, *"As Told By..."* Marcel Reid was the Chair of DC ACORN, and is a personal friend and confidant. Marcel believed that ACORN organizers were exploiting the low-income and minority members it purported to serve. Her story provides the frame or lens from which to view ACORN manipulation and exploitation. My story is a case study or prime example that proves her thesis and how right Marcel actually was about the deceit within the association.

This memoir describes my personal journey through two historic episodes of my life: the rise and fall of ACORN, and the historic 2008 Democratic Primary election campaign between Hillary Clinton and Barack Obama, an ACORN lawyer-trainer. In addition to the inside story of ACORN, it also chronicles the Buffalo Soldiers, the Black politicos who supported Bill and Hillary Clinton since their days in the Arkansas Governor's Mansion. These were exhilarating experiences; I met a lot of people both in ACORN and on the campaign trail. However, this memoir uses fictionalized devices to tell a compelling true story.

The book is unique because it is the only book about the association ever written from the membership perspective, by ACORN National Board Members, using meeting notes, board minutes, training transcripts, campaign reports and hundreds of individual conversations with ACORN insiders and eyewitness interviews as primary source materials in addition to news reports and court documents. It is also unusual because it is a deeply personal story that is written from a whistleblower's perspective—-a real life whistleblower tale written by actual whistleblowers.

The book is written from my point of view as a National Board Member of ACORN and as an African-American political operative working against Barack Obama to elect Hillary Clinton as President. These separate and distinct story strands are connected through the common themes of community organizing, labor organizing and political organizing. The unsettling truths I discovered while I served on the National Association Board will be reveled as I introduce the courageous board members who tried to reform the association before its inevitable collapse.

As background, the book explains the historical roots of ACORN within the context of the welfare rights and civil rights movements. It also describes the contributions that organized labor made to the civil rights movement in the 1960s and the role that the FBI played in neutralizing Black leaders and political organizations during that era.

This memoir recounts incredible things about ACORN the way I perceived and experienced them. Starting with a case of commercial mortgage fraud and public corruption in the City of Atlanta on a national landmark hotel, the story begins by describing the mortgage fraud epidemic in Georgia and my desperate attempts to garner assistance from ACORN for a historic case of commercial mortgage fraud. It continues through my indoctrination into ACORN and my rise to becoming a National Board Delegate. In the process, I discovered the association was not living up to the democratic ideals that it espoused.

Along the way I met many passionate and enthusiastic neighborhood leaders and community activists from across the country; some are friends, many are colleagues. I share them all with you, as you experience the fear, apprehensions and insights of conscientious board members as they unravel the mysteries inside ACORN, and struggle with them to regain control over a membership organization that exploits its members.

Organized labor is examined, as are the Service Employee's International Union, and the SEIU's journey to become the premier labor union in the country using trademark ACORN community organizing techniques. I also reveal how ACORN and the SEIU took on the private equity industry—-and lost, four years before Occupy Wall Street or the rise of the 99 percent.

In closing, this memoir details a riveting two-year period of my life and merges several divergent story lines. Such a story is naturally difficult to organize and convey, so I chose to tell it in chronological order. The story lines may seem to skip around at times, but I wrote it as I lived it, and I tell the whole story from start to finish.

Free The Winecoff

Monday, June 19, 2006

Sweat poured from my brown furrowed brow. I could smell honeysuckle and fresh-cut grass as I hurried past a geyser fountain and water-wall at Woodruff Park, one of downtown Atlanta's largest green spaces. Located in the heart of the city's financial, entertainment and academic districts, the historic park featured a panoramic view of the turn-of-the-century Flat Iron Building, Historic Winecoff Hotel, picturesque Italian-inspired Muse's Building, Georgia-Pacific Tower, and quaint Soho-style storefronts.

Fidgeting, I straightened the pair of *Bill Clinton* signature-inscribed cuff links I wear on special occasions. They were embossed with the Seal of the President of United States, and today was a big day. I anxiously eyed my sterling square-faced watch, still unsure of the exact rendezvous point for our protest. I had come to the park to take part in a Juneteenth demonstration, a coalition of civil rights and community groups gathered to celebrate the 140th anniversary of the Emancipation Proclamation.

I spied Courtney Dillard through the gathering crowd. An athletic, charismatic man of forty-three and dutiful husband, Courtney was on the real estate fast-track. In 1998, when he purchased a historic hotel and founded the Dillard-Winecoff, a small minority development firm, Courtney began living the American dream—a lakefront home, chrome motorcycle and a fire engine red Honda NSX. Together, we led a symbolic march down Peachtree Street, past the national historic landmark which sat catty-corner from the Ritz-Carlton and next to the old Macy's Department store building. The theme of the event was *Financial Freedom by Proclaiming Freedom from Predatory Lending and Mortgage Fraud.*

We were joined by Reverend Frederick Douglass Taylor, sixty-four, a venerable gray-haired activist and the Director of Direct Action for the Southern Christian Leadership Conference, and Joe Beasly, seventy-one, a white-haired orator and the Southern Regional Director for the Rainbow/Push Coalition.

The group assembled in front of Macy's and marched down Peachtree Street through the Gateway to Historic Auburn Avenue which was marked with the West African symbol—Sankofa. It read, "Know your past so you can understand the present and direct the future," meaning, learn from the past, a fitting sentiment for the day's Juneteenth Celebration. Loud call-and-response protest chants rang out, while 300 demonstrators marched down Peachtree Street towards Woodruff Park.

"Stop Mortgage Fraud."
"Free The Winecoff."
"Stop Mortgage Fraud."
"Free The Winecoff."

We passed beneath a 25-foot, bronze sculpture of a woman being lifted from flames by a phoenix in flight, perched above the Five Points entrance at Woodruff Park. The phoenix rising from the ashes symbolized Atlanta's postbellum rebirth after a devastating fire during the Civil War.

Following the symbolic march, the demonstrators gathered around a park pavilion and spacious courtyard containing a water sculpture, flanked by a glass-domed gazebo-styled performance stage. The custom design featured a ceramic fitted glass dome supported by an open strut cornice assembly. Today, it was the podium for the Juneteenth March and Rally.

"Magic Man" Myron Gigger, forty-two, a smooth-talking, mocha-skinned Atlanta radio personality, welcomed the media covering the event and the special dignitaries and guests. He spoke, "We have with

us today, two stalwarts of the civil rights movement, Joe Beasly the Southern Regional Director for the Rainbow/Push Coalition, and Reverend Frederick Douglass Taylor, the Director of Direct Action for the Southern Christian Leadership Conference."

Joe Beasly, a silver-tongued orator, prayed aloud and gave the occasion with this insight: *"Juneteenth Celebration*, as it is better known in the African-American community, is a tradition commemorating the date when news of the Emancipation Proclamation finally reached Blacks in Texas, when the slaves learned they were actually free."

Myron added, "We also have new voices from the movement, Dexter Wimbish, Esq. the General Counsel for the Southern Christian Leadership Conference, and Deacon Dana Williams the chair for Georgia ACORN.

"But the next voice you will hear is Michael McCray, Esq., a lawyer and CPA. He's a Partner and the Corporate Counsel for the Dillard-Winecoff—the victim of the worst case of commercial mortgage fraud in Georgia, but I'll let him tell you about that."

At thirty-eight, I stood 6'3" with rugged good-looks and wood-framed Cartier glasses. I cleared my voice to speak, "Courtney acquired the Hotel Winecoff, then an abandoned convalescence home and developed the first financially feasible plan to restore it into a five-star luxury boutique hotel.

"Courtney was a health and beauty aid professional and once owned the first Black nightclub in Buckhead. And he studied Donald Trump's first book *The Art of the Deal* in order to fashion the Winecoff transaction.

"The Hotel Winecoff is infamous for a tragic fire in 1945 that claimed the lives of 119 people. It was the Atlanta home for Clark Gable during the premier of *Gone with the Wind*. Back then African-Americans were not allowed to stay in the Hotel Winecoff when it operated.

"Donald Trump began his real estate empire by purchasing *the Commodore Hotel* in New York City. But the Winecoff Hotel was a Trump-like commercial development opportunity in downtown Atlanta."

The crowd cheered. "You mean he's a Black Donald Trump!" shouted an energetic onlooker.

"That's right," I responded. "A Black developer was the first person to develop a plan to restore the Hotel Winecoff to her former glory. Plus, he had received funding commitments from MARTA and the Atlanta Development Authority. Unfortunately, mortgage fraud turned his American Dream into a Georgia nightmare.

"Georgia's mortgage fraud epidemic destroyed Courtney's business and nearly cost him his family. InterBank, his lender and development partner, orchestrated a loan-to-own scheme and conspired with Kelco Management and Development, to steal his innovative development plans, his historic building and our taxpayer dollars to fund their fraudulent scheme.

I continued, "Mayor Shirley Franklin and Assistant City Attorney Stacey Abrams convinced the Atlanta City Council to approve city funding for Kelco/FB Winecoff, now the Ellis Hotel, despite the fact the hotel was in litigation and that the actual ownership was being disputed, by a seven to two vote, and thwarted our civil action and requests for a criminal prosecution."

"This scam cost us the opportunity of a lifetime, a $25 million development and $750,000 in personal debt. As a result, Courtney suffered serious financial problems and struggled on the verge of bankruptcy. He lost the faith and confidence of his wife and children. Courtney began drinking heavily and was depressed until he joined New Birth Missionary Baptist Church."

The crowd cheered in unison for his struggle and redemption: "Amen Brother! That's right! Praise the Lord!"

I concluded, "We have waged a legal war with InterBank since 1999. We've fought this legal battle from Atlanta, Georgia, to New York City. Our legal struggle has gone from Fulton County Superior Court all the way to the Georgia Supreme Court, where our company, the Dillard-Winecoff, made new law in Georgia.

"Not only that, the United States Securities and Exchange Commission shut down InterBank Funding Companies in 2002 for committing securities fraud and operating an unlicensed investment company. So what started as one man's struggle, has blossomed into our crusade against predatory lending and mortgage fraud. That's why we're here today!"

The crowd cheered and a thunderous applause filled the open space in the city park. Reverend Frederick Douglass Taylor patted me on my back as I left the podium, "Well done son!" he proclaimed.

I beamed with pride and shook his hand—with both of mine. Reverend Taylor was a living legacy of the civil rights movement; he had marched with Martin Luther King, Jr. in the 1960s.

Dexter Wimbish, thirty-seven, the towering 6'4" General Counsel for the Southern Christian Leadership Conference, took the microphone, "Georgia leads the country in Mortgage Fraud. According to the FBI, 26 states report serious mortgage fraud problems and Georgia ranks first in the nation."

The crowd jeered in disbelief, "Oh my God—we're the worst!" declared a startled demonstrator.

"Unlicensed investment bankers and crooked real estate developers from New York are preying on poor Georgia residents, like Courtney. And they're not just stealing houses anymore—they are stealing businesses and hotels too."

Dexter pounded his fist. "This madness has got to stop! A similar hotel fraud occurred in New York a few months ago, when someone tried to steal the SoHo Grand Hotel in New York City. The only difference in the attempted SoHo Hotel theft and the actual Winecoff Hotel fraud was the way New York deals with title records versus how Georgia handles them."

The startled crowd gasped, "Say that again. . . What do you mean brother?"

"New York, like most states, requires a person to prove the validity of title documents before they actually file them in county records. In the SoHo Hotel case, the county clerk rejected the faulty deed four times before calling the authorities on the culprit.

"But he would have gotten away with this scheme in Atlanta, because Georgia allows non-judicial foreclosure. That means anyone, even criminals, can foreclose on any property without ever having to go to court—and actually prove that they have the legal right to foreclose. Worse, the Atlanta Police Chief Richard Pennington and Paul Howard, Jr., the Fulton County District Attorney, won't do a damn thing about it!"

The crowd jeered in dismay, "Are you serious? That can't be right."

"Essentially, Georgia title records are on the honor system—but there is no honor among thieves. Most states, like New York, make criminals prove they have the right to foreclose. Instead, Georgia makes victims fight to re-claim their property," concluded Dexter.

The crowd cheered as Dexter left the stand. He congratulated Courtney Dillard, and shook hands with Joe Beasly and Myron Gigger.

Deacon Dana Williams, fifty-four, the Chair for Georgia ACORN, a labor activist with a bald head and a crooked smile, took the podium next. A community leader working in rough areas of Atlanta, Dana was hard smart.

He began, "I only have a minute to talk, and this is not what we usually do. But Georgia ACORN got involved with this case because if this type of predatory lending and mortgage fraud can happen to a small business on a commercial project, then it can happen to anyone, our seniors, our children, first-time home buyers and our churches. No one is safe from these types of practices, and the City of Atlanta should not let this stand."

Dana concluded by charging up the crowd with a traditional ACORN call and response chant:

"We're fired up."
"We ain't taking no more!"
"We're fired up."
"We ain't taking no more!"

The crowd had dwindled during the afternoon, and the remaining 180 protestors ended the rally with Courtney Dillard leading a march back up Peachtree Street to symbolically take back the Winecoff Hotel.

Local media covered the event where Courtney Dillard, Dexter Wimbish, Reverend Frederick Douglass Taylor, Deacon Dana Williams and I led protestors past the International Peace Fountain and formed a human-chain around the Historic Winecoff Hotel—to the shock and dismay of the construction site foreman and dozens of confused construction workers at the work site.

Rules for Radicals

Saturday, June 24, 2006

Following the demonstration in Atlanta, I returned home to Arkansas and shared hundreds of photos with Neal Blakely, a seventy-year-old, reflexively loud and boisterous man. His worn hands retrieved an ornate bottle from a purple velvet sleeve and poured two glasses of Crown Royal, his favorite bourbon. I sipped amber liquor as I displayed the pictures from the Juneteenth rally on a glass coffee table.

After touring Europe as an Army M.P., Blake had been a jazz connoisseur, a veteran community activist and my personal mentor. A retired teacher schooled in sociology, Blake epitomized a 1960s era community organizer. He had organized migrant farm workers who chopped sugarcane down in the *muck* of Belle Glade Florida, and urban youths in Atlanta while he studied at Clark-Atlanta University. "These are some impressive pictures." He commented. "How did you all pull this off?"

"We had a lot of help, Blake—and we spent a lot of money."

"Yeah, I'm sure you did."

"We hired a Public Relations firm to handle the local logistics and we reached out to the SCLC."

Curious, Blake's eyebrows raised, "The SCLC? Are they still around? I thought they were going out of business."

"They've had some hard times lately, which is probably why we were able to get their attention. Hell, the NAACP didn't bother to return our phone calls."

Blake sipped his bourbon and nodded, "This is a good turnout, but do any of these protestors know anything about mortgage finance?"

I was surprised by his question, "I don't know. . . why do you ask?"

"Are these people concerned about your issues or are they just props? Did you provide any educational or training sessions on the issues before your protest—or are they just making noise and holding signs?"

"We didn't conduct any formal training on the specific issue, if that's what you're asking, but I'm sure Donald Fields, our P.R. coordinator told them about the purpose of the march."

"Who's he?"

"He's fierce and flamboyant," I laughed. "A grassroots advocate with a Ph.D. in communications, Don runs the Millicom Group—our P.R. company."

"How did you find him?"

"He orchestrated a highly visible but nasty campaign for Black night-club owners against a town ordinance in Sandy Springs, Georgia.

"The city tried to change the times after-hours bars and restaurants could operate which adversely affected the minority business community. All I can say is Don Fields was pure hell on the city of Sandy Springs—it was all over the local news."

Blake asked, "So what would've happened if the news reporters had interviewed a protester instead of your speakers? They wouldn't know what to say."

"Oh no, we told the demonstrators not to speak to the press directly, but to send the reporters to the speakers or media coordinator."

I turned up the volume on the compact disc player. I preferred Miles Davis or John Coltrane, to popular music and Blake was a fellow jazz aficionado. *"If* we can keep the pressure up, we might get a chance to take the hotel back." I said.

"I hear you Michael, but don't count your chickens—yet!"

Blake fanned a deck of playing cards across the coffee table. "You play spades, right? Of course, you play spades." He confirmed.

"Yeah," I nodded.

"How do you play? Straight up or with wild cards?"

I recited the hierarchy of the trump suit, "Big joker, little joker, deuce of diamonds, deuce of spades, ace, king, queen, jack."

"You throw out the two of hearts and the two of clubs—to make the deck count, right?" asked Blake.

"Correct."

"The cards represent medieval society. In early Renaissance Italy, the playing cards showed swords for the nobility. The word spade comes from the Italian word for sword. The Chalices, which became hearts, were for the clergy. Diamonds for the merchants, and Clubs were the symbol of the peasants." Blake laughed, "The poor always have to club their way."

"Okay, I follow you."

"So you play a game, where any spade—*the rich,* can defeat the highest card from any other suit, meaning the rest of society, simply because they are spades. . . they're rich."

"Wait a minute. . . "Say it again?"

"Since you play with wild cards, which means even the lowest merchant—*deuce of diamonds,* or the lowest elite—*deuce of spades,* can defeat any other suit."

"Damn! I see what you mean."

"Worse. . . the way you play, the lowest peasant—*deuce of club,* and the lowest clergy—*deuce of hearts,* aren't even included in the game."

Blake stared in my eyes. "So you tell me Michael, which card are you... and which cards are they?"

"Humph," I rubbed my chin.

"You had a good demonstration, but how long can you afford to generate this much publicity?"

"We're off to a good start. We lit the match, and I hope the SCLC will help us fan the flames."

Blake was skeptical. "Interesting approach, but don't put your faith in traditional civil rights organizations."

"Why not?"

"The SCLC couldn't pay their light bill last month. What do *you* think it would take to buy them off?"

"I thought the SCLC was the best civil rights organization to call. They've done everything we've asked—so far, and we didn't have to deal with any huge egos like Jesse Jackson or Al Sharpton."

"All of those organizations are about the same, useless—including the NAACP. You can buy them off, or scare them off. . . with a quarter and a phone call."

I mumbled under my breath, "Yeah, the civil rights groups aren't what they used to be."

"The only civil rights organization I know which will stand up for poor people and won't back down from bankers, politicians or corporations—is ACORN."

"ACORN?" my voiced raised.

"The Association of Community Organizations for Reform Now. They started here in Arkansas, twenty-five or thirty years ago. They are the only civil rights group I know which will stand up and actually fight for low income people."

"Really?"

"*If* they take on an issue, or start a fight—they won't let go!" Blake reared back, both hands behind his head. "Which is what you want, ACORN goes into the housing authorities and projects to organize people the bourgeoisie Negroes in the NAACP or the SCLC won't bother to speak to. They will even march down to the utility companies and demand they turn on their members lights or heat back on in the winter."

I said, "Other groups help too."

"The other groups talk a lot, write letters and such. Anything to make themselves feel important, but when the shit hits the fan—they run like the wind."

"Wow, that's high praise."

"You need someone who is going to stand up and fight! Because the rich New York developers you're fucking with have enough money to buy the whole city."

"You've got that right."

Blake warned. "They won't be constrained by the rules—this ain't about right and wrong. This is about winning and losing."

"So what should we do?"

"Your tactics depend on you, and the strength of your coalition. Power is not only what you have but what your opponent thinks you have."

I nodded slowly, trying to grasp what Blake had said.

A twinkle crossed his eyes. "Tactics mean doing what you can with your resources. What you're concerned with is the tactic of taking, how the poor can take power away from the rich. Saul Alinsky kept it simple; he said our tactics are written all over your face—your eyes, ears, and nose."

"You just lost me, and who the hell is Saul Alinsky?"

"First, the eyes. If you've already organized a vast mass-based people's organization—show off. Parade around before the enemy and openly display your power.

"Second, the ears. If your organization is small in numbers, then do what Gideon did. Conceal the members but raise such a ruckus and clamor so people believe your organization numbers many more members than it does.

"Finally, the nose. If your organization is too tiny to be heard—then stink up the place."

I stopped him, "I get the first two, like we just did with the Juneteenth rally—and our email blasts, but what does he mean by stink up the place?"

Blake smiled like a Cheshire cat. "Cheat! Fight low-down and dirty— even rotten, if necessary. Once, when we were fighting a grocery store or neighborhood bodega for not hiring enough Black workers, Alinsky sent folks in with pockets full of mice to release in the produce section—to run the stores customers off."

In disbelief, I responded, "You're not serious, are you?"

"Yes. In a street fight—anything goes."

"You can't do that. You would never get away with it. They would just call the police and arrest everybody."

"They did!" quipped Blake. "Alinsky got arrested all the time, especially when he was organizing behind the Chicago stockyards. The meatpackers declared him a subversive menace."

"I'll bet they did."

Blake laughed. "Martin Luther King, Jr. went to jail for raising awareness by staging non-violent protests. Alinsky went to jail for raising hell!"

"But it was his arrests, notoriety and the hysterical reaction of the establishment which strengthened his street credentials in the Black community—we were always suspicious of whites."

I reflected on the implications of what Blake said, "So the ends justify the means?"

"Think about it. The enemies' means, used against us, are always immoral—and our means are always ethical and good. Nietzsche said we have no right to make the bird of prey accountable for being a bird of prey.

"The sheep says the hawk is a low down rascal because they swoop down and kill baby kids. The hawk simply says, I was hungry—I eat sheep. You can't call beasts of prey *evil*, merely for their utilizing their own strength."

"Who the hell was Nietzsche?" I asked.

"Friedrich Nietzsche was a 19th-century, German philosopher who wrote critical texts on religion, morality, contemporary culture, philosophy and science.

Nietzsche challenged some of the key presuppositions of the old philosophic concepts like self-consciousness, knowledge, truth, and free will—explaining them as inventions of the moral consciousness."

"Wait a minute; hold on Blake. Nietzsche didn't believe in Good or Evil?" I asked.

"No. Nietzsche went *Beyond Good and Evil*. He argued the desire for power is the explanation for all behavior, and he denied any universal morality for all human beings.

"Where you stand depends on where you sit. The thief says, I'm a hustler—I live by robbing the rich. The rich say, I'm a banker—I live by robbing the poor."

Blake stood up and walked over to a bookshelf. His trembling hands reached for the tattered, dog-eared copy of *Rules for Radicals* (Vintage Books, 1971) he kept tucked away on a shelf.

"Read this," he said, and tossed the book to me. "It's the bible on community organizing."

My eyebrow arched, perplexed. "Community Organizing? How does that work?"

"At its core, community organizing is all about challenging the establishment. It's about building a power base and learning how to fight the system. Simply put, you need to build an army."

"How do you do that? How do you build a grassroots army from scratch?" I asked.

"In the beginning the organizer's first job is to create the issues or problems. Policy follows power."

"We definitely have an issue. Georgia leads the nation in mortgage fraud and predatory lending."

He wiped brown liquor from his lips. "Mortgage Fraud is a good issue. We need to focus more on Economic Justice, rather than Social Justice."

"What's the difference between the two?"

"Social Justice refers to social rights, like the right to vote, right to peacefully assemble, fair housing, and the right to be free from police brutality. Also, Social Justice is actually in the gospels, so it's easy for church leaders to support social justice issues."

"Which is what the SCLC and traditional civil rights groups focus on?"

Blake nodded. "Economic Justice, on the other hand, refers to economic issues like access to capital, collective bargaining, red-lining and fair lending. It refers to people's ability to make a living. It's not about getting rich, but it is about having a fair opportunity to participate in American capitalism."

He paused for emphasis, "Capitalism is the engine of Democracy."

"What do you mean? The right to vote is the basis of our Democracy."

Blake laughed aloud. "Shit. . . Saddam Hussein and other Middle East Dictators get elected with over 98% of the vote. Yes, it's an election—but that's not Democracy."

"Why not?" I asked.

"These societies operate from caste systems. . . You are, whatever you were born—as in, if you were born rich, you were rich. If you were born poor, you stay poor—there's no social mobility.

"What capitalism does is give you a chance to change your position in society. That's what makes you free—not an education or the right to cast a vote in a meaningless election."

"Humph. I never thought about it that way. So what should we do next?" I asked.

Blake sipped his bourbon. "The moment the organizer enters a community he lives, dreams, eats, breathes, and sleeps only one thing, which is to build the mass power base—or the army. Until he develops a base of power, he shouldn't confront any major issues because he doesn't have anything to confront them with."

"Okay, that makes sense."

"Through action, persuasion, and communication, the organizer makes it clear that organization will give them the power, the ability, the strength, and the force to be able to do something about these particular problems.

"Until he develops the means and power instruments, *his tactics* are different from power tactics. So every move revolves around one central point—how many recruits will this bring into the organization? Whether by local organizations, churches, service groups, labor unions, corner gangs, or as individuals."

"That's where we are now," I said. "We're building our army in Georgia."

Blake nodded.

"So how do you recruit the army?" I asked.

"Ultimately, it's a trade off." Blake said, and took the book from my hand to read aloud. "A good organizer understands each person or block has their own hierarchy of values. Let's say we are in a minority community where everyone supports civil rights.

"One man bought a small house when the neighborhood was first changing, and he wound up paying a highly inflated price—more than four times the value of the property. Everything he owns is tied into his house.

"Through eminent domain, the city is threatening to come in and take it on the basis of a low-value appraisal, which would be less than a fourth of his financial commitment. He is desperately trying to save his own small economic world."

"Okay, I get the picture."

Blake continued to read, "Organizing around civil rights would get him to a meeting once a month. Maybe he'd sign some petitions and maybe give a dollar here and there, but for a fight against eminent domain or urban renewal's threat to wipe out his property—he would give money and come to meetings every night.

"Next door to him is a woman who is renting. She is not concerned about urban renewal. She's raising three small girls, and her major worry is the pushers and pimps who infest the neighborhood and threaten the future of her children.

"She is also for civil rights, but she is more concerned about community policing and public safety, and she wants better schools for her children. Those are her number one priorities."

"Oh, I see."

"Next door to her is a family on welfare—their top priority is more money. Across the street there's a family who can be described as the working poor, struggling to get along on their drastically limited budget. To them, consumer prices and local merchant's price gouging are their highest priorities—and so on."

"So you seek out different people with different problems?" I asked.

"In a multiple-issue organization, each person is saying to the other, I can't get what I want alone and neither can you. Let's make a deal. I'll support you for what you want, and you support me for what I want. Those deals become the program. House by house, block by block—that's how you build a grassroots army.

"However, the acceptance of an organizer depends on his success in convincing key people and many others; first, he is on their side and second, he has ideas and knows how to fight to change things.

"He must establish that he's a winner. It's not enough to persuade them of your competence, talents, and intellect—they must have faith in your ability and courage. They must also have faith in your courage to fight the oppressive establishment—courage they, too, will begin to get once they have the protection of a power organization."

I paused as his words filtered through my mind, and I skimmed through the contents of the book, "Who was this Alinsky guy anyway?"

Blake laughed. "The Chicago Tribune called him a public enemy of law and order, Alinsky was a *radical's radical*. He was so bold, he dedicated his book to the devil himself, which sums up his philosophy."

"No way! You can't be serious."

Blake read the dedication aloud, "Lest we forget at least an over-the-shoulder acknowledgment to the very first radical: from all our legends, mythology, and history—the first radical known to man who rebelled against the establishment and did it so effectively that he at least won his own kingdom—Lucifer."

"Wow, that's provocative. So it's better to be a lion for a day, than to live your whole life as sheep."

"It's all about freedom and controlling your own destiny." Blake smiled, "Alinsky founded an ideology and concepts of mass organization for power. His work in organizing the poor to fight for their rights as citizens is internationally recognized."

"So, he was an author, a scholar or what?" I asked.

"Alinsky was a straight-up gangster my friend. He was friends with Al Capone and Frank Nitti."

"He was what?" I inquired.

"I'm not saying he was actually in Capone's gang—but he was someone Capone and Nitti were comfortable having around. So, he wasn't no boy scout."

"That's amazing."

"Alinsky was a real live gangster, and he wrote *–the–* book on community organizing. He was almost like a Jewish Malcolm X."

"Malcolm X—really?"

"Oh yeah, I loved Malcolm. He didn't play around. Whenever *-He-* came to town there was going to be some action. Malcolm wasn't just about talking slick or giving speeches. Malcolm X was about action, immediate and direct action for the people—all the time."

"How so, what do you mean?"

"If you were able to get Malcolm X to agree to visit your neighborhood, he would come with busses full of demonstrators with him. He would meet with the people, give his speech but before they left town they would go somewhere and mobilize a demonstration that same night."

"Is that right?"

"Malcolm X believed in immediate direct action, which had a huge impact on people in the 1960s—especially for young Black men standing up and leading their communities. Which is why the Federal Government targeted him and other Black Nationals using counter intelligence measures."

"What do you mean?"

"Prior to his death, Malcolm X had expanded his concept of Islam beyond Black Nationalism; he stressed Pan-Africanism. Malcolm X believed Black people needed a cultural revolution; they must return to Africa culturally and spiritually, if not physically.

"Alinsky was a radical's radical. He was all about power and winning— damn the rules. The end is what you want. The means is how you get it. To him, the most unethical of all means—was the refusal to use any means."

"So, Alinsky was a radical because he believed in social change like Malcolm X said—by Any Means Necessary."

Blake nodded, "Exactly, Alinsky was a pragmatist. A good organizer is a man of action. He viewed the issue of means and ends in pragmatic and strategic terms. Alinsky believed in power. Organizing was his philosophy."

"Wow, that's heavy!"

"Rules for Radicals is all about being an effective community organizer. It's about winning, and that has nothing to do with fighting fair. It's about successfully waging war with the limited resources you have."

"So how can we fight them?"

"You can't, right now—you need more power."

"How do we build more power?"

"Read the book. Power either comes from money or masses of people. They've got all the money—you need to build a base of power with the people."

"That's a lot of work, and we're doing okay in court; at least they haven't kicked us out of court." I said.

Blake replied, "Don't be fooled by silly clichés like *the law is the law* or *knowledge is power*—bullshit. Power comes from two sources, money and people. Good lawyers know the law, but great lawyers know the judges— and the judges know them."

"Humph." I pondered his words.

Blake sat up straight. "Don't forget; the courts don't care about your individual rights. You need to organize a broad coalition and build a public awareness campaign to win. A mass movement expresses itself through mass tactics. When fighting against the sophistication and finesse of the establishment, the poor always have to force their way.

"Forget about the law. If you're depending on the facts or the law— you'll always end up getting screwed by the system. Lacking money, poor people have to build power from their own flesh and blood."

Deflated, my eyes dropped as I considered the ramifications of what Blake said.

"The only issue is how will any action increase the strength of the organization. If by losing in a certain action an organizer can attract more members than by winning, then victory lies in losing, and a good organizer will lose—every time."

I contemplated his words.

In a word, Blake was irreverent. His sympathies went out to the weak, the suffering, and the poor. He detested dogma, defied morality, rebelled against authority. Blake was challenging, insulting, agitating and discrediting—he naturally stirred unrest.

Blake could teach sociology or power structures with a deck of playing cards or loose pocket change. He had traveled around the country organizing minority communities on behalf of the Winthrop Rockefeller Foundation.

Blake twisted the ornate cap back on to the Crown Royal bottle and returned it to its purple velvet sleeve. After listening to Blake's admonition, I resolved to catch up with Deacon Dana Williams and get more actively involved with the Georgia ACORN chapter, once I returned to Atlanta.

Freedom Riders

Sunday, April 3, 2005

"Hell no! I'm not going... and you shouldn't go either," thought the forty-nine year-old Marcel Reid as she stood before a group of DC ACORN members. Raised to be a proper Black woman by a strong southern bell, Marcel was taught to never curse—at least not in public. Her heart pounded, because Marcel was terrified at public speaking due to a childhood struggle with a stammering-lisp and dyslexia; she couldn't read or speak growing up. Marcel focused intensely on her words, and the room faded away except for the sound of her alto voice.

A spry woman with a man's name, Marcel had arrived in Washington, DC to join other ACORN chapters from Philadelphia, Baltimore, and southern Maryland. They were preparing for the next day's action and had assembled at the DC ACORN office for an intensive orientation before the next day's bus ride. The training included role-playing exercises, and song and chanting practice, but Marcel wasn't satisfied with the plan of action. The group prepared to embark on a protest to challenge the usurious and predatory fees imposed on poor and working-class people through high-interest Tax Refund Anticipation Loans. Marcel liked to call it a Poverty Tax.

Marcel stood a defiant 6'0" with sweat glazed palms as she placed them on a tabletop lectern worn from years of discussion and debate.

She cleared her throat. "This foolish action is ill-advised and against my wishes. So I'm not going to Virginia Beach."

She looked out into a sea of blank, staring faces.

"Why not, Marcel? What's wrong with the plan?" asked Louise Conway, a seventy-four, tall, feisty woman with roots in the Urban League. Louise had been a proud homeowner in Southeast DC at a time when most blacks either wouldn't or couldn't purchase there.

"Don't be scared, Marcel," chided James Washington, a baby-faced, forty-three year-old DC ACORN member. Standing 6'1", James was tall, dark, and fond of the ladies. "We are ACORN; this is what we do!"

James doesn't know me that well, Marcel thought to herself. *I was raised in Compton California and I went door-to-door through the roughest neighborhoods in America.* "Scared... don't live here!" she replied.

"So what's the problem, Marcel?" asked Louise.

"This is not a good plan. Successful campaigns require strategy and tactics. This action has not been thought out."

Louise rolled her eyes. "What do you mean?"

"For starters, Virginia is a Commonwealth. It's not a regular state."

James rolled his eyes. "So what?"

"We have no idea what we're getting into," Marcel said. "Come on, people. We're about to attempt a militant demonstration in the cradle of the Confederacy and no one thought to call a lawyer first?"

James leaned back in a rickety, plastic chair less certain, as fresh thoughts crossed his mind.

Marcel said, "This isn't New York, Philadelphia or Baltimore—places we are familiar with. This is southern Virginia. The laws are different, the people are different, and the attitudes are completely different."

She paused and stared at the puzzled faces. "I don't think we've thought this through."

"Well, Janice organized it," said Rachel Pope, seventy-three, a short, plump, pretty woman with silver curls. Extremely witty, Rachel was quick to laugh, loyal, and kind.

"Another problem," Marcel said. "I don't trust Janice."

"Why not?" asked Rachel. "She's the Head Organizer; that's her job. She put it all together."

"None of this makes any sense. Janice is the Head Organizer for ACORN, a militant community organization—*while* she's still in the military? Does this make sense to any of you?"

"No, it doesn't," answered Louise.

Marcel said, "She was in the Navy and we're planning a militant action next to one of the most important Naval installations on the East Coast."

"Good point, Marcel," said Louise.

"So what should we do?" asked James.

"I don't know what to do, but we shouldn't go on the action tomorrow." Marcel said.

Speechless, the group still looked unsure.

"Look, the stuff we do is serious business. The protests, the demonstrations and calling out the press—this stuff has consequences. Serious consequences."

"So are you saying we should stop protesting?"

"No, I'm not saying that at all, James. But I do believe we have to be sure we're right before we rush in and disrupt people's lives and businesses.

"We have to learn the law, study our target and only engage in actions our members actually endorse. We can't be running around the country starting protests and demonstrations, just because some staffer tells us to. People can get hurt, people can get sued, or even go to jail!"

Pocahontas Outlaw, seventy-two, and the chair for DC ACORN, stood up to address the group. Regal, and impeccably dressed with silvery hair, Pocahontas was a natural-born leader. She remained excited about the upcoming action despite Marcel's critical remarks. She was flanked by Will Ward, thirty-three, the stocky DC Head Organizer. Will stood 5'8", Irish looking with red hair and freckles. He wore ornate rings on each finger. Will debriefed the group about the ongoing national campaign. From coast to coast, ACORN organized thousands of demonstrators who clamored in front of the local offices of Liberty Tax Services in sixty cities across America.

Pocahontas began, "We've organized coordinated protests at a national tax preparer's offices in the U.S. and Canada, during the first two weeks of February, and we've demanded the company reform its marketing and sales practices for Tax Refund Anticipation Loans."

Will said, "The protestors warned potential customers about the unfair practices of Liberty Tax and told them about free nearby tax preparation at VITA sites and ACORN-run centers in forty-five cities."

Deeply concerned over the safety and welfare of the low-income and minority membership, Marcel feared ACORN organizers were not serving their best interest.

Consumed by growing angst, her throat tightened and voice cracked. "I've got a bad feeling about this. Our leaders and organizers have to think these actions through. If they haven't planned it out, we shouldn't go— period. We're the membership. The organizers are supposed to support us. It shouldn't be the other way around. Bottom line, I'm not going tomorrow, and I don't think you should go either."

The Association of Community Organizations for Reform Now achieved its goals by building community organizations with enough power to win changes through direct action, negotiation, legislation, and voter engagement. Liberty Tax threatened ACORN with legal action, but DC ACORN members vowed to continue their campaign until the company improved its practices.

Liberty Tax Service had become the fastest growing international income tax franchise ever, with 3,000 offices in the U.S. and Canada. Liberty Tax Services ran nearly all of its business operations through individual franchises, but the company was actually owned by John Hewitt its founder and Chief Executive Officer.

Miffed after being rejected by Pocahontas Outlaw and the DC ACORN membership, Marcel Reid stormed out of the storefront office and shook the plate-glass window. The muscular scent of motor-oil and sewer-grease emanated from the adjoining gutter and alleyway.

James Washington rushed after her, careful not to overexert himself. He had an ailing heart and was already collecting social security disability payments.

"Don't feel bad because we didn't agree to go along with you, Marcel," stated James. He tried to console Marcel, and walked her to the car.

Marcel twisted the keys in the door of her silver Cadillac and deactivated the alarm.

"I agree with you Marcel," said James. "But the organizers are so persuasive, and the members, we seem to listen to them. We're ACORN. Direct action is what we do best!"

Marcel climbed into her car. "Direct action is why I joined ACORN. But right is right, and smart is smart."

James closed the car door behind her. "Goodnight Marcel," he said and jogged toward the Capitol Hill Metro Station. He could hear the underground trains approaching.

James was bright, affable, and a long-time rebel to his core. He had held mid-management positions in small businesses and city government, but never for more than a year or two. Marcel watched James walk away and marveled at how naive he could be at times. ACORN preyed on that.

Monday, April 4, 2005

John Hewitt sat at his desk reviewing quarterly projections and pro forma financial statements. He smiled, anticipating a record-breaking year. Most Americans dreaded tax season, but for people like him, tax season meant Christmas in July—or rather April. Hewitt stood to make millions from needy and desperate working-class people through Tax Refund Anticipation Loans or RALs. These products generated 400% to 800% interest or more.

Elsewhere, ACORN demonstrators split into groups before the 9:00 a.m. scheduled departure time. DC and Maryland left from the DC ACORN office. Philadelphia and Baltimore left from the Baltimore ACORN office, while North Carolina ACORN chapters departed from the south.

James joined the group and sat near the rugged but sophisticated Pocahontas. They joined Janice Mowery, forty-eight, the Head Organizer for Virginia Beach. Athletic, she stood 5'6" with close-cropped, sandy brown hair. Janice had finished a 22-year stint in Naval Intelligence.

The departures were uneventful, and the road trip was lively and fun. Less than four hours later these financial Freedom Riders encountered intense violence near the Naval Aviation Station in Virginia Beach. The women wore dresses and tennis shoes; they never wore heels. Most men wore coats and ties, and they all wore ACORN's trademark blood-red color—complete with buttons and badges.

Restless members played spades and bid-whist to pass time on the trip, while Janice described the local actions which led up to this demonstration. "Virginia Beach ACORN members protested at the Liberty Tax Corporate Headquarters and requested a meeting with company owner John Hewitt. But he refused to meet with us. Instead, Mark Baumgartner, the Chief Financial Officer met with us to discuss our concerns."

"That's right!" the riders cheered, "We don't want the henchmen—we want the boss."

Janice said, "Portland ACORN members negotiated with their local franchise owner and convinced him to take down all of the signs advertising RALs and high-cost next-day refunds at his store. He even took down his Lady Liberty mascot's RAL advertisement sign, and faxed ACORN's list of demands to Liberty Tax's corporate headquarters."

Yvonne Stafford, sixty-two, a tall, thin woman with curly brown hair, and the chair of North Carolina ACORN was loud and boisterous, but her bark was often worse than her bite. She said, "North Carolina ACORN members convinced our local Liberty Tax store manager to fax a letter of ACORN's demands to John Hewitt.

"We warned the customers and employees about Liberty Tax's misleading practices—and one Charlotte employee decided to quit on the spot."

Janice said, "And California ACORN members rallied at a South Los Angeles Liberty Tax office, chanting and singing until the branch manager put John Hewitt on the phone with a local leader to discuss ACORN's demands directly."

To liven up the ride, James grabbed a bullhorn and practiced protest chants:

"Sound off."
"One, two."
"Once more."
"Three, four."
"We are."
"ACORN!"
"We are."
"ACORN!"

Not wanting to be outdone, Pocahontas fired up the demonstrators, "From May until November 1961 more than 400 Black and White Americans risked their lives by traveling together on buses and trains.

"They were called Freedom Riders. They deliberately challenged the Jim Crow laws and endured savage beatings and imprisonment. The Freedom Riders traveled from Washington, DC to New Orleans to promote social justice and equal rights; they changed America.

"Today, we're traveling from Washington DC to Virginia, the cradle of the Confederacy, to promote economic justice for working-class families. We are on a modern day Financial Freedom Ride."

"Fired up."
"Fired up."
"Ready to go."
"Ready to go."
"Fired up."
"Fired up."
"Ready to go."
"Ready to go."

The interracial group of demonstrators engulfed the Liberty Tax building. To their surprise, they were set upon by a mob of angry workers and security guards. Hewitt bolted to the window of his corner office concerned about the growing clamor downstairs. They started to chant, harsh words were spoken, pushes became shoves until a protester got sucker punched. Pandemonium broke out. The demonstrators were beaten by the security guards, tax workers and police. The protesters were kicked and stomped into submission—even the elderly women.

James ran over and dropped to his knees along side of a fallen female ACORN member. Her hair mussed and her face bloody, she had been badly beaten by the mob. Impending doom washed over James, and his heart raced at an irregular pace. He became nervous and anxious with his skin cold and sweaty.

An intense pain spread through his shoulders, neck and arms—like a burning sensation or a heavy weight. James fell to the ground sweating, nauseous with shortness of breath. He clutched his chest, dazed and lightheaded from the pressure, fullness, and pain in the center of his chest. The discomfort spread from his chest, to his neck, and inside his shoulders and arms.

James had a heart attack, while other protesters were beaten and left lying in the street. For what seemed like an eternity, the mob attacked the ACORN protestors unabated before the Virginia Beach mounted police stepped in.

Local television and news reporters covered the attacks and stated: "These demonstrations against the Virginia Beach based firm are part of a larger national campaign by several hundred ACORN chapters during the heart of the 2005 tax season. ACORN is the nation's largest community organization of low and moderate income families, with over 150,000 member families organized into 700 neighborhood chapters in 65 cities across the country."

A number of the demonstrators were hospitalized during the melee along with Liberty Tax employees. Following the physical clash, Hewitt reported the incident to Virginia Beach Police Officers. "All of sudden, four bus loads of homeless people pulled up in front of our headquarters," exclaimed Hewitt.

"They came pouring into the building like a Mongolian horde—clawing, screaming and fighting. Two employee were rushed to the emergency room after being bitten and scratched."

All of the protestors were arrested for trespassing, unlawful assembly and other alleged offenses. The Virginia Beach Police ultimately issued over 124 summonses to the demonstrators. The Liberty Tax criminal complaint was eventually dropped except for one protestor who was wanted in another jurisdiction.

Hewitt also filed a SLAPP suit against ACORN. The Strategic Lawsuit Against Public Participation was a civil action designed to silence people who spoke out on issues of public concern—a rich irony for an association built on public demonstrations.

New Party

"So what happened?" Marcel Reid asked, as she watched dozens of beleaguered members return to the DC ACORN headquarters, many of whom renounced their memberships following the Virginia Beach spectacle. Dumbfounded, she struggled to comprehend the violent debacle. *These things happen. You used to see them on the news all the time, in the sixties and seventies, but this is a new millennium—it's not supposed to happen now!*

Devoutly religious, she was raised a practicing Jehovah Witness and attended Catholic School. Marcel had hoped and prayed for the protest to be safe and successful.

"I don't understand what happened, Marcel," replied Pocahontas. "We had a long but tolerable drive. We pulled up, got out and all hell broke loose.

"Right on schedule, our charter buses arrived at the Liberty Tax Headquarters. We were met by Virginia Beach Mounted Police and a mob of angry employees."

They knew we were coming, Marcel thought to herself.

Will Ward added, "It was covered extensively on local television and ended with hundreds of arrests. Some people didn't even get a chance to get off the buses. The police swarmed in and we were beaten and surrounded."

James said, "By the time the first group reached the front door we were attacked by security guards and angry employees. I fell to the ground, grabbed my chest and woke up in the emergency room."

Relieved, Marcel smiled, "I'm glad to see you're alright, James."

James averted his gaze from her. He had been released following a week of treatment on the cardiac ward at Howard University Hospital. Naturally amiable, he became surprisingly agitated towards Marcel following the Virginia Beach conflict.

"I don't care what you all say." Willie Flowers, a seventy-nine-year-old, tall man with athletic build, commented. A good man from the neighborhood, Willie understood battle. "We got our ACORN asses kicked!"

"I've never seen an action like this before; hell none of us have," said James.

A petite eighty-three year-old with boundless energy, Edra Derricks wore a close cropped silver natural. An old school teacher, Edra decried, "Why did we have to go there anyway?" as the motley group looked at each other until one-by-one, each head turned toward the head of the table.

Pocahontas looked uneasy, as she glanced toward Will, who hesitantly stepped forward and answered. "We started this campaign for economic justice and financial security last year against H&R Block, the largest tax preparer in the country."

Tawanna Baker, forty-six, the youngest person on the board, asked, "What's so bad about tax preparers?" A chain smoker and neighborhood girl, Twanna possessed a quick wit and a basic intellect, but was street smart.

"It's not the Tax Preparation Services," said Pocahontas. "It's the Refund Anticipation Loans. RALs are extremely predatory loans with effective interest rates which exceed 400% or more."

Marcel replied, "Low income people can't afford those fees! But minorities have to accept them because they need their money. That's what I mean by a Poverty Tax!"

Modestine Snead, fifty-six, 5'4" pint sized and high strung, genuinely cared about the community having worked with youth in parks and recreation. She nodded in agreement. Modestine possessed a Master's

Degree from the University of the District of Columbia and took in visiting boarders for ACORN from time to time. "I bet most people don't understand how much RALs actually cost."

"That's right," said Will. "So we concentrated on predatory practices and the disclosures about the costs of RALs, and other issues. Our negotiations resulted in a series of meetings last year at H&R Block's training center in Kansas City."

Marcel asked, "Pocahontas, did you know about this?"

Pocahontas's gaze dropped toward the floor as she shook her head.

Will said, "This was followed by a series of conference calls in March. And we had a final session at H&R Block's world headquarters last spring."

"Did you know about that?" Marcel asked again.

"No I didn't, Marcel."

Easing the tension James inquired, "So how did we do?"

Pleased, Will beamed. "The meeting resulted in a final agreement which we used to move on the rest of the tax preparation industry."

"Okay, so what does it mean for us?"

"It means, H&R Block dropped its fees from the RALs," said Will. "This one reduction alone saved $200 million for tax filers during the next year."

"Two hundred million? That's amazing."

Will explained, "Chris Connors, H&R Block's CEO and chairman, didn't believe in RALs for lower-income taxpayers, but he insisted his company could not afford to stop offering them as long as its top competitors continued to push them."

"That's a shame," said James. "H&R Block didn't want to be the only one to do the right thing."

"That's right!" Will said, "But this additional insight convinced us we were right on target, which gave us our next target, Jackson Hewitt, the second largest tax preparer and then Liberty Tax Services, the third largest.

"H&R Block set the pattern for subsequent industry agreements.

Jackson Hewitt began negotiating by late 2004, and after a few actions we had hoped to sign an agreement by the end of the 2005 tax season.

"Once Jackson Hewitt and H&R Block negotiated agreements with us we shifted our attention to Liberty Tax, which is why we went to Virginia Beach. We started the campaign with demand letters, and continued with protests against their corporate offices across the country."

"Including Virginia Beach," Pocahontas, chimed in. "But everything turned out terribly wrong."

"So why didn't we know all of this before we got on the buses? Did the national board know? And if they did, why didn't you, Pocahontas?"

"I don't have all the details," she replied. "We constantly fight for economic justice and we have Financial Justice Centers to help, but I didn't receive any details about these actions or our negotiations."

Will said, "Those negotiations were on a strictly need to know basis Marcel."

"You can kiss my need-to-know ass." Marcel fumed under her breath and marched out of the second floor conference room. She was done with this meeting.

Tuesday, April 12, 2005

One by one, the remaining DC ACORN members filed into the store front office for their regular monthly meeting. The southeast DC ACORN offices near Capitol Hill depicted the contradictions, which lay within the venerable association. Capitol Hill was the home of the federal government, complete with all the trappings of political power and wealth, which simultaneously existed in Southeast Washington, D.C., the section of the city infamous for low income, high-crime and poverty—with a majority African-American population.

This spatial intersection of political power with race and poverty was the very essence of ACORN. Unapologetically confrontational, the militant group always used pressure and demands to advance its agenda.

By the next DC ACORN meeting, the magnitude of the Virginia Beach defeat weighed heavily on Pocahontas's mind. Pocahontas stood before the group and cleared her voice. "This isn't the best time to do this, but I'm stepping down as Chair for DC ACORN—effective immediately."

"What? Why now Pocahontas?" asked Modestine, "It's not because of Virginia Beach, is it?

Pocahontas's eyes dropped, "I'm not going to lie, Virginia Beach helped me make my mind up, but I've been thinking about this for a long time.

"Maybe if I didn't have so much going on in my personal life and responsibilities on my real job, I could have recognized how flawed our action plan was."

"Don't blame yourself," begged Tawanna. "Marcel was the only one who thought about that, and we wouldn't listen to her."

"I appreciate the support, and what you all are saying, but it's time for me to go."

Edra exclaimed, "But you can't leave now, Pocahontas! We still need a leader."

Willie stiffened and leaned forward. "What about you Marcel? You tried to stop us from making that terrible mistake. And you were the only one who figured out the problem with our plan."

"That's right," said Edra.

"Plus, you were strong enough to stand up to the organizers and try to stop the action," declared Tawanna.

Willie moved, "That's why you should be our new leader, our new chair."

"I second that motion." said Tawanna.

"Hold on guys; wait a minute. I'm not seeking leadership. I was just trying to help."

"We believe you, Marcel," said Modestine. "That's why you should be our new leader."

Marcel hesitated wondering what her mother might think of this. Her mother Miriam, always prim and proper, white gloved, hair perfectly coiffed, was the most influential person in Marcel's life.

A natural born leader, Miriam led everything she ever joined. Consequently, Marcel was raised to be strong, independent and proud— a proper Black women. *She remembered she had been with ACORN four short years when her mother passed away leaving a terrible void in her life. Miriam was her best friend, and so the women of ACORN became her confidants and surrogate mothers.*

"Okay, ok. I'll consider it under one condition."

"What's that?" asked Modestine.

"I'll do it, if Pocahontas stays on with me as Vice Chair."

All heads turned and looked toward Pocahontas. She fidgeted in her seat. "It's just too much for me right now."

Marcel stood her ground.

Meekly, Pocahontas asked, "How about Secretary?"

"Okay, it's settled then," prompted Tawanna. "We have a motion, and we have a second."

"Call for the question," said Willie.

"All those in favor of Marcel Reid serving as Chair of DC ACORN say aye."

Every hand rose in unison; it was unanimous.

Marcel Reid became the elected Chair of DC ACORN by the unanimous acclamation of the membership, the first time ever, to the chagrin of Will Ward, who nervously twirled the rings on his fingers. That wasn't supposed to happen; he squirmed after the vote. Will thought this election was a mistake because it violated ACORN organizer's unwritten rule: control the membership and promote NO strong or independent community leaders.

Will came from a family of union organizers and trained under Wade Rathke, fifty-six, and his common-law wife Beth Butler, fifty-five, in New Orleans. As the Head Organizer for DC ACORN, Will reported directly to Wade Rathke, the Chief Organizer for ACORN.

Until that day, the Head Organizer had appointed all the DC ACORN board members and chairs. Marcel Reid was the first elected Chair of DC ACORN—ever, and her election was undisputed. Marcel pulled Pocahontas aside after the meeting had adjourned. "Thank you for believing in me. You are a great leader and I'm going to call on you often."

Pocahontas flashed a twisted smiled. "I'll help and support you all I can, but be smart, be wise and be careful, Marcel."

Puzzled, Marcel asked, "What do you mean?"

"Look, I work for the federal government and I've noticed some things which make me uneasy."

"Things like what?" Marcel asked.

"You'll see," replied Pocahontas. "I can't afford to get mixed up in any foolishness at ACORN, especially considering my position at HUD."

Suddenly, Marcel felt concerned. A blank stare washed over her face, and a wheezy sensation filled the pit of her stomach.

"Don't worry, Marcel, I'm not sure if anything is wrong, but I just think certain things aren't right." Pocahontas turned and walked away before Marcel could press her for more information. Within a week Marcel received a letter from Pocahontas, which declined the position of Secretary for DC ACORN.

Cadillac wheels sped down the picturesque George Washington Parkway along the banks of the Potomac River toward Old Town Alexandria. Steeped in history, Mount Vernon was a thriving business community coupled with tidy neighborhoods and parks. This was a place where Marcel Reid devised strategies she employed in the hardball political arena, called the District of Columbia.

Marcel arrived home, turned on her television and watched in shock and disbelief. The persistent coverage of the violent action drew national attention to Liberty Tax Services' usurious rates and predatory practices. Sipping herbal tea, Marcel reflected on her experiences in ACORN.

I sure have come a long way since growing up with a lisp and stammer in Compton. Chris Leonard, forty-five, the previous Head Organizer for DC ACORN, recruited me to join the group in 1999, the same year Rhode Island sued paint makers for selling lead paint long after they knew its hazards and attempted to cover up the threat of lead poisoning.

As a fresh new recruit, I sold a life membership to Tony Augusta, the General Manager of WPFW radio station, for a $300 cash payment, and an ACORN membership to a local police officer in Ohio from the back of his squad car. Regular member dues totaled $120 per year, but local organizers often pressured the low-income members to have $10 to $20 a month drafted directly from their checking accounts.

Katy Fitzgerald, fifty-eight, a petite woman with a short natural, was the Chair of DC ACORN back then. A former post office employee, Katy was dedicated and smart but easily manipulated by Chris Leonard, the DC Head Organizer. Tall and thin, with chestnut hair, Chris wore blue jeans and glasses. Despite his Bachelors Degree in English, Chris spoke in a slow deliberate drawl, almost patronizing at times.

Chris appointed me to the local board due to my salesmanship and chutzpah. No one had ever sold a lifetime membership before. He also listed Katy as the President of the New Party, and me as the Secretary/Treasurer—unbeknownst to either of us.

The New Party, a regional political party formed to help low income and working people educate themselves politically and have an active voice in legislation and political policies which affected their daily lives, was the forerunner to Washington DC's Working Families Party.

Although the Virginia Beach protest was a dismal failure, the violent reactions it provoked bolstered the credibility of the Association of Community Organizations for Reform Now as fierce advocates and placed ACORN at the vanguard for social and economic justice.

Despite the recent debacle, Craig Robbins, forty-eight, the Deputy Field Director and Northeast Regional Director, remained undeterred. Tall and slender, Craig was smart and understated—much like Chris Leonard except Craig was much more calculating.

Craig continued to put pressure on Liberty Tax Services for a settlement and coordinated street canvasses in Virginia Beach. These sustained actions convinced the company there would be no peace without an eventual settlement. As a result, John Hewitt signed a long-term agreement to pay $50,000 a year to a related affiliate. The same year, ACORN created a Community Labor Organizing Center to build and foster partnerships between community activists and organized labor. More importantly, the violent spectacle proved ACORN actually fought for the rights of poor and working-class families.

Marcel Reid attended the national board meeting in Charlotte, North Carolina following the clash in Virginia Beach. ACORN General Counsel Steve Bachmann, fifty-four, standing 5'9" with graying sandy-brown hair was also present. The Harvard educated attorney gave up Wall Street or big law firm practice to work for the anti-poverty group, and developed the byzantine legal structure of ACORN—to vest ultimate control with the Chief Organizer, Wade Rathke. Dale, his fifty-five year-old younger brother, managed CCI which controlled the finances for the group.

An organic genius with piercing grey eyes, albino blond hair, and alabaster skin, Wade and Dale looked like twin caricatures of 1960s era diabolical scientists. A loyal friend and long-time consigularie of the Rathkes, Bachmann announced, "After Virginia Beach, ACORN will no longer pay any costs associated with any future arrests."

Flanked by Zach Polett, ACORN Political Director and Mike Shea, the Executive Director for ACORN Housing, Wade Rathke addressed the national board members in Charlotte, North Carolina. Wade began, "Over the last ten years, ACORN's Financial Justice Center has been able to focus on developing campaigns against the predatory practices of financial institutions, tax preparers, credit card companies, payday lenders, mortgage companies, and loan servicers, which are mostly no longer banks.

"During these hard-fought efforts, the Financial Justice Center has found not only that change is possible, but also that it is possible to create a different and better world. We want to model good behavior and make the most of the surprising paradox that has emerged from many ACORN campaigns around financial justice and wealth creation."

Mike Shea cleared his throat and added, "The absurd gap between rich and poor in the United States was featured in a story on CBS about the status and wealth envy in Manhattan between the mere million-aires and the mega-millionaires. Meanwhile, there are 300 million other Americans, and at least 32 percent of them are low and moderate income.

"These families are being dropped from health insurance coverage at accelerating rates, and they are unable to finance higher education for their children. For lower-income families, the question of whether or not they hold any wealth at all often begins and ends at the front door. Among low-income homeowners with household incomes pegged at less than $20,000 per year, 72 percent of their wealth derives from home equity. For lower-income families with incomes between $20,000 and $50,000 per year, home equity accounts for 55 percent of total wealth. For those who rent, the median wealth of a low-income family is one-twelfth of that of a low-income homeowner."

"That's astonishing, so what did we do about it?" asked Yvonne Stafford, the Chair for North Carolina ACORN.

Wade stood and said, "In the last thirty years, the great story of build-ing community wealth has been the fight to win equitable rights to home ownership for minorities. And it all starts with the fight that led first to the passage of the Community Reinvestment Act (CRA) in 1977, and then to the long campaign for the act's implementation."

Marcel Reid raised her hand. "Pardon me for asking, but exactly what is the CRA?"

Zach poured water into a cup and replied, "The CRA was passed to deal with a very real problem: entire neighborhoods, usually minority areas of lower-income and working families, were essentially 'red-lined,' meaning that banks refused to lend in these areas and therefore spurred full-scale disinvestment in many inner-city neighborhoods.

He sipped his water. "None of these effects happened by accident, particularly racial discrimination. The Federal Housing Administration made it clear that segregation was required to maintain housing values, as a matter of policy, arguing and I quote, *'If a neighborhood is to retain stability, it is necessary that properties shall continue to be occupied by the same social and racial classes. A change in social or racial occupancy generally contributes to instability and a decline in values.'*"

Wade's gaze traced the ceiling. "I remember the *'Save the City'* organizing drives initiated by ACORN in Little Rock in 1972. A difficult campaign centered on the Oak Forest neighborhood at what was then the east—west borderline between working neighborhoods and more middle-class and upper-income areas to the west across University Avenue.

"Oak Forest was majority white at that time, and the organizing committee suddenly found that the only subject people wanted to talk about, a concern echoed loudly at house after house, was the onslaught of scurrilous real estate agents who were trying to *'blockbust'* the neighborhood by creating a wave of panic selling."

"Oh my goodness, did we stop them?" asked Yvonne.

Wade sighed. "Their method was deadly and efficient. Working families had almost all their resources tied up in these tidy little bungalows in Oak Forest. They were being told that black families had just bought into the area on this block or that block, and that if they did not list their houses for sale immediately they were going to be stuck riding the value of their houses down to dirt as the neighborhood became increasingly black. We fought back furiously."

"How so?" asked Yvonne.

He smiled with satisfaction. "ACORN signs that said *'This House Is NOT For Sale'* went up everywhere in Oak Forest. We enlisted Carroll O'Connor (*Archie Bunker from television*), Ryan O'Neal, and Jack Nicholson to do radio public service announcements letting people know that "blockbusting" was against the law thanks to the Fair Housing Act of 1968 that banned discrimination in housing based on race, color, religion, or national origin."

"What happened next?"

Wade continued, "You can still visit the Oak Forest neighborhood more than a generation later and be impressed with its stability and the fact that there still remains some measure of diversity. Unfortunately, such real estate wars are ones of attrition that many local communities cannot win.

"The fight to get Congress to pass the Community Reinvestment Act ran much along the lines of the Oak Forest effort. As citizen and community organizations focused on rebuilding the urban core and creating stronger neighborhoods in the inner city, the programs that had fueled redevelopment and investment in the 1960s were largely gone or exhausted."

Zach explained, "The Nixon administration's shift of aid dollars to Community Development Block Grants meant that less money was available from federal sources, and communities in the future would depend on their ability to leverage private dollars into recovery and development. The refusal of banks to participate based on the perceived credit risks of lending to lower-income and racially diverse families meant that without that leverage our neighborhoods were caught in a cycle of decline.

"Community groups of various persuasions, such as ACORN, the National Tenant Information Center (NTIC) and its feisty leader, Gail Cincotta of Chicago, NTIC organizer Shel Trapp, and policy experts from the Center for Community Change and other think-tanks and advocacy groups tried to navigate our way around Washington like immigrants in a foreign land, with few resources and little D.C. savvy or capacity."

Wade cut him off. "The critical tactical breakthrough came with the passage of the Home Mortgage Disclosure Act of 1975, which spelled the beginning of the end for bank redlining practices, because now we would be able to prove that banks were disproportionately receiving deposits from lower-income and minority communities while investing poor people's money in safer investments in richer areas while refusing to make even minimal loans in the redlined areas."

Marcel asked, "What happened once they passed the new laws, CRA and HMDA? Did they work?"

He replied, "As hard as CRA was to enact, the corresponding challenge was to implement the full spirit of the CRA and make it work for urban communities, and this meant the kind of hand-to-hand combat from city to city that an organization like ACORN specialized in undertaking.

"The two most significant cases that showed both the gains possible from CRA and the act's limits were brought by ACORN and led to Federal Reserve Bank hearings, the first involving Boatman's Bank in St. Louis and the second involving Hibernia National Bank in New Orleans."

Yvonne asked, "So what happened?"

Wade explained, "Thirty years after passage of the CRA there still have been very few Federal Reserve Bank hearings into lending practices, but the Boatman's Bank hearings were the first, coming fairly quickly after passage of CRA. The bank's name alone seems to evoke memories of a lost, almost quaint, era of community banking in America.

"But there was nothing quaint about the failure of Boatman's to lend in low-income neighborhoods throughout St. Louis, and this was at a time when the city's neighborhoods were not just migrating from the river to the suburban counties but were galloping away to depopulate the city. ACORN protested the merger within the comment period, and in a precedent-setting move the Federal Reserve Bank of St. Louis agreed to hold a hearing."

Yvonne said, "So we forced them into a congressional hearing?"

Wade glanced down and smiled. "Not exactly, but the prospect of a Federal Reserve hearing convinced Boatman's to negotiate with ACORN representatives. The agreement that followed was groundbreaking for both ACORN and its future, especially in creating citizen wealth, as well as proving to community groups throughout the country that CRA, for all of its blemishes, offered organizers the leverage they needed for successful campaigns.

"The delays that could come with CRA hearings meant that the higher cost of delayed transactions, particularly in the 1970s when interest rates were rising dramatically, could alter the entire economics of a deal. Additionally, in the consumer deposit—driven era of community banking in the 1970s, issues of reputation were also critical, and there was no way to avoid the fact that a Federal Reserve hearing gave real legitimacy to ACORN charges that there was de facto discrimination at work in a bank's lending, or rather non-lending policies."

"That's great. So we can force the banks to listen to us by using the CRA." Yvonne asked, "What happened next?"

Shea replied, "The negotiations led to the creation of a $50 million loan commitment to St. Louis neighborhoods and the establishment of a review committee to oversee the investments. Both ACORN and Boatman's wisely embraced the agreement. A Boatman's spokesperson at the time said, 'We're being held up as the heroes, and that's super. That's the kind of publicity we love. And we're not making any loans we feel are bad.'"

Wade added, "The fight with Hibernia was more difficult and actually went through a full-blown hearing at the offices of the Federal Reserve Bank in New Orleans. ACORN had less leverage in this case because we were challenging Hibernia's purchase of a smaller bank in Louisiana, a bank that was very conservative and 'southern' to its core in the insulated way that has been common to New Orleans businesses.

"Nevertheless, ACORN proved its charges against the bank in its complaint. The Office of the Controller of the Currency (OCC) had rated Hibernia as 'satisfactory' on its CRA performance, but when the Federal Reserve Board investigated it found the bank's performance 'woefully inadequate' without even 'proper records' to support an evaluation."

"So we shut them down." replied Marcel.

Shea leaned forward in his seat. "The Federal Reserve Board did end up approving the Hibernia acquisition, but it did so on the condition that Hibernia develop and submit a plan to improve its performance under CRA, which ACORN felt at the time was a victory.

"Agreements like the ones forged by ACORN with Boatman's Bank have been duplicated over and over around the country with the emergence of interstate banking and the array of mergers resulting in larger and larger money center banks or superbanks. This wave of bank consolidation has been a mixed blessing.

Wade clarified, "The existence of fewer small community banks means that it is harder to create tailored agreements more closely fitting specific needs in distinct communities. On the other hand, ACORN's agreements with larger institutions have over time become deep, multifaceted partnerships funded in the millions, committing and delivering literally billions of dollars' worth of home mortgage money to impacted low- and moderate-income neighborhoods."

"We began pitched battles in the mid-1970s against the banks that were exploiting our neighborhoods. We have not only seen the passage of programs that make a difference, like the Community Reinvestment Act in 1977, but we have also seen some of our opponents in these campaigns gradually changing course and becoming partners.

Wade motioned toward Mike Shea. "For instance, ACORN's partnerships with Citibank, Bank of America, J.P. Morgan Chase, and others have created the resources allowing ACORN's sister organization, the ACORN Housing Corporation, to devise a loan counseling program for lower-income families focusing on more than thirty ACORN cities."

Marcel Reid's eyes widened, "Oh, so through the CRA, you want ACORN to become the *Good Housekeeping Seal of Approval* for all commercial banks."

Wade and Zach were dumbfounded. They looked at each other quizzically and stared back at Marcel in stunned disbelief. That was exactly what they meant, but they hadn't expected Marcel or any other ACORN board member for that matter to grasp the strategy or summarize their plans so quickly.

Over the last two decades, hundreds of thousands of our members and neighborhood residents in inner cities have moved into first-time home ownership. The impact of CRA has had the desired effect of significantly increasing the home ownership percentages of minority households and therefore of creating huge amounts of bottom-line citizen wealth. By mid-1997, twenty years after its passage, CRA agreements had produced total commitments for over $215 billion of increased loans and investments in underserved areas.

Marcel had a knack for slogans and language. She was adroit at breaking complex topics down into sound bites and catch phrases that were easily understood by everyday people. Message and communications were the building blocks for community organizers.

Wade had noticed Marcel prior to this association board meeting since she participated in actions dressed in banker's suits and tennis shoes. Marcel didn't wear the low-income garb most ACORN members wore.

Wade asked, "You're the one who donated five computers to DC ACORN. So how did you get involved in all of this?"

Marcel blushed. She had convinced her employer to donate surplus computers to the Washington, DC ACORN office.

"Craig Robbins has told me all about *you,* Marcel." Wade continued, "Where do you live? Do you think we can get your neighbors to join ACORN?"

Not wanting to disclose too much about her personal life, she replied, "I don't know about that, Wade. I live right over the bridge in Northern Virginia."

Wade explained, "Well we need to broaden our base of support. We could use more members like you Marcel, people who get lifetime memberships and donated equipment—-maybe your friends and neighbors."

She and Wade always discussed marketing, branding and how to attract new members; they never talked about poor people or poverty. Marcel was a quick study and a fast learner, but she may have been too astute to suit Wade or his brother Dale.

Dressed in dungarees and cowboy boots, Wade Rathke, rugged and strong, jealously guarded his privacy and maintained a low public profile. However, Dale was much more effeminate and flamboyant. A regular in the society pages of the New Orleans *Times-Picayune,* Dale Rathke visited New York and shelled out $2,000 to stay at the Waldorf-Astoria, including $700 for fancy meals at La Cote Basque, and various credit purchases to shop at Gucci and Neiman Marcus.

Poison Paint

Marcel's foot tapped incessantly while she waited for the meeting to start. She was anxious because this was her first national action since becoming a member of the ACORN national board of directors as the chair of DC ACORN.

Marcel Reid felt a familiar surge of adrenaline as she joined a group of ACORN members gathered at the Service Employees International Union Hall in Cleveland, Ohio. They planned to confront the CEOs of all the major paint companies about the lead poisoning of thousands of inner city children. She paced in the back of the union hall.

The union hall was packed with hundreds of ACORN members from dozens of cities across the country. Stale doughnuts and burnt coffee were the breakfast order of the day—Spartan accommodations, because ACORN ran a lean and mean operation.

The low-income members and minorities genuinely desired to improve the conditions of their families and neighborhoods. They paid monthly dues for the privilege of forming the all-volunteer army for demonstrations and protests.

A small feisty woman with short, brown hair took the podium before the group. The National Campaign Director for ACORN, Amy Schur, thirty-nine, was pretty and petite. She possessed a natural affinity for organizing Blacks and Latinos. "Lead-based paint had been banned in the United States since 1978, long after the scientific community established it was dangerous for children," she asserts.

"Lead paint flakes and dust can cause brain damage in children who ate or inhaled it. The harmful effects included learning disabilities, speech problems, and behavioral disorders. Worse, highly elevated levels of lead poisoning can even cause death."

"Who pays for these costs now?" asked Marcel.

"Great question," Schur said. "American taxpayers pay the entire bill for addressing the problem of lead poisoning, and these costs are enormous."

"Costs like what?"

Schur replied, "Cities, states and the federal government pay hundreds of millions for testing children and testing homes, health care and special education costs, plus the costs for subsidizing lead hazard remediation."

Sunday, October 26, 2005

Marcel Reid sniffled and coughed from the cold air and carbon monoxide exhaust, which spewed from beneath the yellow school busses packed with protestors. They charged towards the Renaissance Hotel—Cleveland's landmark social and business address. Built in 1918, the hotel's architecture reflected the city's unique style and rich history. The historic landmark featured vaulted ceilings, high arched windows and a beautiful marble fountain. The hotel offered an abundance of elegant event space and a magnificent Grand Ballroom. The massive hotel was connected to Tower City Center's exclusive boutiques, restaurants and cinema.

The demonstrators quickly assembled outside Public Square near Progressive Field, Quicken Loans Arena and the Rock & Roll Hall of Fame. They converged upon the luxury hotel from every direction.

Marcel's heart pounded as she felt a lump form in her throat. She eagerly joined the loud call and responding chants as they pierced the tranquil atmosphere.

"Everywhere we go."

"Everywhere we go."

"People want to know."
"People want to know"
"Who we are."
"Who we are."
"So we tell them."
"So we tell them."
"We are ACORN."
"We are ACORN."
"Mighty, mighty ACORN."
"Mighty, mighty ACORN."

It was 1:00 PM, when the protesters and demonstrators startled and frightened many of the visitors and guests of the luxury hotel as they rushed through the upscale lobby and fine dining establishments.

Over 250 ACORN members swarmed the building, pushing and shoving their way into the expansive conference area and adjoining meeting rooms. Fear and anger gripped the pinstriped executive's faces, including Chris Connors, forty-eight, the CEO of Sherwin-Williams along with fifty other CEOs at the National Paint and Coatings Association board meeting. It was a look which often followed any confrontation between low income Blacks or Hispanics and upper class Whites.

The protest chants grew louder and intensified.

"Poison pigment."
"Poison paint."
"Sherwin-Williams."
"Get the lead out."

The demonstrators rushed into the closed boardroom where the startled Connors asked, "What's going on here? Who the hell are you people?"

"We are ACORN!" The group shouted.

Outside, a gaggle of news reporters descended upon the hotel lobby following the action. A local reporter gravitated towards Marcel because she was tall and animated.

John Jones the fifty-three year-old Chair of Washington ACORN stood 5'10" with tan skin and a bald head. He had an affinity for colorful suits and garish outfits—almost like costumes. John and his Vice-Chair Heather, a 6'1" towering blond, joined Marcel with the reporters.

Heather stood beside them while Marcel spoke to the reporters. She waved a report from the Department of Housing and Urban Development in the air and declared, "Even though lead-laced pigment was taken off the market three decades ago, one in every four homes in the U.S. still contains lead paint or dust. Homeowners have spent millions of dollars to remove lead from their properties because untold numbers of children have been poisoned by the substance. Everyone is paying the price—except the poison paint companies."

Heather joined in. "Like the asbestos and tobacco industries before them, the paint industry has managed to escape responsibility for decades. Sherwin-Williams has not owned up to its responsibility to help the hundreds of thousands of children hurt by its poison paint.

In fact, our report shows the company is a repeat offender which is abusing the environment and using lobbying and lawsuits to undermine health and safety standards."

"So what do you want them to do?" a reporter asked.

Marcel said, "ACORN demands Sherwin-Williams establish lead clean-up funds for cities with high rates of lead hazards. We insist that Sherwin-Williams provide lead-detection kits to households in high-risk neighborhoods.

"And some of Sherwin-Williams' manufacturing facilities have dangerously polluted the surrounding communities. We want Sherwin-Williams to meet with local community representatives of ACORN and help make our neighborhoods lead-safe."

Marcel thought to herself. *Professor Karenga would be so proud to see his skinny teenage prodigy command television news reporters and make demands on corporate executives.*

Heather spotted James Andrew Doyle, forty-eight, the President of the National Paint and Coatings Association, as he scurried away from the news reporters and demonstrators. The pair followed Doyle past the jeering crowd of hyped-up protestors. Heather was right behind Marcel. They walked toward him, the pace quickened as Doyle walked faster and faster. The duo matched him stride for stride into the lobby bar.

Cornered and flustered, Doyle relented and reluctantly agreed to meet with ACORN at their request. Marcel added, "But I need it in writing." Doyle acquiesced to the proposition and slipped Marcel a handwritten note using his business card as stationary. He agreed to meet with ACORN no later than November 30, 2005.

Liz Wolff, the forty-five year-old National Staff Researcher and Craig Robbins, the Northeast Regional Director, watched Marcel's impromptu lobby meeting. Wolff was thin, with thick, black hair and horn-rimed glasses; she looked almost quakerish at times. But she was extremely shrewd, smart, and deceptively unassuming.

Craig Robinson and Liz Wolff leapt into action. They pulled Heather aside and immediately chastised Marcel. Craig was weary, if not fearful, of independent ACORN members. Wolff asked, "What the hell do you think you're doing, Marcel?"

Perplexed, "I was delivering our demands to Sherwin-Williams—like I was supposed to do." Marcel said.

"You never, ever, engage the target alone!" Wolff exclaimed. "There are no big chiefs and little Indians around here Marcel!"

"I'm sorry, I didn't know the rules for this."

Wolff said, "ACORN is a mass membership organization, this is a mass membership demonstration, and at ACORN the members negotiate together in mass; that is what we do!"

Monday, October 27, 2005

Marcel Reid packed her bags and road the hotel van to the airport along with a half-dozen other members with early morning flights. Her first national action was an exhilarating experience. A warm feeling of satisfaction flooded her body, especially since she was able to corner the paint and coatings executives and schedule the follow up meeting herself.

She boarded an early morning plane, still miffed from her "discussion" with Liz Wolff and Craig Robbins. Tired but relieved, she flew back to Washington the day after the Cleveland action and returned to the DC ACORN offices.

A young black woman nervously drove to the ACORN store front office in Southeast Washington, DC. The woman exited her truck and reported for her first day at work. Ashawnita "Anita" MonCrief, twenty-six, an almond skinned corpulent woman, had applied for a staff position with ACORN. But upon arriving for her first day of work, Anita was actually hired to work for Project Vote, a non-profit organization, which shared office space with ACORN in both Louisiana and Washington, DC.

Anita assisted S.W.O.R.D., the Strategic Writing and Research Department for ACORN, where she worked on a broad range of research projects including grant administration, drafting grant proposals and creating power point presentations.

Overworked, underpaid and under constant pressure to recruit new members, Wade Rathke maintained iron-clad control over all the ACORN organizers and staff. Short on cash, Anita MonCrief borrowed money from Project Vote and other DC Office staff in order to make ends meet.

A political science and history major from the University of Alabama, Anita arrogantly snubbed ACORN's uneducated and low-income membership. But, Belinda Ferrell, the new Head Organizer for DC ACORN, a forty-seven year-old, single mother of three girls, lent Anita money to help her pay for childcare and rent.

Monday, December 5, 2005

Marcel Reid woke up early excited about what this day had in store. She put on a white silk blouse, ruby lipstick and a gray flannel pant suit. Marcel didn't want to wear African shells or a dashiki like other Black activists; it's a dated look from organizers in the 1960s.

Marcel believed organizing and negotiating should be conducted in a modern and professional way. Looking strictly business, she placed an ACORN button in her purse—to complete her ensemble.

Today was the day ACORN assembled a team of local leaders and staff to negotiate with the National Paint and Coatings Association, following the Cleveland action. The NPCA headquarters was not a high-rise commercial building, instead it was a gothic, three-story stone structure which could have easily been located on embassy row. The historic building suited the powerful association. The NPCA was established over a century ago, and the opulence of the headquarters reflected its rich heritage.

Marcel arrived at 9:45 am, professionally dressed in her two-piece pant suit, silk blouse and a bold ACORN button. As Chair of DC ACORN, she was joined by Reverend Gloria Swieringa, sixty-seven, the almond-skinned blind minister was the Chair of Maryland ACORN. National staff members were also there, Helene O'Brien, forty-one, the National Field Director, a good-looking woman with brunette hair, and Mitch Klein, thirty-four, the Head Organizer for Maryland ACORN.

Helene was calculating and intelligent with a disarming smile. She could assess any negotiating situation in a fraction of a second. A pudgy man with curly raven hair, Mitch often resembled a Hasidic Jew. He was young, aggressive and a Black Belt in Martial Arts.

Mitch put Baltimore ACORN on the map in 2002 when he organized protests outside the home of Baltimore Mayor, Martin O'Malley and dumped garbage in front of city hall to protest the lack of services in low-income neighborhoods. He dropped his head and smiled when he saw Marcel, "You sure look nice today Marcel, you should be our facilitator." The rest of the group agreed. They walked around the circular driveway, and entered through the double doors under a solid stone carousel canopy.

"Good morning, Gloria. Are you ready for action?" Marcel asked. Reverend Gloria was a persuasive and sympathetic figure.

Parading little old ladies in front of the public was a quintessential

ACORN tactic. The public face of ACORN was always stern, iron-faced, little old ladies from low-income neighborhoods and communities; a blind, black, woman, minister was a potent weapon.

The ACORN team met with James Andrew Doyle, President of National Paint and Coatings Association and Thomas Graves, fifty-three, their General Counsel. Marcel opened the meeting. "Sherwin-Williams is the largest paint manufacturer in the country, but they are poisoning little children and babies in Black and Brown communities all across America.

"According to the Centers for Disease Control, the number of children with elevated lead blood levels has steadily decreased from 1997 to 2004. But Black children still have higher rates of lead poisoning than White and Latino children."

Reverend Gloria added, "Your paint is poisoning our children! So what are you going to do about that?"

Marcel injected, "And high levels of lead can damage kidneys and the nervous system. Lead exposure can also lead to learning disorders, mental retardation and sometimes death. Lead poisoning primarily affects children because their systems more readily absorb the heavy metal, and they are more likely to be exposed to lead particles on the floor or ground."

Doyle paused for a moment, "This is a bad situation, but it's not the paint manufacturer's fault. It's the condition of the paint that's the problem, not the paint itself."

"Oh, no!" Marcel wasn't falling for that line. "Sherwin-Williams knew about these hazards as early as 1904. They knew lead paints were poisonous for the workmen and for the inhabitants of the houses painted with lead colors."

Reverend Gloria said, "And it's well documented that the paint flakes which come from the friction of opening and closing windows and doors is potent enough to seriously poison a child."

"This is total nonsense, lead-based paint has been banned ever since 1978," quipped Doyle.

"That's not good enough," Marcel argued. "European countries banned lead paint back in the 1920s. But U.S. manufacturers continued to sell lead paint in the United States well into the 1950s."

Reverend Gloria added, "The U.S. banned the sale of lead-based paint in 1978, but the problem is far from over. Each year, some 400,000 children under the age of five have lead poisoning."

Marcel said, "And 38 million homes still have lead-based paint on their walls. The problem is still hazardous in roughly 25 million of these homes."

Graves replied, "In 2003, the NPCA negotiated an agreement with the Attorneys General from 50 states and jurisdictions to fund an education and outreach program called Lead Safe Training. This program provides education and training on potential exposure to lead dust during the remodeling or renovation of buildings containing old lead-based paint."

"That's not good enough," Reverend Gloria leaned forward. "We want better information at the point of sale. And we want them to reach into those deep pockets, or we're going to encourage our chapters to continue to pressure these companies, and if necessary—litigate."

"Whoa ladies, litigation is not the answer," snapped Doyle. "These companies are not responsible for risks today from a product made so long ago."

Graves crossed his arms. "The companies, which once manufactured lead paint or lead-based pigments, have continued to win court rulings after court rulings—from Milwaukee, Santa Clara County, California and Chicago. The courts have found no evidence of any conspiracy to defraud, and the judges are rebuking plaintiff's by citing the statute of limitations in dismissing the suits."

Marcel said, "I'm not a lawyer, but I can tell you this. First of all, their products are poisoning more children every day, and will continue to do so until lead hazards are abated. Second, there is renewed hope that the paint industry will be held accountable for their role in the lead paint problem. For the first time, we are seeing courts uphold these cases and charge these companies for knowingly creating a public nuisance, and juries are holding them liable."

Exasperated, Doyle rubbed his brow, "But we're doing our part. The National Paint and Coatings Association and the paint industry started a non-profit to help. It's called CLEAR Corps and Sherwin-Williams contributes several hundred thousand dollars to this program each year."

Undeterred, Marcel insisted. "That's not real reform. That is only a token attempt to give the appearance of real action. The companies are funding small projects that don't even scratch the surface of the real problem."

"So, what do you guys really want?" asked Doyle. "What do we have to give you to make you guys go away?"

Mitch looked nervous, his eyes darted and his foot shook. On cue, without hesitation the ACORN staffers, O'Brien and Mitch, held up a huge 4-by-8 foot poster of a check for $38,000,000,000—made out to ACORN.

"You want what?" Doyle rocked back and forth in his chair stunned and confused by the boldness of the demand. "You can't be serious. There is no way that we. . ." Their voices faded away as Marcel lost her focus on the meeting due to the staggering demand that ACORN had made.

Dumbfounded, Marcel silently fought to comprehend the sheer magnitude of the number and what she had witnessed. *"What have I gotten myself into? A $38 billion demand for ACORN is ridiculous. It's one thing for a city or state to sue for millions or even a billion dollars for lead paint remediation. But how can a grassroots organization be able to demand nearly $40 billion for it? This is crazy."*

An unsettling truth sank into her mind. *Is this even legal—what is ACORN? What kind of grassroots organization can demand a billion dollars from major corporations?*

But with that realization, Marcel knew her life had changed forever. She couldn't look at ACORN the same way, but she didn't know enough to compel change—yet.

Public Nuisance

Sunday, January 22, 2006

One frigid winter night the lawyers for the nation's largest paint manufacturers gathered in rented office space in downtown Providence, Rhode Island. Dressed in monogrammed shirts and tailored suits, they settled around a mahogany conference table littered with ashtrays and coffee cups for a long debate on the night before their opportunity to present a defense in the case. Following three months of intense testimony, the high-priced lawyers strategized about how to counter the state's contention that their clients were responsible for the decades-old, lead paint contamination problem.

Almost a quarter of the nation's housing stock contained lead paint, and the country had been grappling with the ramifications for three decades. Millions of children had been treated for lead poisoning, and billions of dollars had already been spent.

Rhode Island's lawyers argued the corporate predecessors of the paint companies manufactured and marketed lead-based paint long after its dangers were known, causing harm to hundreds of thousands of children. For almost two decades, paint makers had successfully fought off all lawsuits which contended their products contaminated homes with lead. Not once in all those years had the industry ever lost, or even settled, a large suit like this one. The previous Rhode Island trial in 1999 ended in a hung jury.

Charles Moellenberg, Jr., a lawyer for Sherwin-Williams thought the state's case was flawed. "I can't believe it's so weak." He asserted. "They can't close a case based on nothing but sheer speculation."

Thomas Graves, the National Paint and Coatings Association General Counsel, wondered whether the state was holding back more incriminating evidence for some unknown strategic reason. "I don't know; they've got to have something else, something more. What are we missing?"

Other lawyers were concerned about jury fatigue. They'd been there three months already, for nothing. Did they really want to add months and months for a technical defense when the jury was already weary enough?

By the end of the night, the defense team decided not to call a single witness—confident the jury would conclude their clients did nothing wrong.

Marcel Reid set her stainless steel convection oven to 500 degrees. The oven must be preheated before the biscuits go in. Before getting started, she washed her hands thoroughly and prepared the ingredients in advance to work quickly and efficiently.

The most important ingredient was flour; not all flours are created equal, she thought. Southern, all-purpose flour was better suited for quick breads, such as biscuits, cakes and muffins. Marcel reached for her old faithful Pillsbury, Gold Medal, a national brand bleached, all-purpose flour. She memorized her mother's recipes by heart.

1 1/4 cup cake flour
3/4 cup all-purpose flour
1 1/2 teaspoon baking powder
1/2 teaspoon baking soda
1/2 teaspoon salt
1/4 cup butter, cut into small chunks
3/4 cup buttermilk

Spoon the flour into measuring cup and level with a knife. Measure the flour into bowl. Cut in butter until the mixture resembled coarse crumbs. Blend in enough buttermilk until the dough leaves the sides of bowl. Knead gently two or three times on a lightly floured surface. Cut with large biscuit cutter. Place on pan with biscuits touching. Brush tops with melted butter. Bake at 500 degrees for 8 minutes or until golden brown. Cool for a few minutes and then eat.

Marcel often reminisced about friends and family during Christmas and New Years. The holiday season also included Kwanza, when Marcel often reflected on the core set of principles she learned from Dr. Ron Karenga. She wondered what her college professor would think about all this ACORN stuff.

Professor Karenga always insisted on the culturally-rooted and the ethically sound. His philosophy -Kwaida- was summed up in the three principles of service, struggle and institution building.

The daughter of a southern bell, with roots in Alabama, Marcel decried the lost art of home cooking. *It's such a shame women quit making buttermilk biscuits from scratch after canned biscuits came out,* Marcel thought, as she often loved to bake when she was under pressure. Nothing like the old adage, *"If you can't stand the heat stay out of the kitchen."* For Marcel, the greater the heat, the more she cooked—and she had a lot to think about this Sunday morning.

Miriam Reid had lived with Marcel for ten years before she passed away in 2003. *Miriam was a pillar of restrained strength and rectitude; she never raised her voice, never lost a fight and never backed down—ever! Miriam never found an enemy she didn't best, except cancer.*

Always the dutiful daughter, Marcel stood by her mother's side while she battled the dreadful disease. Self-reliant, she learned early on she didn't have to go along to get along, and she didn't have to fit in. Cooking made her feel closer to her mother's memory, and Marcel often baked to relieve stress.

Baking was a bonding ritual with her mother when she was growing up. Marcel thought of her love for her mother with sadness and longing, as she wiped beads of sweat from her brow with floured hands. She whisked together the flour, baking powder, baking soda and salt in a medium-large bowl until everything was blended. Lost in thought, she cut the butter in small chunks and tossed the butter cubes in with the flour so they were all well coated.

Marcel dusted the counter and dough with all-purpose flour, and dumped the mixture onto the floured work surface. She contemplated while she kneaded the dough until thoroughly blended. *Professor Karenga believed the task was to love each other in the midst of the hatred directed toward us, to defend and give power to the vulnerable, to bear witness to truth to love justice, to hate wrongdoing, and to always try to do what was right and good.*

With floured hands, Marcel cut the biscuits, and carefully placed them on the baking sheet so they gently touched each other. She quickly brushed the tops with melted butter, and placed the baking sheet in the middle of the preheated oven. Marcel felt the searing 500-degree heat rush across her face and baked the biscuits for 8-10 minutes until golden brown, before scuffling them on a wire rack to cool for a few minutes.

But how does this reflect on what I just learned about ACORN? "Thirty-eight billion! Oh my God!" Marcel thought to herself, *I look good my ass—Helen and Mitch set me up! They used Gloria and me to make these ridiculous demands, and they knew it all the time. I've been involved with community organizations all of my life, but I've never seen anything like this. A grassroots organization demanding $38 billion—and meaning it. Was this a legitimate protest or legalized extortion?*

Wednesday, February 22, 2006

"The verdict was in—guilty, Guilty, GUILTY!" Six jurors filed into Rhode Island Superior Court, four weeks after the paint companies' lawyers decided to close without calling a single defense witness. The four-man, two-woman jury decided the lead contamination of homes was a public nuisance unleashed by the paint companies, which violated the public's right to clean health.

The jury foreman, Gerald Lena, sixty-four, a security screener at T.F. Green International Airport, believed the state had not presented enough evidence about who made the paint that was causing the problem, and whether property owners themselves might be responsible for the paint flaking off. "They could have brought their own witnesses up there," Gerald had said. "The fact is, the person you hear last leaves a lasting impression, but maybe they couldn't dispute anything.

"Once we finally started our deliberations, we spent more than a day reviewing the judge's instructions. Then we took an informal vote to see where everyone in the room stood. Like the first jury, we split four-to-two in favor of the paint companies."

Other jurors were swayed by the defense arguments: if lead paint was well maintained, lead poisoning was rarely a threat. The condition of the paint, but not the paint itself, was the problem. Two jurors believed the state had proved its case.

Robert Merwin, thirty-seven, a juror who worked as an editor for a group of community newspapers said, "It was well documented that the lead companies knew it was a toxin, a poison, and they continued to sell it."

Another juror, Mary McGowan, sixty-nine, a retired bookkeeper declared, "The state said the companies manufactured and sold 80 percent of the paint sold in the country. It was up to the paint companies to say no, but they didn't furnish the jury with anything. All they had to say was no, but they didn't because they couldn't."

"We deadlocked. Frustrated after almost three days of deliberations," Gerald said. "The judge asked if we could reach a verdict through further deliberations."

"Oh my God! We've been here five and a half months. Let's try to go back and get a verdict," Gerald thought. "So we went through the whole processes again and then we went home early."

The next morning, he returned to the jury room and declared, "I've changed my mind."

"Just like that?" The other jurors looked at him in stunned disbelief.

"I reread the judge's instructions," Gerald said. "But I still think that property owners are a part of the lead-paint problem."

After that, a young woman who had sided with the paint companies, announced she had also changed her mind. She went up to the board and gave a detailed breakdown of how she reached her conclusion.

"That's what started the process of breaking the deadlock," Mary said. "When one person changed their mind, you could see how it affected the other jurors. They gave their reasons, which got others thinking."

With some reluctance, after several more days of intense deliberations, the remaining jurors decided lead paint was a public nuisance in the state, and three of the paint companies were responsible for it.

Patrick Lynch, forty-one, Rhode Island's Attorney General proclaimed, "The verdict is not limited to states. There are other cities and towns that could file suits."

"Other states are sitting and waiting for the Rhode Island decision to come out. This gives them a good sign," declared Liz Wolff, a researcher for ACORN.

In so doing, the State of Rhode Island won the first-ever verdict against the makers of lead-based paint, with a jury deciding that three companies must clean more than 300,000 homes of lead contamination and may be forced to pay billions of dollars in damages.

"The lead-based paint industry's products contributed to decades of debilitating health problems in millions of American children, most of them living in poor neighborhoods," declared Stephanie Cannady, at forty-five, the chair of Rhode Island ACORN. "The companies failed to step up and clean up the problem they created. The legal process has held them accountable and said they can't duck and run. As long as we have housing stock with lead paint, we will continue to have children at risk in certain communities. It's devastating for these kids."

The paint companies disputed the verdict and the accusation of knowingly selling a harmful product. Chris Connors, the CEO of Sherwin-Williams declared, "We continue to believe the facts and the law are on our side. The court still has to rule on various remaining issues before the next steps in the legal process can be determined."

The paint companies' stocks tumbled, which wiped out billions of dollars in market value in one afternoon. Sherman-Williams plummeted 18% losing $1.3 billion overnight, and NL Industries fell 8% the same day.

Wall Street analysts reported that damages could range from zero, depending upon appeals, to boundless amounts, if additional states decide to hop on the lawsuit bandwagon. Credit Suisse suspended its ratings on Sherwin-Williams stock entirely.

Monday, June 12, 2006

Democratic Presidential Candidates John Kerry and John Edwards attended the Democratic Take Back America conference. ACORN Political Staff members had prepped Marcel Reid along with neighborhood activists and community leaders from across the country who had gathered before meeting the prospective candidates.

Early speculation about the 2008 Presidential Election had begun immediately after the results of the 2004 presidential elections became known. Marcel welcomed Stephanie Cannady, a strikingly beautiful and passionate woman with big brown eyes and flawless skin. Marcel asked, "Zach, please explain what these meetings are all about."

Zach Polett, fifty-six, the Executive Director for Project Vote, who stood 5'9" with wooly hair and a slight-build, replied, "It's a full field this year Marcel, so here's a chance to hear what the candidates say for themselves. John Edwards has probably courted ACORN support the most. He's been the most visible on income disparities and issues of poverty."

Stephanie leaned forward. "That's right. Edwards has worked tirelessly with Katrina survivors in the Lower Ninth, and he always talks about race and poverty—two Americas."

"What about Obama?" asked Toni.

"What about—Obama!" Marcel replied. "I mean, it's great that he's Black and all, but we don't know anything about him, other than he gave a hell of a speech at the DNC convention in 2004. At least -I- don't know anything about him."

Toni Foulkes, forty, a Chicago ACORN community leader said, "Obama is a lawyer who took on the Illinois motor voter case for us, ACORN vs. Edgar, the Republican Governor—and we won."

"So he represented ACORN as legal counsel, but he actually worked for Project Vote?" asked Marcel.

"Not exactly," Toni said. "We invited Obama to attend ACORN leadership training sessions to run the sessions on power every year, and, as a result, many of our new community leaders got to know him before he ever ran for office."

She described Barack Obama's U.S. Senate Campaign, "Obama successfully ran the voter registration project with Project Vote which made it possible for Carol Moseley Braun to win the Senate in 1992.

"Project Vote delivered 50,000 new registered voters in that campaign, while ACORN delivered about 5,000 of them. Obama's campaign theme was, It's A Power Thing. . . You Wouldn't Understand."

"Right on!" Zach smiled.

"What does Madeline think of him?" asked Marcel.

Toni replied, "Carol Mosley Braun asked SEIU Local 880 and ACORN to play a major role in her voter registration and get-out-the-vote efforts for her Senate run. She and Keith flexed their political muscles."

Madeline Talbott, the Head Organizer for Illinois ACORN, initially considered Obama a competitor, but she became so impressed with his work she invited him to help train her staff. Thus, Barack Obama's Chicago political mentor was a fierce ACORN organizer, who was married to Keith Kelleher, a top SEIU Organizer.

"Oh, so he was legal counsel and an ACORN trainer—but never a regular member."

"Exactly, Marcel!" Toni said, "It was only natural for many of us to volunteer in his first campaign for State Senate and then his failed bid for U.S. Congress in 1996. So by the time he ran for U.S. Senate, we were old friends."

"And now he's running for President," declared Stephanie.

"That is something," Zach said. "But I'm more of a Clinton man, myself."

"Why?"

"Because ACORN has had a long and successful history with Arkansas and the Clintons."

Stephanie chided, "Well you're from Arkansas, so you don't count."

Marcel replied, "I'm for Hillary myself, and I'm from Compton. In the end, DC ACORN endorsed both Barack Obama for the Democratic nomination—*and* John McCain for the Republican nomination."

They all laughed together at the thought.

Take Back America

Wednesday, February 22, 2006

After opening mail and reviewing office paperwork, Anita MonCrief first weighed and then forwarded the mail using the new Pitney Bowes postage machine. She hated the bitter taste of postage glue, but Anita was the registered user of the postage meter. Her husky fingers sliced envelopes and removed various donation checks.

Next door, ACORN political staff continued to prep Marcel Reid, Stephanie Cannady and other local community leaders from across the country to meet prospective Democratic Presidential Candidates, John Kerry and John Edwards in the second floor office suite.

The Executive Director for Project Vote, Zach Polett who also served as the Director of Political Operations for ACORN, ordered, "Have Anita make 50 copies of the briefing books for the ACORN board members." Anita was abruptly summoned into the adjoining conference room.

A boisterous diva around the Washington D.C. offices, Anita looked down on regular ACORN members. However, she treated ACORN organizers as equals and she respected the national board members, and Marcel Reid as the Chair for DC ACORN. Her main duties consisted of opening mail, recording charitable donations, and other purely administrative tasks—although she considered herself to be a member of the political operations staff for ACORN.

Marcel Reid reached out to congratulate Stephanie Cannady, who was now chair for Rhode Island ACORN, following the recent landmark court decision. "We heard about the victory, Stephanie. Rhode Island rocks!"

"I know. Can you believe it?—Amazing," Stephanie smiled. "It was a surprising and devastating verdict for the paint industry. The reaction was swift and severe. Investors feared the clean-up costs could total billions, and the paint industry might face a tidal wave of litigation, like the tobacco, asbestos and pharmaceutical industries."

"So what happened?"

"It was just like the movies," Stephanie said. "Attorney General Whitehouse wanted to file a lawsuit based on public nuisance laws for some time, so he hired Motley Rice to try the case."

"Who is Motley Rice?"

"Not who, but what. Motley Rice is a South Carolina-based law firm. They were involved in the litigation against tobacco companies in the 1990s."

"Oh, so they beat big tobacco?" asked Marcel.

"Yep! And the paint companies hated them," Stephanie giggled. "The paint companies attacked the suit, arguing it had been shopped around to other states by Ronald Motley."

Marcel nodded, "I bet they did."

"The paint companies complained that he was on the hunt for his next corporate victim—after making a killing in the tobacco wars."

"He made a killing?" Marcel voice rose.

"Ronald Motley is a famous whistleblower," said Stephanie. "He was portrayed in the movie *The Insider* as the heroic litigator who took down evil tobacco companies."

Marcel beamed. "I saw the movie; it's a great film."

"And his firm raked in hundreds of millions of dollars in fees and controversy for leading the landmark $246 billion tobacco settlement. In the 1998 agreement, the tobacco companies agreed to pay 46 states to cover their cost of treating people made ill from smoking."

"Two-hundred and forty-six billion?" Marcel stammered in disbelief.

She thought to herself, *Maybe a $38 billion demand was not so unreasonable after all.*

"Right. I know," replied Stephanie. "So the paint companies argued Motley Rice had a sinister agenda which went beyond cleaning up lead paint in Rhode Island."

"What agenda?" Marcel asked, "Besides money?"

"They argued the firm had taken the case in exchange for 16 or 17 percent of any settlement or judgment. Which is silly because all lawyers work for money!"

"I know that's right," said Marcel. "They took a difficult case on a contingency basis. They fought hard and they won! Plus they made new law. So they deserve to make some money."

Stephanie whispered, "But it started off bad, Marcel. Most of the accusations against the paint companies had already been dismissed, including product liability and conspiracy."

Marcel's eyes widened with surprise. "Dismissed! Completely?"

"When opening arguments began, only one issue remained. Did lead paint constitute a public nuisance in Rhode Island? The verdict could have easily gone in favor of the paint companies. The jury started off split, in favor of the paint companies."

"What happened?"

"They lost because of in fighting between the defense lawyers and their courtroom strategy. Three of the six jurors were surprised and disappointed because the defense team did not offer a single witness to rebut the state's central argument."

"Which was what?" asked Marcel.

"That simply by having been in the business of making lead-based paint, their companies contributed to what is now a pervasive public nuisance."

"So what does it all mean?"

Stephanie said, "For the first time a court found three paint manufacturers guilty of having created a public nuisance. The Attorney General finally won his suit against Sherwin-Williams, NL Industries, and

Millennium Holdings. "And the verdict makes the paint companies fund the decontamination of more than 300,000 Rhode Island homes. The lawyers said this may cost over a billion dollars."

Marcel flinched. "A billion dollars?"

"Yes! And the judge still has to decide whether the paint companies will pay punitive damages," Stephanie said, "and how much that amount will be."

Marcel clarified, "So the jury ruled three paint manufacturing companies created a public nuisance by selling lead-based paint and ordered the companies to clean up homes with lead hazards. Why did they let the other paint companies off?"

Stephanie said, "The jurors didn't blame the fourth company, Atlantic Richfield Co., because they decided most of the lead pigment they sold between 1936 and 1946 was probably used for the war effort during World War II rather than for painting homes. DuPont had already settled with Rhode Island for $10 million for lead paint clean up, removal, and education funding."

Marcel asked, "Do you know what this means? ACORN can organize around this issue all around the country because, you guys, Rhode Island led the way. We can work with the local governments to improve our communities."

The door swung open and the corpulent Anita MonCrief returned with bound and collated copies of the briefing materials for the Take Back America conference.

Anita placed the books on the conference table, "Here you are, Zach. Can I get you anything else?"

"Thank you, Anita. These look great," Zach said. "How about getting some cokes and coffee for our guests?"

Belinda Ferrell was the new Head Organizer for DC ACORN. An experienced union organizer who grew up in the District of Columbia, Belinda wanted to work in the DC court system.

She burst into the upstairs Project Vote offices, "I know times are still hard—but I need my money Anita," declared Belinda.

"I am so sorry it has taken so long for me to pay you back Belinda," Anita said. "I don't have the money right now, but I can write you a check—if you can hold off until next week to cash it."

Belinda rolled her eyes, exasperated and repeated, "I need my money Anita." Then she walked back downstairs.

Relieved, Anita wiped her brow, and then quickly completed an application for public assistance—but without Rachel's knowledge, Anita used Rachel Pope's address to apply for Washington, D.C. benefits, although Anita actually lived in Maryland.

Thursday, June 22, 2006

A red truck careened to a stop near the front gates of the Marine Barracks on Capitol Hill, which supported both ceremonial and security missions in the nation's capital. An irritated Anita MonCrief honked her horn in a frantic attempt to park near the historic barracks. The south and east sides of the Marine Barracks quadrangle were used for offices, maintenance facilities and living spaces for troops, and a building on the west was the officers' quarters. Ironically, the DC ACORN offices were located adjacent across the street.

Marcel Reid walked past the growing altercation on her way to the DC ACORN office. She entered the storefront office and called out. "Belinda, were you able to follow up with DC City Council on our lead paint campaign? We're going to urge more city and state governments to file lawsuits."

Belinda Ferrell stared out the plate-glass window at the argument brewing in front of the Marine Barracks across the street. "I'll get right on it Marcel. My family has a personal relationship with Marion Barry."

At 2:04 PM, Belinda turned her attention away from the escalating conflict outside her window and feverishly typed a letter to the DC City Council members, which read:

"Currently, the health and safety of DC residents is at risk, because our city lacks sufficient funds to significantly reduce lead-hazards found in housing. Here in DC, as well as across the country, children are essentially being used as lead testers. It is when we discover that a child has been poisoned that we then work to deal with the lead hazards. When sadly, it is too late, at least for that child. For example, Webb Elementary has the lowest scores in the city; this could be tied to the environmentally hazardous paint, mold, as well as other usual suspects.

We need a more proactive, preventative approach, which seeks to reduce lead hazards in homes before children are poisoned. To do this we need homeowners and landlords to be getting their properties tested, housing code inspectors to be identifying the problems, and then we need funding to help low and moderate-income homeowners remove lead hazards.

The State of Rhode Island's successful suit against several paint manufacturers, including Sherwin-Williams, is expected to deliver billions of dollars from the companies which sold lead-based paint, when they knew it was poisonous, to the state in order to make their housing units lead-safe.

The basis of Rhode Island's lawsuit was these companies had created a public nuisance that is still poisoning children today. Sherwin-Williams, along with several other companies, made and sold a product that is poisoning children every year here in D.C. We think it's time that we discuss this issue and explore whether or not there is an opportunity to hold them accountable and secure much needed resources to help us, finally, eliminate the threat of childhood lead poisoning."

At 2:21 PM, Donna Rouse responded back on behalf of the DC City Council. "Good Afternoon: Please provide me with available dates and times. I will check the calendar and arrange a meeting. Thanks."

Meanwhile, Anita MonCrief was engaged in an animated argument with two young Marines from across the street. Propped in a ghetto lean, and an intoxicated rage, Anita accosted the pair of armed soldiers guarding the front gates of the Marine Barracks.

"Fuck you, sailor boy!" said the angry black women, neck popping, and finger snapping—with one hand propped on her fat hips.

The puzzled Marine looked back towards Anita in disbelief and utter confusion as she cursed him out from head to toe.

"You can't park here now—Ma'am!" said the young Marine wearing dress blues and white gloves who sternly motioned for Anita to move her truck.

"And, why the hell not?" Anita challenged. Always a diva, anyone who got in her way, including the sailors standing guard near the entrance of the Marine Barracks, she would confront.

"We need this area clear for our evening parade, Ma'am" replied the Marine. "Move along!"

Anita ranted. "I'm a single mother, I'm late for work and I need that fucking parking space!"

His pupils tightened as the young Marine stared back at her in rage and disbelief.

"Who the fuck are you looking at soldier boy?" She bellowed, reflexively confrontational. Anita cursed more than a dozen sailors and lambasted the Marine for standing guard.

Instinctively, the young Marines gave Anita the 1,000-yard stare forged from desert combat. If looks could kill, this would have been a double homicide. Frustrated, and confused, the Marine braced himself, clinched his teeth and balled his fists in anger.

Anita burst into the DC ACORN office like a real-life *"Sapphire"* from Amos and Andy, and exclaimed. "He ain't crazy. He wouldn't dare put his hands on me!"

Belinda suggested that she check herself. "This is crazy Anita. You've got to pull yourself together."

Frustrated, "You just don't understand, Belinda. Money is tight and I need this job. I was running late, but he wouldn't let me park," replied Anita.

Front Runner

Marcel Reid hurried past black cast-iron gates while a sharp military cadence bellowed over the barracks wall. Thunderous sound pierced the vanilla sky with a garnet and tangerine glow at dusk. Sunset Parades were a universal symbol of the professionalism, discipline, and Esprit de Corps of the United States Marines.

"Fired up."
"Fired up."
"Want some."
"Fired up."
"Here we go."
"Wanna go."
"Fired up."
"Fired up."

The ceremony started promptly at 6:00 PM with a concert by the United States Marine Band. The parade showcased the ceremonial prowess of Marines, and the musical eminence of the U.S. Marine Band using the resplendent setting of the Barracks and the Marines flare for showmanship. The parade drill was precise but without any fancy theatrics.

The one hour and fifteen minute performance featured music and precision marching. Following the military parade that night, Marcel Reid returned to the office at 6:45 PM, just prior to the monthly DC ACORN chapter meeting.

Belinda rushed to tell Marcel about Anita's earlier confrontation.

In stunned disbelief, Marcel asked, "She cursed out a Marine?"

Belinda pointed across the street. "She sure did Marcel, right over there in front of the barracks."

Marcel smiled with her eyes, "I guess if you can't have a Marine, you can curse a Marine."

Belinda laughed out loud.

"Anita must have lost her mind!" Marcel said and then asked, "He was a real life, Semper Fi, Devil Dog... Marine? He could have killed her—by accident."

Charles Turner, a fifty-seven year-old DC ACORN member stood 5'9" with a medium build, bald head and darting eyes. He walked through the office during the verbal exchange and flashed a quick easy-going smile. "Are y'all talking about Anita?" He commented. "I almost had to beat her ass last week myself."

Marcel glared, "Charles! What are you saying?"

Charles was smart, street wise and savvy as he spoke with conviction. "A few of us were meeting in the conference room, and Anita stormed in and told us to shut up!"

"Shut up?" asked Marcel.

"Yeah. We thought she was crazy," Charles said. "We told her to go back in her office and mind her own business.

"She was in the next room listening to music or something—and then she stormed in on us talking about she couldn't hear herself think."

"So what did you say?"

"We told her to go to hell, Belinda—and she broke bad and cursed us all out."

The trio snickered and laughed aloud.

"She did what?" asked Marcel, testing Charles to see if he would repeat himself.

"That's right, she cursed out everyone in the room. I held it together when she went off on me, but I jumped bad when she started cursing out the older women in our chapter. The bitch went too damn far!"

Marcel scolded him. "Charles! Don't call her a bitch."

"That's what she is. An uppity crazy bitch," Charles said. "And I can't stand her ass!"

"I agree with Charles. We all know she's stuck up. We can all agree to that, but I think she was drunk."

"Why do you say that, Belinda?"

"You know how it is when you have a hangover, Marcel?"

"No Belinda. I *don't* know about that. I don't drink." *Not much anyway.*

Turning away, Belinda said, "Charles, -*You*- know how it is when you have a hangover, right. When every little sound or noise gets amplified in your head."

Charles agreed. "Yeah, that's right, which explains a lot about the way Anita acts around the office."

Belinda laughed. "You have a point. I don't know about Anita; she seems strange to me too, Charles."

Marcel replied, "Let's not start any rumors. Clearly, she's having a bad day. But she is a young Black woman, like us, and we don't want to make it any worse than it is, or damage her reputation."

Saturday, June 24, 2006

Buzz, buzz, buzz—the sleek slim profile of a Motorola Blackberry vibrated to indicate an incoming email. The message was from Amy Schur.

The text message read: "Marcel, I don't know who will see this before the call, and who can open the Adobe Acrobat attachment, but I just received this draft of the report back from the graphics person working on it, and wanted to send it along. I think it looks pretty snazzy (and hopefully the content is good too)! Talk to you in a few – Amy."

Wednesday, June 28, 2006

"Sherwin-Williams knowingly covered our country's homes in poison paint," declared Maude Hurd, the sixty-eight, scrappy, and mahogany-skinned National President of ACORN. "Now it is time to ask Sherwin-Williams to use some of its profits to help make housing in our communities lead-safe. We need to prevent more children from being poisoned."

In the wake of Rhode Island's successful suit against Sherwin-Williams and two other paint manufacturers, local ACORN leaders called upon their city and state officials to sue the company in order to secure needed funding to deal with the lead paint problem.

ACORN released its own study—Sherwin-Williams: Covering Our Communities with Toxics—and called on local and state governments to file lawsuits and take other actions, including the divestment of public pension funds, to force the company to help fund lead paint clean-up.

ACORN's report documented how Sherwin-Williams knew in the early 1900's that lead-based paint was poisonous, and how they acted to cover up this fact and deceive consumers. The report further detailed much more recent cases of Sherwin Williams' environmental abuse, from polluting manufacturing plants to the company's efforts to prevent further state regulation of certain paint emissions called Volatile Organic Compounds, which contribute to the ozone and smog problem.

Marcel admired the striking graphic imagery on the ACORN report cover, which made a mockery of the well-known red and blue Sherwin-Williams logo while she was lost in thought. *The cover was a black and green picture depicting Sherwin-Williams covering the world, not with paint, but with poisonous toxins instead. The imagery was both funny and shocking. Humor is an essential tool for a community organizer and successful campaign. The establishment can't stand to be ridiculed.*

Sunday, October 8, 2006

After finishing a piping hot buttermilk biscuit, Marcel Reid typed a quick message to Marc Borbely a local member on DC ACORN School Modernization and Oversight Committee from her Motorola Blackberry, which read:

"Mary asked me to forward some information to you about the

ACORN Lead Paint Campaign. This campaign has been going on for a few years now and we have won a major victory in Rhode Island which will result in a settlement of over a billion dollars.

Read the report, and I will answer any questions I can. We have been in the negotiations with Sherwin Williams and the National Association of Paint and Coatings President.

However, our negotiations with Sherwin Williams have hit a snag that has forced us back into the streets. We will continue to picket Sherwin-Williams stores until we are back in meaningful negotiations – F, H & C... Marcel."

Tuesday, October 10, 2006

The suspension roared on Marcel Reid's Silver Cadillac as she turned and cornered down Pennsylvania Avenue. She was anxious and tense. ACORN members were waiting to continue the national action on Sherwin-Williams.

Buzz, buzz, buzz –- the sleek slim profile of Marcel's Motorola Blackberry vibrated to signal an incoming email. The message was from Amy Schur. The subject line read "Sherwin-Williams Action in Cleveland."

The message read, "Hi Marcel. I am in the airport but wanted to catch you. We are having a conference call tomorrow at 7:00 p.m. to discuss the plan for an action this Saturday. Are you available? – Amy"

Feverishly texting while driving, Marcel clicked in a careful response. "Have a safe trip, Amy. I will be in Ohio on Thursday a day early. Yes, I will do the call in and I will see you soon – F, H & C... Marcel."

Friday, October 13, 2006

ACORN launched a nationwide campaign to force Sherwin-Williams to help clean up the problem of lead paint. The action was timed to coincide with an ACORN national board meeting the next day. Marcel Reid joined the campaign to pressure paint companies to increase funding for lead-paint clean up, as ACORN continued to protest at the offices and stores of paint giant Sherwin-Williams. We were equipped with picket signs and helium balloons. Hundreds of cardinal-clad protestors flooded Prospect Avenue in Cleveland, Ohio in front of Sherwin-Williams Headquarters.

She joined a phalanx of reporters positioned in close array during the Cleveland action. "Sherwin-Williams Company is guilty of a pattern and practice of environmental abuse," Marcel announced. "ACORN's report documents how Sherwin-Williams profited from the sale of lead-based paint for decades, when they knew it was poisonous.

"We are calling on our local and state elected officials to help force Sherwin Williams to help cleanup the lead paint mess and explore the feasibility of a city or state lawsuit, like the successful suit in Rhode Island. We want public hearings on this issue and to divest all Sherwin-Williams stock held by local or state pension funds."

An eager reporter asked, "Why focus on Sherwin-Williams? Aren't there other companies which sold lead-based paint?"

Marcel cleared her throat. "There are other companies that sold lead-based paint prior to the 1978 ban, including DuPont, NL Industries, American Cyanamid, Atlantic Richfield, Duron, ConAgra and Millennium Holdings.

"But we are focusing on Sherwin-Williams first because they are by far, the largest paint manufacturer that is responsible. They own the Dutch Boy brand, which had belonged to NL Industries, and they bought Duron in 2004.

"And they're the ones who made money off of this and manipulated the public opinion and political system and spent lots of money doing it. So it only seems fair that they should be part of the solution. Sherwin-Williams is covering Black communities with toxins and poison paint."

The reporter followed-up, questioning, "Sherwin-Williams claims they stopped making lead-based paint back in 1938. Is this true?"

"No. That's not true," quipped Marcel. "From 1910 to 1947 Sherwin-Williams manufactured and sold paints containing very high concentrations of white lead carbonate for both interior and exterior usages.

"After 1947, Sherwin-Williams stopped manufacturing white lead carbonate themselves, but instead bought it from other companies like National Lead Company, today called NL Industries, the former maker of Dutch Boy brand paints.

"They continued to sell house paint containing white lead carbonate well into the 1970s and their own internal company memos say they intended to deplete their existing stock of lead pigments before implementing the 1971 standard of lowering lead content."

Another reporter asked, "Didn't a number of cities and states file suits years ago that were thrown out of court? What's different now?"

Marcel replied, "Earlier lawsuits focused on product liability claims and had to deal with difficult legal issues about assigning blame when the product was sold 30 or 40 years ago and you can't prove which company actually made the paint on the walls of any particular homes.

"But a landmark Rhode Island case broke new ground, arguing that the product created a public nuisance by poisoning thousands of children and contaminating hundreds of thousands of homes."

Another question sounded. "Sherwin-Williams says they have been willing to meet with ACORN to resolve these issues. Is this true?"

"No. That's not true." She responded. "ACORN has met with their trade association, the National Paint and Coatings Association. But the NPCA was only prepared to discuss small pilot projects and was not willing to discuss more global resolutions to the problem.

"We've asked Sherwin-Williams for a meeting, and they refused. Right now ACORN is focusing our attention on Sherwin-Williams, to start, but we think all responsible paint companies should help in the clean up.

"We are starting with Sherwin-Williams because they were one of the largest sellers of lead-based paint, and they are the largest ones still in the paint business today."

A Saturday morning ritual began in every hair salon in the District of Columbia. A young hair stylist concentrated on difficulties involved with doing black hair braids, which was a time-consuming project, because of the uniqueness of the hair. She was an expert with perms, oils and sheen and knew Black hair can be elegant, relaxed and or easy-going braid styles.

A consummate perfectionist, the stylist wanted to be able to do all hairstyles with ease. Since practice makes perfect, the stylist allowed her girlfriends to coax her into trying weaves, extensions and braid styles on them. She unpacked a duffle bag of black hair products.

Anita MonCrief, had thick, kinky-hair which looked a hot mess this morning—it stood all over her head. The stylist sprayed the braids thoroughly with the water bottle to wet the hair, using the water as a lubricant. She applied a small amount of detangling conditioner to the braid to ease removal.

The stylist took the first braid in her hand and carefully removed the elastic band, which secured the braids, by clipping it with the scissors. Starting at the end of the braid, she used the pointed end of the rat-tail comb to work the braid free, stopping as needed to loosen any tangles with her fingers.

Once the braid was completely unwound, she combed through the hair with the wide tooth comb and then secured it at the top of Anita's head with the clip, so it didn't become tangled again. The stylist removed Anita's braids, then brushed and combed her hair.

"What style should I get this time?" asked Anita.

The stylist said, "There are so many different styles, Afro kinky hair or the Marley braid. Of course you have the most common styles—weaves, simply braided or corn rows. Nowadays you can find a lot of people using synthetic hair.

I don't think any style is as unique or more admired in the end as black hair braid styles. As long as we have it, I say we do our best to have great looking hair, no matter what the type."

Anita rolled her eyes. "You're a lot of help."

The stylist smiled. "Of course, using the right hair care products goes a long way in keeping the hair looking good and beautiful."

It was a Saturday morning ritual, but this was not a beauty salon. It was the second floor office of DC ACORN. By the time they were finished, the room looked like someone had pulled the pin on a black "hair grenade" which exploded all over the upstairs office, to the surprise and dismay of the other ACORN staffers in the office.

Marc Sidel, a scruffy twenty-seven year-old with a young wife and a younger newborn, was bright but clumsy. He made mistakes but his heart was in the right place. Pat McCoy, sixty-five, stood 5'9" with brownish hair; he wore wire-rimmed glasses and was an unassuming but deft attorney.

Pat was a long time organizer with ACORN and possessed a natural affinity for the people. He never raised his voice, was never discourteous but never showed his hand. Anita's supervisor Karyn Gillette, thirty-five, was tall and shapely.

Anita's co-workers became completely unhinged at the sight. Synthetic hair, weave and extensions were everywhere, scattered all over the upstairs office. Marcel Reid discovered the staffers in the office were completely shocked by this spectacle.

In a stern tone reminiscent of her father, an Army drill sergeant, Marcel tried to rationalize what she had just learned to Belinda Ferrell. "You can't get your hair done in the office. It's so unprofessional."

Belinda replied, "Anita said we ain't paying her enough to make her work weekends -*and*- miss her hair appointments. She had to get her hair done."

Exasperated, Marcel said, "The white staffers here don't know about or understand Black hair. They didn't know if she was getting a hair weave or having a bone placed through her nose! Project Vote could be a tremendous opportunity for Anita. She's a Black woman, with a college degree in political science. I hope and pray she doesn't blow it!"

Saturday, October 14, 2006

Marcel Reid eagerly prepared for the National Board Meeting in Cleveland, Ohio the headquarters of Sherwin-Williams. Maude Hurd, the ACORN National President, called the National Board Meeting to order at 1:25 p.m.

Mary Keith, fifty-two, the Chair for Cleveland ACORN, an ebony skinned woman with short platinum blond hair, presented a progress report on the recent actions and our demands for negotiations. "We delivered the demands and will send additional letters to Chris Connors, the CEO for Sherwin-Williams. Even more demonstrations are scheduled for Little Rock, Arkansas; Atlanta, Georgia; and Hartford, Connecticut. Plus Toronto and Vancouver, Canada; Tijuana, Mexico; Lima, Peru and Buenos Aires, Argentina."

Saturday, February 10, 2007

A seasoned political operative, I eagerly watched the coverage of the upcoming presidential campaign season. The Democrats had regained majorities in both houses of Congress in the 2006 mid-term elections, and early polls showed Senators Hillary Clinton and Barack Obama as the most popular potential Democratic candidates.

John Edwards, fifty-four, had announced his candidacy for the presidency on December 28, 2006. This run was his second attempt at the presidency. Senator Hillary Clinton, fifty-nine, had announced her intentions to run in the Democratic Presidential primaries on January 20, 2007.

I sipped bitter French roast coffee as I eagerly flipped television channels to watch the CNN coverage of today's historic Presidential announcement. Senator Barack Obama, forty-five, announced his candidacy from his home state of Illinois. The announcement, from a chilly outdoor stage in front of the Old State Capitol in Springfield was tinged in symbolism for the first black candidate with a realistic chance of obtaining enough broad-based support to secure a major party presidential nomination.

It was amazing how beneficial instant celebrity status had been to Obama's political aspirations, an outgrowth of the national stage that beckoned following his keynote address at the 2004, Democratic National Convention. Using the home of Lincoln's famous *house divided* speech as a backdrop, Obama announced his historic entry into the 2008 presidential campaign and presented himself as a symbol of a new generation of leadership and politics.

The formal announcement by the state's junior Democratic senator launched a three-day wave of campaign events in Iowa, New Hampshire and a Chicago fundraiser in between. *The Washington Post* listed Clinton, Edwards and Obama as early front-runners, leading in polls and fundraising and well ahead of the other major candidates. CNN/WMUR polls of New Hampshire Democratic primary voters found 67 percent of them holding a favorable impression of Senator Obama, slightly below the 74 percent favorable ratings held by better-known rivals, Senator Hillary Rodham Clinton and former Senator John Edwards of North Carolina.

Interestingly enough, none of the candidates received a significant bounce in their poll numbers after their official announcements. But the media speculated on the prospects of several other candidates, including Al Gore, the runner-up in the 2000, election; Senator John Kerry, the runner-up in the 2004, election; John Edwards, his running mate; Delaware Senator Joseph Biden; New Mexico Governor Bill Richardson; Iowa Governor Tom Vilsack; and Indiana Senator Evan Bayh.

I began my career in politics and public service as a student organizer in the 1992 Clinton Campaign. Once heralded as the first Black President, Bill Clinton arrived on the national scene with a cadre of black compatriots, including Ernie Green, Rodney Slater, and Carol Willis.

I had traveled to Washington, D.C. with the Clinton Administration and began my community development career working on the Federal Empowerment Zone Initiative. In this capacity, I toured the country conducting technology training and speaking engagements at White House Empowerment Zone Conferences and Regional Enterprise Community Conferences across the country.

I was one of many Blacks who got their starts in politics from working on Clinton Campaigns, within the Clinton Administration or Clinton's Democratic National Committee. During the Clinton re-elect, former Representative Alan Wheat of Kansas City was the Deputy Campaign Manager and Director of Constituent Outreach. Theodore "Ted" Carter was the Deputy Campaign Manager and Chief Operating Officer. State Directors included Katrice Banks, Georgia; Gordon Gant, Louisiana; Heyward Bannister, South Carolina, and Marvin Randolph, Maryland.

State Political Directors included Jacqueline Andrews, South Carolina; Thomas Dortch, Jr., Georgia; Fred Humphries, New Jersey; Opal Jones, Florida; Vivian Jones, Alabama; Tonya Lombard, Louisiana; Mark Mays, Tennessee; Charles Monroe, Missouri; Bruce Moore, Arkansas; Rodney Shelton, Oklahoma; Aaron Ward, District of Columbia; and Sherri White, North Carolina.

Field Operations were Rodney Capel, Maine; Etharin Cousins, Illinois; Lawrence Daniel, Ohio; Tawanna Dukes, Texas; James Franklin, North Carolina; Michael Frazier, Pennsylvania; Toni Harp, Connecticut; Freeman Hendrix, Michigan; Orson Porter, Rhode Island; Glenn Rushing, Mississippi; Kelvin Simmons, Missouri; Wallace Williams, Virginia, and Donna Brazile, Washington, D.C.

During the Gore campaign, I worked for Carol Willis in the DNC Community Outreach Services as the National Coordinator for Faith Based Community Outreach. Willis had been a fixture in Bill Clinton's campaigns since the 1980s and was a senior adviser on minority voters at the Democratic National Committee.

I traveled to Florida to organize grassroots support during the Gore/ Bush controversy. As it unraveled during the November 2000 general election, former Secretary of State James Bake flew to London for an exclusive function at the posh Lanesborough Hotel to explain the Florida election controversy to a group of wealthy attendees.

Meanwhile Dale Rathke, the comptroller for Citizen's Consulting Inc., flew on the Concord for champagne and chocolate filled junkets to

Paris, France with a male assistant—his own personal valet. Dale's profligate spending included shopping at luxury stores, riding in limousines, and frequenting five-star hotels and restaurants.

New Delegate

"Click". . . I pressed *enter* on my metallic, Gateway laptop and downloaded the rules for the primary elections from the Democratic National Committee website. I was very interested in working on the upcoming presidential elections, and the Democratic Party had published the 2008 rules which governed the convention.

The Democratic Party allowed only four states—Iowa, New Hampshire, Nevada and South Carolina—to hold elections before February 5, 2008. The early primaries and caucuses were considered the most critical components of the nomination process. Most candidates who lacked support dropped out after doing poorly in the Iowa caucuses and New Hampshire primaries. These state results often shifted national preferences.

I continued reading; 3,409 pledged delegates—those committed to vote for a particular candidate—will be selected by primary voters and caucus participants, as will 823 unpledged delegates, or super-delegates—who are free to vote for any candidate. So, with roughly 4,233 total delegates, it requires 2,117 votes for a majority.

By the end of 2007, both political parties adopted rules against states moving their primaries to an earlier date in the year. For the Republicans, the penalty for this violation was supposed to be the loss of half the state party's delegates to the convention. The Democratic penalty was the complete exclusion from the national convention of delegates from any state that broke the rules.

My cell phone vibrated then rang with a Muddy Waters, jazz/blues ring tone. I noticed the -404- Georgia prefix and immediately answered the call. A familiar voice surfaced, "Michael, I'm not going to be able to make it to the Legislative Caucus in Washington, DC this week." Deacon Dana Williams, the chair for Georgia ACORN, continued, "But Georgia still needs to be represented. I need you to step up and help out—if you're still going to be in D.C."

"No problem, Dana," I replied. "I'm here for whistleblower week anyway. I'll do whatever I can, if you think it will help."

"Great! The Atlanta Board already voted you in as the official alternate for the national board of directors from Georgia."

"Really?" I choked. Dana caught me completely by surprise.

"Congratulations, Michael! It's a two-year term."

Hesitantly, I responded, "That's great. What do I need to do?"

"Don't worry; you'll do fine," said Dana. "The first thing you need to do is to contact Ronald Sykes."

"Who's he?" I asked.

"He's a good man and one of our members from Georgia ACORN working on fellowship in Washington DC with the ACORN National Staff."

"Where do I find him?"

"He's working out of the DC ACORN Office on Capital Hill."

"I'll look him up." I replied

"The next thing I need you to do is give the campaign report for Georgia."

"Okay, I know about the Mortgage Fraud campaign, but what else should I present?"

"You definitely need to talk about our environmental justice campaign, and I'll send you all the briefing materials and campaign reports you need. I'll also send you Ron's number along with our briefing materials. Don't worry; you'll do fine. And while you're there, see if you can talk to someone about replacing our organizer."

"What's wrong?" I asked.

"They sent us these inexperienced guys completely untrained. They don't know nothing, and they don't want to go out and do anything."

"Is that what you want me to say?" I responded, looking for confirmation.

"Organizing is hard work," Dana complained. "A good community organizer must solve organizational problems, analyze power dynamics, deal with communications, develop conflict tactics, develop community leaders, and introduce new issues. I've been doing his job since he got here."

"Yeah, Dana. I guess you're right."

"The only issue we need to concern ourselves with is how we can increase the strength of our organization," Dana quipped. "Change comes from power, and power comes from organization."

Sunday, March 11, 2007

Joe Lewis, Louise Davis, Pat Williams, Marcel Reid and I felt the rush of adrenaline when a government issued Lincoln Town car pulled up to the splendid lawn in the affluent -*gold coast*- neighborhood of Washington, DC. The Mayor, Adrian Fenty, thirty-six, well-dressed and pale-skinned stepped out of the black town car parked directly in front of a small picket line of DC ACORN protestors.

Surprised by the news cameras at his home, Mayor Fenty greeted the protestors with a tight-lipped smile. He extended his hand to Ronald Sykes, forty, an athletic but well-manicured man who stood on the lawn before the small group of protestors. Active and fit, Ron was ex-army and a fierce advocate who snubbed the Washington Mayor on camera. Ron paraded in front of the jeering crowd and chanted:

"No handshaking."
"No ass kissing!"
"No handshaking."
"No ass kissing!"

Following the local action in front of the new mayor's Washington DC home, Ronald Sykes and I returned to the ACORN Legislative Conference. We walked through the concave driveway in front of the Washington Plaza Hotel. The nine-story resort-like property was designed like the Fontainebleau and Eden Roc in Miami Beach and featured curving corridors, with a shimmering swimming pool.

White painter's tarp and floating dust particles filled the air near the hotel lobby front desk. You could feel the sense of excitement and smell fresh paint and new carpet. Preparations for a new hotel renovation had already begun.

I was eager to meet with the local leaders from across the country because I wanted to learn the inner workings of ACORN first hand. Shirley Burnell, Fannie Brown, Ina Mason, America Alfaro, Stormy Henry, Stephanie Hughes, Marquina Wilson stood near the entrance way.

The ACORN Legislative Policy Conference was an unforgettable experience: meetings, trainings, actions, and other functions. Following our arrival and registration, Ron and I joined other ACORN delegates, Coya Mobley, Elizabeth Ratliff, Herbert Morris, James Moreland, Sharon Patterson, Leroy Ferrell, Tina Martin Brown, Sharon Dirocco and Mary Scott, at a buffet dinner from 5:00 to 6:30 p.m.

The working dinner included the Opening Sessions, Agenda Review and Conference Goals. The session introduced ACORN issues and spokespersons, and reports on local campaign victories. I delivered the Georgia ACORN campaign report.

My report featured the Dillard-Winecoff Mortgage Fraud Campaign, and the Lea O'Neal case of environmental racism, and the chronology of sewer and flooding problems on Hermen Circle.

I also discussed a lawsuit brought by ACORN, Project Vote/Voting for America, the Georgia Coalition for the People's Agenda and the Georgia State Conferences of NAACP against Cathy Cox the Secretary of State for Georgia, for violating the National Voter Registration Act of 1993.

I closed with, "Georgia ACORN is also fighting the proposed

AT&T Bell South Merger. If allowed, this merger would create the largest communications monopoly in the country, and monopolies are not constrained by competition. They can raise prices on poor people with impunity. Georgia ACORN hopes the FCC will put the public interest before AT&T's interest."

Monday, March 12, 2007

The alarm went off at 6:05 AM. I walked downstairs and joined Roslyn Dodge, Joseph Sherman, Bonnie Mathias, Derrick Richardson, Rosa Lewis, and Angela Butler for breakfast. We ate at the Number Ten Thomas Restaurant from 7:00 to 8:00 a.m. At 8:30 a.m., I joined the other ACORN members and participated in various training sessions concerning the issues of the next day's actions. The Learning the Issues break-out sessions included: Issue No.1, ACORN's Working Families Agenda; Issue No.2, ACORN's Response to Katrina; Issue No.3. ACORN's Comprehensive Immigration Reform; and Issue No.4, Fighting Predatory Lending and Foreclosures.

The Learning the Issues sessions were an essential element in developing ACORN leaders. The issues training sessions were necessary to provide the membership with a uniform understanding of the issues they were fighting for, since ACORN was involved in multi-issues and multiple campaigns across the country. ACORN members are not paid protesters instead they pay annual dues to demonstrate. A well-informed member is a motivated protester.

At 1:00 p.m., I eagerly loaded into a rented yellow school bus, along with Adrianna Jones, Billie Jo, Yolanda Warden, Ledora Gary, Yvonne Woods, Rose Robinson, Lashon Campbell, and Frankie Robinson. I pressed my knees snuggly against my chest as I struggled to fold my 6'3", 250-pound frame into a three-foot rectangular bus seat, which was spaced less than 18-inches apart.

Lunch was served on the yellow school buses en route to the next action. The boxed lunches consisted of turkey, ham and cheese cold cuts, served on day-old stale bread. A small bag of potato chips, a crisp apple and bottled water completed the meal. It was like summer camp, except this one was for adults.

Our buses arrived at the Federal Emergency Management Administration (FEMA) Office in Southwest Washington, DC, promptly at 1:30 p.m., on Capitol Hill. Vanessa Gueringer, fifty-two, from the Lower Ninth Ward office, led the rally at FEMA to Rebuild New Orleans in response to Katrina.

Local news cameras filmed Sarah Lott-Edwards, Veronica Edwards, Terrell Walker, Jamie Wilson, Erica Rambo and Bruce Cooper, as we symbolically rebuilt a *new house* made of paper maché bricks in front of FEMA Headquarters.

On cue, screaming ACORN protesters began to chant to the theme of Old McDonald:

"This is the way."
"You build a house."
"Build a house."
"Build a house."
"This is the way."
"You build a house."
"So early in the morning."

Following the FEMA action, our buses returned to the Washington Plaza Hotel, just in time for late afternoon and evening training sessions on Predatory Lending and Foreclosure Fraud Prevention. I met Jordan Ash, forty, the Director of ACORN Financial Justice Centers. A pudgy but pugnacious man with wire-framed glasses, Jordan was committed and smart. He always anticipated the next action or the next campaign ACORN should undertake.

Jordan opened the training session addressing the issue of reclaiming our homes and neighborhoods from foreclosure and predatory mortgage lending. "ACORN Financial Justice Centers were created in 2001, to respond to the financial needs of low and moderate income families. It plays a key role in ACORN's campaigns to fight predatory mortgage lending and abusive tax refund anticipation loans.

"Well before the explosion of subprime lending, ACORN financial justice campaigns had targeted what we believed were the predatory practices of three companies—Ameriquest, Household Finance, and Wells Fargo. Our strategy is simple and straightforward. We go after the largest subprime lender, and then number two, then three, and so on.

"We are currently in a campaign to protest Money Mart's predatory payday lending practices. The typical interest rate on a payday loan from Money Mart is 456%. Money Mart claims payday loans help people in a one-time emergency. But we think payday loans are set up so people can't pay them back and so are forced to repeatedly renew the loans and pay additional interest."

Chris Jones, a stout fifty-seven year-old man, stood before the group. He was from California ACORN, with worn suntanned skin, and long white hair cut in a "shag"—tapered in the front but thick in the back. Chris possessed an easy going and laid back demeanor, like an ex-surfer dude who became a labor and community activist.

Chris described ACORN's Fight Against Predatory Lending and ACORN's Direct Action Campaigns against Wells Fargo Finance and Household Finance. "Wells Fargo was the main target of 1,500 marching ACORN members through downtown Los Angeles during the ACORN National Convention back in 2004.

"Maude Hurd stood on the sidewalk in front of the Wells Fargo building, within sight of the newly opened Walt Disney Concert Hall, and issued our demands."

Chris continued, "But these were not our usual demands to negotiate. This demand was for Wells to stop its predatory practices and to meet ACORN in court.

"Maude handed a copy of a lawsuit we filed that day to the highest Wells Fargo executive standing on the sidewalk challenging the bank's predatory practices."

Everyone in the banquet hall burst into laughter and cheered out loud. Chris laughed himself. "So can anyone tell me, exactly what is predatory mortgage lending?"

Puzzled looks crisscrossed the banquet hall, but no one offered an answer.

He answered himself. "It's the use of predatory practices to rob citizens of their home-based wealth, and they are not difficult to spot."

Chris outlined a litany of *warning signs* for consumers to identify predators, "High interest rates, way above those of prime lenders;

"Excessive points, late charges, and prepayment penalties which block people's ability to refinance out of a predatory loan without huge transaction costs;

"Credit insurance packing, in addition to other useless and discretionary products;

"Asset-based lending, a pernicious practice designed to strip away equity with a loan that is not based on the ability of the consumer to pay;

"Material misrepresentations, which essentially are a bait-and-switch tactic at closing;

"Loan flipping or multiple refinancing which pushes borrowers into a refinancing cycle with rising rates and closing costs they can't afford;

"Balloon payments, with a large *death sentence* payment due at the end of the loan;

"High closing costs paid by wrapping excessive fees into the loan, forcing interest payments to be made on them;

"Deceptive loan servicing, unsatisfactory loan statements that leave payments and accounts a guessing game;

"Bogus home improvement loans;

"Loan broker fees which siphon commissions from the loan proceeds, often without borrower notice or understanding;

"Signing over the deed, a gratuitous offer to protect the homeowner from foreclosure, but often intended to rob the owner of the house;

"Stop-payment advice, recommendations to stop payments, jeopardizing the note and forcing foreclosure; and

"Plain old discrimination, charging of different rates to women, older adults, and minorities for loans."

"Predatory practices run the range of the imagination, as unscrupulous, often unlicensed and unsupervised brokers see a pile of money for the taking in the form of built-up equity." Chris said.

"And what's worse is the refusal of corporations or the government to protect citizens against the abuse. Jordan lamented. "But we are ACORN; that's what we do. Ameriquest was the centerpiece of the ACORN National Convention in Philadelphia in 2002, and we forced them into a settlement, but Chicago-based Household Finance was a much harder target."

Chris commented, "Household was a longtime player with a broad product line, including credit cards. They specialized in subprime lending, and for all of the billions of dollars worth of mortgages they handle, there are predatory issues with far too many. Their attitude toward our actions was to stand and fight, so this campaign was long and drawn out."

Jordan said, "We threw the kitchen sink at Household Finance with actions at lending offices all around the country. We collected cases of actual predatory practices and turned them over to consumer advocates and attorneys general all over the country.

"But William Aldinger stood his ground, despite everything we did. We could not budge Household's Chief Executive, either through the front door or behind the scenes."

Chris said, "So in a last ditch effort, we went to court with a class action suit in various jurisdictions. After us, a group of attorneys general from a number of states filed suit, using many of the cases in their states that ACORN had initiated."

Claudie Harris, fifty-four, stood 5'6", a dark skinned woman with close-cropped salt and pepper hair. The Chair from Kansas City ACORN had an infectious smile and wore designer glasses. She joined in. "How does predatory lending affect our communities?"

"It is devastating Georgia!" I shouted. "The average bank robber in America gets away with less than $5,000 in cash. But people can steal $40,000 to $50,000 or more, from the bank or a homeowner at the closing table. And they can do it 15 to 20 times a month."

Claudie motioned for me to come up and take the microphone. And

I fired up the audience by telling the story about InterBank Funding Companies and Georgia ACORN's Mortgage Fraud epidemic. "Predatory lending is giving loans to people under terms when you know they can't afford them. Predatory lending is wrong, but Mortgage Fraud is a crime."

Sharon Dirocco, fifty-one, and chair from Providence, Rhode Island ACORN, discussed current predatory practices and equity stripping. "Predatory mortgages strip homeowners of their wealth by financing exorbitant fees and prepayment penalties into the loan," she said. "Congress should adopt the policy currently in effect in several states which limits points and fees to 5% of the loan amount."

Claudie discussed lenders making loans people can't afford to pay back. "Lenders should not put families into loans they cannot afford to pay back, either from the time the loan starts or when the interest rate increases and the payment goes up."

She said, "Legislation should require that lender's verify the borrower's ability to repay the loan."

Chris discussed steering borrowers to worse loans than they qualify for. "Too many borrowers with good credit, especially African-Americans and Latinos, are being charged higher rates and fees than they qualify for and deserve."

He said, "Legislation must prohibit lenders from steering a borrower into a worse loan than what they qualify for."

Karen Inman stood. A seventy, a silver-haired lawyer, teacher and former union organizer, Karen was the Secretary from Minnesota ACORN. "There is no limit to the types of scams that predatory lenders will think of, so we need legislation that will cover any predatory practices that they come up with in the future."

She said, "We need to require loan officers and brokers to have a duty of good faith and fair dealing to conduct their business honestly and carefully, and not to harm the customer."

The President of ACORN Housing, Alton Bennett, fifty-two, stood 5'10" with brown skin and a bushy mustache. The former Treasurer of ACORN said, "Half of all people who lost their homes to foreclosure never talked with their lender or servicer. "These people feel powerless and frightened. A housing counselor can help them find affordable solutions. ACORN Housing found that many foreclosures could be prevented." Bennett concluded, "There needs to be a major, ongoing funding commitment to support housing counseling for people at risk of foreclosure."

Karen agreed, "Federal Legislation is a new opportunity for Congress, but any legislation needs to address both current and possible future practices, and fund foreclosure prevention counseling."

Immediately following the evening training session, Maude Hurd and Jordan Ash convened the financial justice team to discuss the pre-action strategy for the Mortgage Banker's Association. They asked me to join the group.

"The plan of action is our tactical attack plan. It defines the logistics and objectives," Jordan lamented.

The shapely Julie Smith, forty-four, and a community leader from Cleveland, joined in. She stood 5'6" with red hair and freckles. "The address is 1919 Pennsylvania Avenue, and we are going to arrive right after the Capital Hill March. It's a large commercial building with limited street access," She said.

Jordan replied, "They don't own the entire building, so we can't pull up outside and start protesting."

Julie retorted, "The Mortgage Banker's Association is on the eighth floor. So we've got to figure out how to get enough of our folks all the way up there, if this is going to work."

Jordan said, "We scouted the building today. Security is light; there are only one or two security guards at one central station in the lobby.

Chris replied, "The key is to get to these central elevator banks, which are directly behind the guard posts on the Mezzanine level."

Jordan said, "The lobby configuration is a large open atrium space, with glass doors leading out to the street on the north and southwest sides."

Julie pointed at the hand-drawn map. "There is another entrance directly connected from the Starbuck's here on the east. And there may be another entry point somewhere on the north."

Maude replied, "Okay, so here's the plan, the busses will arrive at 3:30 p.m. and park around the corner. We will assemble outside the buses and gather at three or four rally points near the lobby."

"We can completely fill up the Starbucks," Julie said. "And if there's another restaurant or store with a lobby entrance, we can scout it out and gather our members there too."

Chris placed his hand on my shoulder. "We can check that out. And we'll slowly file in and ease our way up to the Mezzanine level at 3:50 p.m."

Jordan eyed his watch. "At 3:55 we will send in two members—a couple of cute ones—to flirt with and distract the security guards."

The team chuckled at Jordan's suggestion.

Chris hastily sketched a diagram of the floor-plan. "If this works, then we should have our initial group properly positioned to get to the elevators and make their way up to the eighth floor."

Claudie said, "At 4:00 p.m. the rest of the demonstrators should flood the lobby from every direction and start to protest inside the lobby and outside the building."

Jordan said, "The key is to distract the guards. If they shut down the elevators before we get enough folks to the eighth floor, then we are sunk."

I replied, "So we've got to make the guards think the demonstration is downstairs or outside, while we slip in enough members to the elevators to make it upstairs."

"That's right," said Julie. "The elevators let out into a waiting area by the reception desk."

Chris said, "If they don't shut off the elevator, we should be able to quietly fill the eighth floor waiting area by 4:15 or 4:20 at the latest."

Maude concluded, "So as each team makes it upstairs, we wait, and sit quietly until the other members join us. We won't move until we completely fill up the waiting area... *and then* we rush back into the MBA offices and cubicles."

Militant Action

Tuesday, March 13, 2007

I gulped hot coffee and stale doughnuts and then joined ACORN protestors who boarded local school buses after breakfast. We rode to Capitol Hill for the National Day of Action with dozens of charter buses filled with ACORN members from Maryland, Philadelphia, New Jersey and New York.

They had been arriving at Friendship Baptist Church from 8:00 a.m. to 10:00 a.m. ACORN organizers passed out pastel colored flyers containing the words of various protest chants. We practiced the songs and chants on the buses like sheet music in a gospel choir. Everything was organized and orchestrated—right down to the songs and the protest chants. Since this was a day of multiple actions, all the materials were segregated and color-coded. The seamless operation was a marvel of organization, coordination and logistics.

The ACORN protest army was a well-oiled machine. The school buses converged on Capitol Hill. Irene Holcomb, Estella Willis West, Maxine Nelson, William Cornelius, Karen Inman, Sunday Alabi, Sherman Wilburn, Daniel Stewart, Betty Jackson and I joined the swelling crowd of thousands of red clad protestors.

We assembled on the porch in front of the Russell Senate Office Building and waited for the introduction of the Healthy Families Act. Senator Ted Kennedy and Representative Rosa DeLauro, addressed the group and announced they had just introduced our legislation on the floor.

The gathering crowd roared:

"We are."

"ACORN!"

"We are."

"ACORN!"

During the rally I noticed two ACORN members wearing Pine Bluff nametags—my hometown. I walked over and introduced myself to Maxine Nelson, who was sixty-four years-old, and a brown-skinned woman with coal-black hair. She was wearing a Pine Bluff ACORN tee-shirt. The National Secretary of ACORN, Maxine stood 5'9" with a medium build; next to her was Irene Holcomb, a sixty-six year-old former school teacher, turned public servant, and whose career progressed according to the four "Cs"— from cotton fields, to college; then classrooms, to City Council.

"Good to meet you, Michael." Maxine said, and paused to study my name badge. "You're Dr. McCray's son. I work with your mother all the time."

My mother had earned a Ph.D in housing and was nationally respected as the Dean of the School of Agriculture, Fisheries and Human Sciences at the University of Arkansas at Pine Bluff. She had worked with community housing groups and community based financial institutions for decades. "If you know my mother, then you know I came to community activism honestly. I'm a second generation community development practitioner," I smirked.

At 1:00 p.m., after the rally, Ron Sykes and I joined a larger group of ACORN protesters, including Karen Mendoza, Nina Nunez, Sherridan Scwartz, Kenneth Clebourne, Eric Henry, Vermadean Griffen, De Phillips, Margarita Alvarez, Beatriz Quinones, Nancy Pyle, Erica Young, Victor Bernal, Lucille Puckett and Yvonne Stafford. We turned at the Russell Office Building and streamed down Massachusetts Avenue to the U.S. Citizenship and Immigration Services.

Eliseo Medina, the Vice President of the Service Employees

International Union, greeted our group and demanded, "Stop the Fee Increase for Citizenship!" Medina addressed the crowd and local media from 1:15 to 1:45 p.m. Afterward, we left the USCIC and marched toward the Capitol Dome. The whole day was a marvel in coordination and efficiency. Dozens of smaller protests in close vicinity combined and culminated with thousands of red clad protesters converging on the U.S. Capital.

In a scene reminiscent of Civil Rights Marches in the south, the streets and sidewalks around the Capitol overflowed with a sea of scarlet-clad ACORN demonstrators. Democratic Congressional Leaders joined the rally at the Upper Senate Park before the gathering, chanting crowd:

"First things first."
"First things first."
"Just say, No!"
"To the Bush budget!"
"First things first."
"First things first."

We exited the Capital Grounds and loaded on the buses at 3:15 p.m., to prepare for the action to Stop Predatory Lending and Foreclosures. All of the previous actions had been street protests or outdoor rallies. This action was different. This action was dangerous; it was the only militant action scheduled during the legislative conference week. This time we were marching into the belly of the beast so to speak and taking on Wall Street, itself. The Mortgage Bankers Association, a trade association, represented the real estate finance industry—mortgage companies, mortgage brokers, commercial banks, thrifts, life insurance companies and other leaders in the mortgage finance field.

At 3:35 p.m., Chris Jones and I walked into a Chinese restaurant adjoining the MBA headquarters building. Nonchalantly, Chris ordered a Budweiser from the bar, while I scanned the premises for a rear exit. A neon exit sign appeared over a silk oriental screen, concealing the door from plain sight. I re-joined Chris at the bar and nodded, indicating we were ready to go. I ordered an Amstel Light beer and waited.

Chris called Julie, and whispered. "Eureka! Send some protesters to the Chinese restaurant on the east side. We've got a rear entrance which leads into the lobby."

"How many people do you think can we stage there?" She asked.

"We could get twenty or thirty folks in here before they start getting too suspicious," Chris replied.

"Okay, we're on the way." Chris hung up the phone, took a sip of beer and looked me directly in the eye. "Here comes the cavalry."

We passed the time talking about community organizing and ACORN, while we eagerly waited for the other protestors to arrive. Chris reassured me, "By the way, you did real good in the training session last night. You stepped up and fired up the room."

"Thanks, man. I wasn't sure if everyone could follow what I was trying to say."

"Oh no. You broke it down," replied Chris. "In fact, you opened my eyes to some new things about predatory loan fraud."

Wiping beer foam from his lips, Chris asked, "Is this your first national conference with ACORN?"

Tentatively, I responded, "Yes. How could you tell?

"Don't worry; it wasn't obvious. I've never seen you before," Chris said. "It's important to attend national conferences because you don't understand the power of ACORN until you've participated in a national action."

"Why not?" I asked.

"Don't get me wrong, local actions are important, but when you see massive, coordinated direct actions, that's when you really understand what you're a part of now."

I sipped my beer, "It all happened so fast for me. We organized a successful action on Juneteenth last year, and a few hundred folks came out to fight Predatory Lending and Mortgage Fraud."

"That's a good action."

"The next thing I knew, Chris, I went from being a brand new dues paying member, to being an alternate delegate for the national board."

Chris paused, "You know what? It's an organizing technique. That's how ACORN works. If you demonstrate you are a worker and you can successfully pull off an action, then your organizer will push you forward in leadership."

"Oh, really?"

"Soon you start to feel like you're on a roll. They send you to state meetings and national conferences, and then you start to feel like you can make a difference."

"That's exactly right. That's how I feel," I replied.

"At least that's what happened to me," Chris confided. "I was sitting at home, out of work, one day, and I got a knock on my door. It was a couple of young kids organizing for ACORN."

"What happened?"

"We talked for a while, and I didn't think much about what they were saying because they were so young. These were kids, you know. So what could they tell me about my neighborhood anyway?

"I didn't sign up on the spot, but I did agree to come to a neighborhood meeting and see what was going on. It wasn't like I didn't have the time."

We laughed together.

"Ok, so what did you do?"

"Once I got to the meeting and I met the members, not just the organizers, and we talked about neighborhood issues. The members were from all age ranges and I related to them more than the organizers. By the end of the night we were planning an action, on some company, for the next week."

I sipped my beer. "How did you feel about that?"

"I was like, man, this is something. I'd never seen a neighborhood go from complaining about a problem to devising an action plan so quickly."

"What happened on your action?"

Chris paused. "It went off like clockwork; it was amazing. And the organizers liked how easily I related to the members and to the press. So they recommended I go on a state action the following month."

"Really?"

"I started thinking like, man, this ACORN thing is for real. In the space of a few months, I had joined ACORN, done my first local action, and I was protesting on the steps of the California State Assembly with hundreds of protesters from all across the state."

"That's simply amazing, and it happened that fast?"

"I was leading the demonstration and found myself confronting the State Assembly and shouting, 'We're fired up and we're not taking it no more.' "Then a television reporter shoved a microphone in my face and asked, 'What is your name, sir?' Nobody in the press ever asked for my name before. And then, 'What do you think about this, Mr. Jones?' Nobody ever asked for my opinion before either. It was great!"

"Sounds like it, Chris," I chimed in.

He said, "This was an adventure. That's why it is so important to get people involved in organizational activities and what the organizer has to communicate to new recruits.

"Not every member will give his name on television, that's a bonus. But for once, because I was working with ACORN, what I was doing meant something."

"You're right, Chris, that is important,"

"It was truly remarkable. Through ACORN, we've got seventeen bills signed into law, which just goes to show—that if you can do the work and demonstrate leadership, you can move up quickly in ACORN. Small victories, immediate success and coordinated direct action keep people motivated. Unlike other groups, ACORN is not just talk."

The restaurant filled with two-dozen eager demonstrators. We checked our watches at 4:05 p.m. We paid the check and slipped out the rear door into the glass atrium lobby, followed by dozens of ACORN protesters.

We joined the group of ACORN protestors who had swarmed the building, pushing and shoving their way to the center elevator bank. Unsure if we would actually make it to the top floor, we fidgeted nervously as we awaited our fate. I took the longest elevator ride of my life filled with anxiety.

ACORN executed its plan of action with military precision. Chris and I worked our way up to the eight-floor Mortgage Bankers Association and waited silently, accompanied by a growing group of protesters.

"Hello, can I help you?" asked a young receptionist. She tried to greet the first set of visitors—Donald Coulter, Merlene Coulter, Linda Scamaccia, Steven Simmons, Claudie Harris, Hana Sabree, Karen Taylor, Kay Bisnath, Julie Smith, Mary Keith and Yvonne Jackson, who all stood deafly mute, and waited for reinforcements.

The receptionist became nervous and concerned by the sheer number and low-income garb of the crowd; she immediately called for management assistance.

The manager, Kirk Faultenheur, rushed out to the reception desk and tried to placate the crowd. "You guys didn't need to do all of this. If you had called first, we could have set up an appointment," he told us.

The ACORN demonstrators began to chant in unison:

"Predatory lenders."
"Criminal offenders."
"Predatory lenders."
"Criminal offenders."

A flustered Kirk asked, "So who is your leader? Who do I talk to?"

The protesters seemed oblivious to his requests, and the chants grew progressively louder.

Sarcastically, like a spoiled child, Kirk taunted. "So nobody wants to talk. You've come all this way and nobody actually wants to talk. You just want to sit here and shout."

The crowd parted as Maude Hurd emerged in the front of the group; she was flanked by Jordan Ash and Pedro Rivas, thirty-three, a young, confident and extremely ambitious Hispanic wearing a long black ponytail, who loved having his picture taken.

"Not one." Maud said. "If you want to talk, you talk to us all!"

The emphatic crowd cheered:

"We are."

"ACORN!"

"We are."

"ACORN!"

"But we can't meet with all of you at once." Kirk repeated, "Who are your leaders?"

Our strategy was to prevent the officials from saying anything, but instead, to get in their face and start banging on the desks and making demands, never permitting them to interrupt or make a statement. The only time we would let them talk was after we got through. With that careful indoctrination, the protesters stormed into the waiting area, identified themselves, and began an orchestrated tirade consisting of militant demands, but refused to let them say anything.

"We want to see either Jonathan Kempner, President and CEO; John Robbins, Chairman; Kieran Quinn, Chairman-elect; or David Kittle, Vice Chair;" said Maude.

Perplexed by our brazenness and visibly flustered, Kirk stood at a loss for words. But he never had a chance to say anything else.

The crowd exploded in a chorus: "And we won't take—NO, for an answer!"

At which point, the financial justice team emerged from the crowd. Maude gestured toward the protestors and demanded, "WE will meet with you, but THEY have to be in the room."

Sandra Wiekerson, Muriel Handy-Jones, Maria Bueno, Jackie Young, Michelle Young, Brian Dunn, Jesus Salcido, Carlos Rodriguez, Eileen Graham, Daniel Arellano, Gwendolyn Adams, Cheryl Diggins, and Earl Fortenberry stood at attention.

Kirk hesitated. And more protestors demanded, "Is it yes—or is it no?"

"Of course it's, yes," said Kirk.

Maude replied, "That's all we wanted to know."

The MBA Executive walked slowly to a large conference room overlooking Pennsylvania Avenue. On Maude's command, the protesters quieted down and followed the MBA Executive into the mahogany boardroom.

Paul Green, fifty-nine, and the SVP of Corporate Relations, along with four other MBA executives joined Kirk and took seats at the head of the table. The ACORN financial team, Maude Hurd, Chris Jones, Ronald Sykes, Reverend Gloria Swieringa, Claudie Harris, Alicia Gaddis, Julie Smith, Marcel Reid, and I, took the remaining seats around the large conference table.

Four-dozen other protesters stood behind them completely filling the excess space; it was standing room only. ACORN protestors overflowed the conference room, filled the hallway and continued the demonstration in the MBA offices and waiting area.

Reverend Gloria began, "We are members of ACORN, the nation's largest community organization of low and moderate income families. And we are here from all across the country. We are from the neighborhoods that have been hardest hit by predatory lending and foreclosure."

Alicia Gaddis, a sixty-two year-old Hispanic woman, with brownish hair, explained. Nervous and quick-tempered, she stood 5'2". "We're here because the United States is suffering a foreclosure crisis. 1.2 million foreclosures were filed last year—way up from 900,000 foreclosures in 2005."

Claudie Harris said, "The problems have gotten out of control. Foreclosures don't just hurt individual families; they hurt entire neighborhoods through increases in vacant homes and the problems associated with that. We are here to foreclose on the Mortgage Banker's Association, like they have foreclosed on so many of us."

Paul Green tried to strike a more conciliatory tone, "The MBA invests in communities across the nation by ensuring the continued strength of the nation's residential and commercial real estate markets; expanding homeownership and extending access to affordable housing to all Americans and supporting financial literacy efforts."

Julie Smith interrupted him. "We want lenders to stop foreclosures! We want a one year moratorium on all foreclosures involving predatory loans—loans made that the homeowner couldn't afford or were set up for the borrower to fail.

"This includes adjustable rate loans where the initial teaser rate qualified the borrower, so-called stated income loans which had no income verification, and loans that were made without escrows for taxes and insurance."

"ACORN is also calling on lenders to change their practices regarding stated income and adjustable rate loans." I added, "And investigate and stop Mortgage Fraud and non-judicial foreclosures for good measure."

Marcel Reid, Chair of DC ACORN added, "We want the Mortgage Bankers Association to agree to a meeting with ACORN and to set a date within two weeks, in writing!"

Reluctantly, the MBA Executives agreed to a follow-up meeting on April 6, 2007. We proudly paraded around the outside of the commercial office building.

On the ride back to the Washington Plaza Hotel, I heard one of the members saying, "That's the way to get things done; you tell them off and don't give them a chance to say nothing."

Wednesday, March 14, 2007

I ate breakfast at 7:00 a.m., along with Ronald Pughbey, Noelia "Nelly" Jimenez, Gladys Conde, Liz Bidot, Beverly Campbell, Eddy Weatherspoon and Tamecka Pierce. We then loaded on buses destined for St. Mark's Episcopal Church. Hundreds of eager demonstrators arrived on Third Street from 8:30 to 10:00 a.m. The ACORN Georgia Delegation, Ronald Sykes, Harvey Glenn, and I, listened to ACORN organizers.

We received last minute instructions for our lobby visits, particularly on ACORN's *First Things First* agenda. "The Emergency Campaign for America's Priorities is a nationwide campaign of national and grassroots organizations committed to reversing the Bush Administration's policy of drastic cuts to programs which primarily benefited the poor and middle class in order to finance tax cuts which only benefited the wealthy and special interests."

Gee Gee Hartman, Erica Miller, Patricia Hollins, Gail Scott, Lorita Jackson, Bianca Garza, Miguel Almaguer, Maria Garcia, Jose Garcia, Thomas Henry and hundreds of ACORN members fanned-out across Capitol Hill from 11:00 a.m. to 5:00 p.m., and visited the Congressional and Senate Offices of our respective states.

Georgia ACORN was pitch perfect when we visited the congressional and senate offices of David Scott (D-GA), famed civil rights icon John Lewis (D-GA), Sanford Bishop (D-GA), Saxby Chambliss (R-GA) and Johnny Isakson (R-GA).

Ron declared, "Our First Things First agenda is a plan to fully meet pressing human needs over five years and assure everyone pays their fair share."

I said, "The First Things First agenda is based on our shared values that every American deserves the opportunity to succeed, to have access to adequate healthcare, food, housing, education and the economic security to live with dignity."

Following the long day of intense congressional visits, Ron and I attended an ACORN reception honoring Senator Ted Kennedy in the Dirksen Senate Office Building at 5:00 p.m., along with Tammie Pursley, Judy Link, Sophia Tesch, Brook Giese, John Roberts, Diana St. Marie, Jeninah Aragon, Yolanda Pena, and Joanna Landreth. We returned to the Washington Plaza Hotel and gave our report on the Congressional office visits from Georgia, prior to the closing banquet at 7:30 p.m.

The Federal Hall featured rich interior décor, with tone-on-tone carpet, in rich shades of burgundy, melon and gold. It was filled with hundreds of ACORN members adorned in bright red ACORN tee shirts. Intermixed within the ACORN crowd were smatterings of royal purple and gold tee-shirts which read S-E-I-U Local 100.

Two-dozen Service Employees International Union members joined in the ACORN Legislative Policy Conference at the closing Banquet. Congressional Representatives Maxine Waters, sixty-nine, and Charles

Rangel, seventy-seven, were featured speakers at the banquet. They were long time ACORN supporters because California and New York were ACORN strongholds.

ACORN National President, Maude Hurd, introduced the special guests, "Maxine Waters has been a Democratic member of the United States House of Representatives, since 1991. She is the most senior of the twelve African-American women currently serving in the United States Congress.

"She enrolled at Los Angeles State College graduating with a sociology degree in 1970. By 1973, Maxine went to work as chief deputy to newly-elected City Councilman David Cunningham, Jr.

"Afterwards, Maxine entered the California State Assembly in 1976, where she worked for divestment of state pension funds from any businesses active in South Africa—until it stopped apartheid. Maxine was elected to the U.S. House of Representatives following the retirement of Augustus Hawkins (D-CA), in 1990."

Maxine Waters took the podium and thanked ACORN for our support, and recounted how she first met Maude Hurd when ACORN protestors disrupted a closed congressional hearing when Maxine was a freshman in congress.

ACORN showed up in force for the hearings, but its members were denied the right to speak by Republican lawmakers who held the majority. Dozens of ACORN members stood in line the night before the hearings and squeezed out paid lobbyists from the seats in the hearing room.

The hearing began at 9:45 a.m. when a female demonstrator interrupted Joe Kennedy and said, "Madam Chair we are from ACORN and we want to save CRA.

Representative Marge Roukema (R-NJ) told the woman she was out of order and tried to shut her down. They tried to clear the room but Maude refused to be silenced. She insisted on speaking at the hearing room. The police grabbed her when she tried to testify, slapped handcuff's on her, and locked her up in the Capitol Hill jail. It was the most

terrifying thing, but in order to cope Maude and three other ACORN
members sang freedom songs.

"They were finally released after a call from Massachusetts representative Joe Kennedy (D-MA) and a rainy day jailhouse visit from yours truly.
As they left a guard told them, "I don't know who you are—but you must
know somebody important.""

"Maude and ACORN protesters defied the congress and continued to
protest inside the congressional hearing room. Brand new to Congress,
I was so impressed by their boldness, I visited them in the Capital Hill
jail. That's how I met Maude and the *ACORN Three*, and I've supported
ACORN every since," concluded Maxine Waters.

Maude stood and smiled, "We are up here rubbing elbows with powerful people. But we are a force to be reckoned with. We're ordinary people
doing extraordinary things."

The enthusiastic crowd cheered and applauded both Maxine Waters
and Maude Hurd. On cue, DC ACORN Chair, Marcel Reid stood to
introduce Representative, Charles Rangel, the next speaker, but before
she took the podium, Marcel whispered a demand to Maude, who then
flashed a tight-lipped smile. "We need a new Head Organizer for DC and
if you don't get us a new one now, DC ACORN is prepared to disrupt
this entire banquet in front of Maxine Waters, Charles Rangel and the
media."

Marcel walked to the podium and introduced the next guest, "Charlie
came to Washington in 1971, succeeding Adam Clayton Powell, Jr. He
is the most senior member of the state's congressional delegation and a
founding member of the Congressional Black Caucus.

"Over the past forty years, Charlie Rangel has led the fight in Congress
against drug abuse and trafficking, agitated for fairer sentencing, worked
to limit the spread and use of illegal guns, and fought for affordable housing, urban renewal, and economic prosperity in his district and across the
United States.

"He participated in the 1965, Selma to Montgomery marches, marching for four days even though he had planned only a brief appearance.

Early in his tenure, Congressman Rangel served as a member of the House Judiciary Committee, during the hearings on the articles of impeachment of the then-President Richard Nixon.

"A member of Alpha Phi Alpha, the first intercollegiate Greek-letter fraternity established for African-Americans, Charlie is a member of the fraternity's World Policy Council, which is a think tank whose purpose is to expand Alpha Phi Alpha's involvement in politics and social and current policy to encompass international concerns.

"Charlie became chairman of the powerful House Ways and Means Committee in January 2007—the first African-American to do so. He was the principal author of the five-billion dollar Federal Empowerment Zone demonstration project to revitalize urban neighborhoods.

"And he is the author of the Low Income Housing Tax Credit, responsible for financing ninety percent of the affordable housing built in the United States in the last decade. He championed the Work Opportunity Tax Credit, which provided thousands of jobs for underprivileged youngsters, veterans, and ex-offenders."

SEIU is ACORN

High-pitched feedback from the public address system pierced the thundering applause while Charles Rangel was being greeted with a standing ovation. The Harlem Congressman took the microphone following Marcel Reid's rousing introduction and stood before a sea of ACORN members and supporters.

Congressman Rangel recounted how he transformed from wayward youth to a public servant, "I was a high school dropout, but I enlisted in the United States Army, and I served with distinction from 1948 to 1952.

"I was a member of the all-black 503rd Field Artillery Battalion in the 2nd Infantry Division fighting a rear-guard action in the Battle of Kunu-Ri during the Korean War. Half of the battalion was killed in the overall battle. I was awarded a Purple Heart for my wounds and the Bronze Star with Valor for my actions in the face of death. After Kunu Ri—I mean this with all my heart. I have never, ever had a bad day since."

Rangel viewed his time in the Army, away from the poverty of his youth, as a major turning point in his life, "When I was exposed to a different life, even if the life was just the Army, I knew damn well I couldn't go back to the same life I had left."

Ronald Sykes and I rejoined the DC and Maryland ACORN members at a banquet dinner table, along with Marcel Reid, and Louise Davis, a seventy-five year-old DC ACORN member. She was a fair-skinned woman with deep and wide roots in the community. Louise had worked at the Dirksen Senate Office Building and had been with ACORN for 20 years.

At fifty, Sonya Merchant-Jones, the co-chair of Baltimore ACORN, was a glamorous but corpulent woman. Always fashionably well dressed, Sonya looked more like a plus-sized, Lane Bryant mode, rather than the typical ACORN member. Along with Mildred Brown, sixty-seven, a handsome and well-maintained woman, she was both lively and gracious. The Legislative Director for ACORN and a former National President, Mildred knew and worked Capitol Hill effortlessly, although she had deep concerns about ACORN.

Ron Sykes worked along with Marcel but he reported to Mildred, as a legislative aid in the DC ACORN Office. Ron whispered, "Mildred was a former National President. She always tried to help the membership. She even stood up to senior management once or twice."

"Oh?"

"Mildred believed she was an actual president," Ron smirked. "She only served one term."

I noticed a group of purple and gold clad visitors as dinner began. They were service workers from the SEIU union. I asked Ron, "Why are they here?"

Ron dropped his fork. "From time to time, various policy groups attend ACORN conferences to show solidarity and to solicit our support."

I followed up. "But Ron, they're a labor union. What do they have to do with civil rights?"

"They're just like us. Service workers are either under-paid or minorities. Besides, Wade is a big shot in the SEIU."

"Why?"

Mildred said, "Let me give you some history. ACORN started in the 1970s organizing welfare mothers; by the 1980s we were organizing workers. In neighborhood meeting after meeting, our members started raising their hands and asking how they could get help on their jobs."

"Once jobs and income became an increasing focus of ACORN's

work, the lack of interest in low-wage workers by traditional unions became glaring."

"But why wouldn't a traditional union want to organize low-income service workers?" I asked.

Marcel replied, "First of all, -No- sustainable labor union business model is based on collecting dues from among those least able to pay them."

I agreed, "Makes a lot of sense."

She said, "The craft and trade unions often ignored poor and minority service workers."

"Why, Marcel?"

"Traditional labor unions are not concerned with organizing low-wage workers. When they talk about organizing the poor it is based on nostalgia, a wistful look back to the labor organizers of the C.I.O. during the great depression," she said.

I conceded, "You may have a point, Marcel. Early labor organizers were revolutionary activists. They were radicals, and the C.I.O. labor organizing drive was one of many activities. People like Powers Hapgood, Henry Johnson, and Lee Pressman organized vast sectors of middle-class America to support their programs."

"They are long gone now. Any resemblance between them and the present professional labor organizer is in name and title only." Marcel said, "Today's professional labor union organizers often turn out to be sorry community organizers. It's not the same thing."

"What do you mean?" I asked.

"Labor organizing is easier because everything is definite. Labor organizing is tied to fixed issues and discussion points, whether it's demands on wages, pensions, vacation periods, or other working conditions. Everything is anchored to particular contract dates."

"That's right."

"Organizing the masses is different. There are no fixed chronological points or definite issues. The demands are always changing; the situation is always fluid. Most of the goals are not expressed in concrete terms of dollars and hours; instead, they are constantly changing and psychological."

"I see what you mean, Marcel."

Mildred said, "Traditional labor organizers lose their minds when they try to organize a community, which is how the SEIU became the fastest growing service union in America—by using ACORN's model. It's not like traditional labor organizers didn't care, but more like they lack the capacity or the background to understand this type of work. Most unions do not have active organizing departments on the local union level, and even on the national or international level in some cases."

Marcel said, "But we're different; we're an organization of lower-income members. Our community organizing method is street-to-street and door-to-door. We already knew how to reach and organize these folks."

"Exactly," replied Mildred. "ACORN helped establish the United Labor Unions, an independent union which organized lower-wage workers in Boston, New Orleans, Philadelphia, Detroit, and Chicago. These cities have all become ACORN strongholds."

"So ACORN started to build independent unions to address the issues our members were having in their workplaces—whether home health workers, hotel workers, or fast food workers. These independent unions later merged into the Service Employees International Union in 1984."

Still curious, I asked, "So what happened to them? Why did they merge?"

Mildred confided, "The ULU was outmatched in financial, legal and political resources, as a result of drawn-out efforts under the National Labor Relations Act and legal delays in creating bargaining units.

"The ULU members voted to affiliate with the Service Employees International Union, which supported lower-wage worker organizing and re-chartered the locals in Boston, New Orleans, and Chicago as SEIU locals."

Ron leaned in. "So that's how ACORN started SEIU Locals 100 and 880 in New Orleans and Chicago?"

"Correct," said Mildred. "SEIU Local 880 in Chicago prevailed before the NLRB which allowed housekeepers and home health aides representation elections. The union won handily."

"That's great."

Mildred said, "Organizing home healthcare workers into unions was essential to our early work in Boston, and later the key to building the local in Chicago.

"Local 880 continued to organize other private-sector home health employers in the Chicago area, knocking on doors in housing projects and working closely with ACORN organizers."

Marcel said, "And the Head Organizer who's responsible for Chicago is a sister."

Surprised, "A Black woman's in charge?"

Marcel replied, "Not a sista—but a white woman. Her name is Madeline Talbot. She's Chicago rough and Chicago tough, and the best strategist and organizer in ACORN."

"Why do you say that?"

"She has spent over 25 years as an organizer for ACORN. She's been a field organizer, lead organizer and head organizer for many ACORN cities. In fact, Madeline Talbot organized Illinois and laid the groundwork which elected Carol Mosley Braun."

"The Senator?" I asked.

"Exactly! Wade may have organized protests, demonstrations and issue campaigns across the country but he's never elected a Black Woman to the U.S. Senate. Madeline Talbot has!

"She and her husband, Keith Kelleher the Head Organizer of SEIU Local 880, ran Chicago. Keith had been a field organizer, lead organizer and head organizer at ACORN, the United Labor Unions and the SEIU for over 20 years."

"So Chicago ACORN is a family affair?"

"True—but only one family counts in ACORN," Marcel whispered. "Once employees of SEIU Local 100 tried to organize themselves into a union, Wade used his wife and brother to plot an aggressive union-avoidance strategy.

I looked towards the purple and gold clad SEIU visitors. "So these guys are members from Wade Rathke's union locals?"

"Right," replied Ron. "They are showing support for ACORN. They are poor and working-class people, but they are well trained organizers."

"That's because we trained them," Marcel said.

"How so?" I asked.

Mildred replied, "ACORN provides support and training services for organized labor, through ACORN Community Labor Organizing Centers. ACLOC is active in Canada and the U.S. where it provides *basic training* for Service Employees International Union recruits in Houston and Boston who are then moved into Organizer Apprentice positions.

"SEIU Local 880 donated $60,118 to ACORN for membership services, because ACORN trained SEIU new recruits and SEIU used the ACORN model for community organizing. ACLOC is the single largest recipient of donations from SEIU to ACORN.

"In fact, SEIU mastered these strategies in ways which built huge memberships in Oregon, Washington, Michigan, Ohio, and Pennsylvania. The SEIU had two million workers in health care including hospitals, nursing homes and home care and government employees."

Due to this unheralded success, Andy Stern, fifty-six, the president of SEIU, tapped Wade Rathke, ACORN Chief Organizer and member of the SEIU Executive Board, to prepare strategies on how to re-envision labor federations and create comprehensive growth of organized labor based on the ACORN model. They shared the fundamental belief that there are alternative and effective models for building worker organizations—if not traditional unions. The reality is, in every meaningful way, SEIU is ACORN.

Thursday, March 15, 2007

The International Lounge offered superb dining options and soft, striped wall covering with custom-designed lighting. The cozy lounge overlooked the city's most celebrated swimming pool and offered spectacular views of Washington, DC.

Yvonne Stafford, the Chair of North Carolina ACORN, met Fannie Brown, sixty-two, thin but strong, and the Chair of California ACORN. A steely woman and former Black Panther, Fannie was unafraid and always spoke her mind. They joined Marcel Reid, Louise Davis, Ronald Sykes, and me by the fireplace and enjoyed the view of a landscaped pool deck, ideal for relaxing and al fresco dining.

Tense and suspicious, Terrell Walker, a young man from Cleveland, leaned towards me and whispered. "Hey man, I've been watching you. So are you a member—or an organizer?"

"I'm definitely a member." I told him.

Relieved, Terrell said, "Good! Man, I was feeling what you were saying about Mortgage Fraud and stuff," he said. "We're having so much trouble with our organizer, we can't get any of *our* issues off the ground."

"I know what you mean," I replied. "We are, too."

"That's a common complaint," said Louise. "A lot of chapters have trouble with their organizers."

"Why don't you fire him?"

Terrell said, "They won't let us."

Puzzled and confused, I asked, "Why not? I thought they work for us."

"They do, or at least they are supposed to," said Ron. "But national assigns the organizers to the local chapters."

Fannie agreed, "The chapters can complain, and they might say they got rid of them, but all they do is send them somewhere else."

"Yeah," Yvonne said, "to screw up someone else's chapter."

They all laughed aloud.

"Marcel is the only one who has ever fired an organizer," taunted Ron. "How did you do it, Marcel?"

Marcel blushed. "We had a young African organizer once. She was extremely elitist and arrogant; her name was Maduh Weisjnecki or something like that. She was from Ceylon, and didn't like poor people or respect the members. Dark skinned and exotic, Maduh acted like an African Princess."

"Anyway, one day she came to me complaining. 'Organizing is difficult. I'm not sure if I want to keep doing this. The fund raising and constant recruiting is overwhelming.'

So, I said, "Okay Madhu, I understand. I know what you mean. We accept your resignation." Madhu stuttered and stammered. 'What a minute Marcel. I didn't mean to...'"

"Don't worry about a thing Madhu, we've got it covered."

I immediately sent out a blast email to the ACORN National Board and Senior Staff officially accepting Madhu's resignation. The next day, Craig Robbins approached me in the DC ACORN Offices. Hesitantly, he asked, "I got your email, Marcel. What does the F, H & C by your name mean?"

"It means, Faith, Hope and Charity in all things," Marcel said. "I sign all my emails that way."

"Faith, Hope and Charity, that's nice." He said, "But you can't do what you said, Marcel."

"Do what?" she asked.

"You can't fire an organizer. Only ACORN National can do that," replied Craig.

Marcel replied, "I didn't fire her, -She- resigned. Besides—what's done is done, let's move on."

"Just to be sure," Marcel said, "I told Maude that DC ACORN was prepared to protest at the podium before the banquet if we didn't get a new organizer. And -she- told Craig Robinson."

Ron laughed out loud. "And that's how DC ACORN terminated their organizer."

I inquired, "So why don't we get a say in selecting our own organizers, anyway? And why aren't there any Black ones? Especially, since we are out here organizing Black communities?"

Ron said, "There are some, very few and they don't last too long. It's so bad, the few Black organizers did an action on ACORN a few years ago."

"You're kidding. What happened?" I asked,

Mildred said, "A few years ago a strong sister from New York, Bertha Lewis, actually led black organizers against ACORN's senior staff. "The Black Organizers were complaining about the working conditions, and the constant pressure to recruit new members in order to meet their membership quotas."

Marcel said, "ACORN's membership numbers drive everything. Our numbers are our strength, which is why we're always organizing."

Mildred said, "Anyway, one meeting started by asking how many organizers had been with ACORN for one month, three months, six months—you know. And we watched the hands go up and down.

The Black organizers started dropping off at six months. By the time they got up to two years -*No*- Black organizers remained. None had been with ACORN for more than two years."

Fannie agreed, "And that's the key; the organizers and staff act like ACORN is their organization—NOT OURS! They take the local leaders for granted and completely disregard the membership."

Yvonne argued, "It's been a constant struggle. We are the ones, as local leaders and state board chairs, who have to speak up and try to do something about it."

"That's right. Otherwise, the organizers won't listen to the local chapters at all," said Fannie.

I asked naively, "But how can they do that, if ACORN is a membership organization?"

"Well, they do it because they can," said Yvonne. "That's how it is around here."

"We represent the membership." Fannie said, "*We* are ACORN. The organizers' goal should be to create power for the members to use. It's about US, the organization membership. It's not about the organizers."

Marcel and Fannie noticed Steve Kest, fifty-five, the Executive Director of ACORN, talking to Jordan Ash and two well-dressed businessmen in the lobby of the Washington Plaza Hotel near the entrance to the International Lounge.

Fannie whispered to Marcel. "Yeah, I see them. There're about to get that money, honey."

Marcel said, "It looks like they are getting ready to meet with some banking or finance folks—probably Wells-Fargo Executives. And if Steve Kest is meeting with them, then they're about to ask for the big bucks."

Fannie said, "They won't know what hit them."

The best time for ACORN to negotiate with their targets is around the National Meetings and Conferences, when ACORN stages mass demonstrations. Which is what Alinsky meant by, "If you've got the numbers, show your strength with huge rallies and marches."

Marcel asked, "Michael in your campaign report, you said Georgia ACORN had joined with Project Vote and the NAACP or SCLC together on a lawsuit?"

"Yeah, we did." I said.

"That's interesting, Michael. ACORN usually won't partner with any other civil rights groups."

"Why not?"

Fannie quipped, "You never see ACORN on actions with civil rights organizations."

Yvonne agreed, "You're right. As a matter of fact, our organizers wouldn't let us collaborate with any of those groups, even if we wanted to."

"But, why not?" I asked. "If there is an issue which is important to the Black community, why wouldn't ACORN work with other groups to solve the problem?"

"We don't need them," replied Yvonne. "ACORN can pressure banks and major corporations into making large settlements. What can the civil rights groups actually do?"

More curious than ever, I asked, "Exactly, how large are these settlements?"

Yvonne replied, "We never know for sure, but ACORN could get millions, if not hundreds of millions in negotiated settlements."

"Really, that much?"

Fannie argued, "Yeah, and that's why ACORN won't collaborate with other civil rights groups—so Wade doesn't have to share the money."

Monday April 9, 2007

I steered my Chrysler Le Baron through darting traffic on my way to visit Carol Willis, fifty-seven, at El Rancho Bar and Restaurant. The Ranch was his favorite Little Rock watering hole, but I wanted to discuss the upcoming Presidential elections. We discussed the prospects for the upcoming campaign, and I stressed the need for Hillary Clinton to get a head start on African-American outreach.

At times a surly man, Willis had saffron skin with red undertones, and was the political consultant and Clinton campaign aide, long considered President Clinton's link to minority voters. He had once been a source of friction between Bill Clinton and black ministers who formed an important base of Democratic Party support.

During the 1996 re-elect campaign, Bill Clinton employed more Blacks in higher posts than any candidate, including the first minorities to hold state director and political director positions. As a result, the country's leading Black ministers and mayors had trended towards the Clinton campaign camp.

However, they did so out of familiarity or fatalism. Charles Rangel, a strong Clinton ally declared, "Of course I would support someone I knew and had liked and had worked with, versus someone I'd never heard of."

"We all knew the Clintons personally, or at least you knew their allies in the community." Rangel pondered, "Who was this Obama guy, aside from the resonant voice and the photogenic smile?"

Democratic Whip, James Clyburn, sixty-eight, agreed, "Being African-American, sure, my heart was with Obama, but I've got a head too. In the beginning, my head was with Hillary Clinton. The conventional wisdom was this campaign was going to be over in February."

Consequently, Senator Clinton consolidated an early lead in the Democratic presidential contest, while Senator Obama challenged her for fundraising supremacy and media attention. Additionally, Senator John Edwards beat her to the punch in introducing big policy proposals. But nothing her rivals did derailed Senator Clinton, which led them to begin aggressive new strategies aimed primarily at her.

Friday, April 13, 2007

I double checked the address as I drove past Little Rock Central High School, the Clinton Presidential Library, Little Rock River Market, and the Arkansas State Capitol before arriving at the Legacy Hotel and Suites.

A National Historic site, the Legacy Hotel had housed several well-known people including Winthrop Rockefeller, former President Bill and Hillary Clinton, Richard Dreyfuss, Woody Harrelson, Al Gore, Muhammad Ali and other reporters and politicians throughout the years.

Today, it was the host hotel for the ACORN National Board meeting. I thought Chris was right; this ACORN thing does take off fast. Last month I attended the ACORN Legislative and Policy conference in Washington, DC and thirty-days later I'm going to my first ACORN National Board Meeting.

My head was spinning by the end of the national association board meeting. Chris was right; over the last six weeks I met far more people than I could remember and learned many things I'd never forget. The sudden immersion into ACORN leadership had been breathtaking, exhilarating—and exasperating. I had met hundreds of community activists form across the country, participated in dozens of actions, both militant and sedate, and advocated to various politicians about numerous issues. It felt like I had been trying to drink water from a fire hydrant on a hot summer day.

I parked my car and walked through the lobby to the scent of fresh ground coffee, which quaffed through the air followed by the sound of hot pressed steam from the espresso machines at Filibusters Bistro & Lounge. The historic building featured tall ceilings, marble floors, deep mahogany molding and brass, which maintained the atmosphere of old world charm and beauty.

The National Board Meeting offered a Financial Training Session from 5:00-7:00 p.m., and New Delegate Orientation from 7:00-8:00 p.m., in the annex adjoining the south end of the hotel in an art deco international styled building. I eagerly attended both training sessions.

ACORN board meetings are a far cry from the banking and corporate meetings which ACORN targeted. In those board meetings, the rooms were filled with participants draped in $200 custom shirts and $3,000 tailored suits.

In contrast, an ACORN boardroom is filled with scores of community leaders and neighborhood activists. Spartan in their accruements, blue jeans and oxfords were the dress of the day for the working-class board members. There's not $3,000 worth of clothing in the room.

My heart raced with anticipation as I nervously entered the New Delegate orientation session. This is it. This is how I'm going to learn about the inner workings of ACORN.

ACORN Treasurer, Paul Satriano, sixty-two, a husky man with pale marshmallow arms, gave a financial presentation during new board members orientation to nearly two-dozen new delegates in attendance.

Satriano discussed the national board composition. "The local chairs of each ACORN chapter are automatically included on the respective state boards from each state. Two members from each state board are appointed to the national board of directors, plus one, the President, to ensure an uneven number of representatives. Since ACORN currently operates in 26 states, there are 53 board members, plus alternates."

Satriano drew five interlocking circles on a large paper flip board and declared, "ACORN, ACORN Housing, Project Vote, AISJ and a handful of small companies make up the ACORN Family." He also stated that the total ACORN budget was three to four million dollars per year and read a financial report, which reflected the financial standing of each chapter. Satriano stopped when he got to Georgia ACORN. "Houston we have a problem," he mocked. "Georgia ACORN seems to be in the red. Can anyone here speak for Georgia?"

Embarrassed, I could feel the blood rushing to my head through my inner ear. My head was spinning after what I just heard. How could this be? I joined ACORN and made it to the national board of directors, but before I can get any assistance, I find out that my chapter is in the red and about to become defunct?

And why didn't Dana warn me? He didn't tell me anything about any financial concerns. Dana said all I had to do was give the campaign reports for Georgia. What the fuck? I've got to pull myself together. But I need some more time to figure all this out.

Nervously, I said, "I'm the new delegate from Georgia ACORN. I have the financial information from our local board, but it doesn't match what you just said."

I did not want to air out Georgia's dirty laundry or financial business in public, "But let's discuss this more after the meeting."

After the meeting, I pulled Paul Satriano aside, "We're also having trouble with our organizer. We need to fire him."

"Hold on. You can't just fire an organizer."

"Why not?" I asked, "It's our chapter and he's not getting out in the community enough. So when we call an action, nobody comes."

Satriano, shook his head.

"Hell, we have to do his work for him, and we don't get paid or anything for doing it."

"Look, ACORN National hires and controls the staff. The organizers report to ACORN National, not the local chapters." Satriano said.

Still confused, "But if they're *our* staff why don't the local members get to say who *we* want?" I asked. "Or how the organizers are performing?"

"National pays the rent, leases your office space and pays your staff," said Satriano. "That's why we have to account for each local chapter's contributions to the association."

I stared back blankly.

Satriano said, "ACORN makes loans to local chapters for local operations and campaigns. Local chapters build credit with ACORN by identifying local grant opportunities and successful actions."

I asked, "So we'll be straight if Georgia ACORN can find local grant donors?"

"Not exactly. All grants and Moines first go to ACORN National, and then ACORN will credit the Georgia ACORN account."

I clarified, "You're telling me *-We-* can't handle, *-Our-* own money?"

Sternly, "Right now you guys aren't pulling your own weight. We are providing staff, office space, and a financial justice center for Atlanta, but we don't have anything to show for it!"

Speechless, I nodded.

Satriano said, "Even if you guys mounted a successful campaign or had an issue we could take across the country—that would be something."

"What do you mean an issue?"

"Local chapters get credit for successfully engaging in winning campaigns or bringing national issues to the board."

"But we *have* an issue," I replied. "Georgia leads the country in mortgage fraud and we have a campaign which highlights this problem."

Satriano paused, "Okay, sounds good. Bring it up to the board. But you've got to find a way to make some money soon, because we can't keep supporting Georgia's expenses forever."

Slowly it dawned on me; ACORN National controls local chapters by controlling the staff and their money. ACORN's financial management was completely top down. The local chapters were not allowed to receive state or local grant funding directly. All financial decisions were made by ACORN National.

I asked, "By the way Paul, how can I get a copy of ACORN's entire organizational charts and audited financial statements to review and brush up on?"

Mortgage Fraud

Friday, April 13, 2007

Muzac soft-music played in the background as I met Marcel Reid, Reverend
Gloria Swieringa and Kevin, the state
Chair from Minnesota ACORN, in
the lobby of the historic Legacy hotel after new delegate orientation. The
Legacy offered well-appointed rooms and suites and featured an intimate courtyard with a gazebo. Tired and hungry, I asked the group, "Is
anybody hungry? Let's go out and get something to eat."

The beautiful lobby created an inviting atmosphere of comfort,
elegance, and style, located close to premier shopping malls, entertainment centers, and popular restaurants including Juanita's Café, Vino's,
Cajun's Warf, and Doe's Steak House.

The group loaded into my car and I followed the road signs towards
downtown. We exited the expressway at Center and Main Street and
proceeded south. We drove to a yellow stucco building with bright neon
lights. The aroma of sizzling grilled meat filled the air.

Juanita's Café, a Mexican cantata restaurant and bar, known for more
than a decade as the best place for live music and great food. A frequent
gathering place for good food, strong drinks and intimate conversation, Juanita's could accommodate 150 diners through a large room and
enclosed patio.

I ordered Juanita's cheese dip, homemade salsa, fresh corn tortilla
chips and southern sweet iced tea while we looked over the menu to

decide. Gloria, the blind Reverend asked, "Okay Michael, what are they known for?"

Always helpful, I read Juanita's menu aloud, "The Fajita Feast—the best Fajita's in town. You get your choice of mesquite grilled beef tenderloin or chicken breast served with sautéed onions and peppers."

Marcel frowned. "You can get those anywhere; everyone serves Fajitas. This looks good too, the Grand Southwestern San Antonio Feast—two soft tacos with shredded beef or chicken and Tex Mex enchilada."

"I think I'll try the Jamaican Jerk Chicken," I said. "A whole grilled chicken breast marinated in tangy Caribbean seasonings with sautéed fajita vegetables, black beans and rice."

"What are you going to have, Kevin?" asked Marcel.

Kevin replied, "I think I'll try the Gulf Coast Dinner: baked Tilapia filets with tomato tequila sauce, rice, and black beans."

Everyone placed their respective orders and waited for the server to respond. Reverend Gloria asked, "Kevin, what's your story? How did you get involved in community action?"

"I'm new to all of this community stuff. After I retired, I had some extra time on my hands, so I started working in my neighborhood with ACORN."

"So you were bored," said Reverend Gloria.

They all laughed.

"Where did you retire from?" asked Marcel.

"I was a research scientist for the Veteran's Administration," replied Kevin.

"Wow? That's different. I don't think we've ever had a scientist on the ACORN board before."

Reverend Gloria asked, "So Michael, how did you get involved in all of this community action stuff?"

"I was a community development specialist and a national speaker on technology and community economic development for USDA. I grew up in Pine Bluff, a distressed low-income community here in Arkansas. My hometown had the dubious distinction of being ranked the worst city in America—two years in a row."

"Is that right?" asked Marcel.

"Being raised there is why I developed such a strong sense of social responsibility and the burning desire to improve the living and working conditions of people living in communities like mine."

"That's good," said Reverend Gloria.

"So, I traveled to Washington with the Clinton Administration and started working in community development on the White House Empowerment Zone Initiative—or the Federal Empowerment Zones and Enterprise Communities Initiative."

Marcel smiled. "Oh yeah, I know all about the Empowerment Zones program."

"It had a great experience helping people. I toured the country conducting technology training to low-income communities," I said. "I was a national speaker at White House Empowerment Zone Conferences and Regional Enterprise Community Meetings across the country, along with other high-profile speakers like Vice President Al Gore, HUD Secretary Andrew Cuomo, and Transportation Secretary Rodney Slater."

"Is that right?" asked Reverend Gloria.

I chuckled, "Yeah, I got a chance to travel across the country, visiting the worst places to live in America."

"So you were a F.O.B.—friend of Bill?" chided Marcel.

"Yeah, right, until I became a federal whistleblower and I reported over $40 million in government waste, fraud and abuse at the USDA."

"Forty million? How did you discover the theft?"

"It was my job," I replied. "I ran the file room and was in charge of securing the applications, so they ordered me to remove the scores."

"What?" asked Marcel. "And you went along with it?"

"I did what they ordered, but I reported it to my supervisor and the OIG."

Reverend Gloria asked, "So what happened?"

"They threatened my life and ruined my career," I said. "That's how I became a federal whistleblower."

"So what happened to your complaint?" asked Marcel.

"A huge cover-up," I replied. "It never got investigated."

"Wow!"

"Mike Espy resigned, and he got away with $40 million for his congressional district, but I got thrown under the bus."

"I thought Espy was cleared," commented Marcel.

"The Clinton White House forced him to resign, but his trial revealed Mike Espy received $30,000 or $40,000 in football tickets and gifts."

Marcel asked, "So he got busted for $40,000—but he got away with $40 million?"

"The things Mike Espy did would have been legal for a sitting Congressman." I clarified, "But not as Secretary of Agriculture—they have different rules."

"What do you mean?" asked Kevin.

I explained, "Congressmen can receive small gifts, tickets to sporting events and such from their constituents; that's okay. And it's congresses' *job* to represent their constituents. They have the power of the purse."

"That's right" agreed Marcel.

I said, "Which includes getting funding for projects in their congressional districts—through earmarks."

"Earmarks?" asked Kevin. "Oh, you mean pork barrel spending."

"That's right," I paused. "One man's pork, is another man's bacon, and you've got to bring home the bacon to get re-elected."

They all laughed together.

I said, "But the problem is this, congressional earmarks are legal, unpopular—but legal. Executive earmarks are illegal."

"Really?" asked Marcel.

"Right! Mike Espy got in trouble because he continued to act like he was still in congress after he became the Secretary of Agriculture."

"The rules are different," declared Marcel.

"Bingo!"

"Why would he do that?" asked Marcel.

"Don't forget Marcel, when Mike Espy stepped down to become Secretary, his brother Henry ran for his vacated congressional seat."

She hesitated, "Oh, so they were setting up a family dynasty."

"Correct," I said. "Don't get me wrong, he didn't win. Bennie Thompson beat him out."

"Ok, Michael."

"But at the time, Henry Espy was running for congress, and his brother, the Secretary of Agriculture, pumped $40 million into the district they hoped he would represent."

"Oh, I get it," said Marcel. "They primed the pump to get the money later."

"Exactly! Congressional campaigns aren't cheap, and we know Henry Espy racked up huge campaign debts."

Rhetorically, "So what better way to clear up any outstanding obligations than to have $40 million sitting in a friendly non-profit in your own backyard?" asked Marcel.

"Which is why the Mississippi Empowerment Zone became such a dismal failure," I said. "It never should have been funded in the first place."

"Wow," said Reverend Gloria.

"It was a taxpayer funded, political slush fund, but the people like me, the ones who tried to stop it, lost everything."

"I never knew," said Marcel.

"They kept it hush, hush for a while, and President Clinton pardoned him after the trial. Mike Espy is untouchable now."

"So he got away scot free?" asked Marcel. "The final Clinton scandal."

I laughed aloud.

"So you're from Arkansas and you bucked the Clinton Administration?" asked Kevin.

"It seemed like a good idea at the time, but I didn't see it that way."

"Why not?" asked Marcel.

"I bucked politics, fraud and corruption," I replied. "The

Administration was trying to do the right thing. The Empowerment Zones Program was designed to empower people."

"Okay," said Marcel.

"I was a hard worker and a true believer, but I got caught up in the politics. So I became a public interest and judicial reform advocate, after I blew the whistle at USDA."

I sipped my lemon flavored iced tea. "Eventually, I joined the No FEAR coalition, which passed the Notification of Federal Employee Anti-discrimination and Retaliation Act of 2002."

I said, "And we're engaged in seeking strong judicial reform provisions to be included in No FEAR II. You know what, Marcel? We should get ACORN to support No FEAR."

"What do you mean?" asked Marcel.

"Think about it. ACORN receives money to support low and moderate income communities, but federal workers and officials are screwing around with the money."

"That's right," agreed Reverend Gloria.

"ACORN should support the brave whistleblowers who are trying to do the right thing for the community."

"I see what you mean Michael," said Marcel. "It makes a lot of sense— DC ACORN could support something like that."

Saturday, April 14, 2007

I joined Marcel Reid after lunch following the morning committee meetings from 10:00-12:00 p.m. Over 50 other chapter leaders and delegates from across the country gathered for the ACORN National Board Meeting.

Maude Hurd gave the welcome and introductions, starting at 1:00 p.m., and a special acknowledgment and thanks to Ronald Sykes, who had completed a Whipple-Bell Fellowship at the end of January.

Yvonne Stafford stood and recommended more flexibility in recruiting Whipple-Bell Fellowships for shorter periods of time which would accommodate more community leaders within the guidelines of the program.

Marcel and I joined other ACORN community leaders at the national board meeting including Vanessa Gueringer, a striking woman with hazel eyes and auburn hair; she appeared exotic and Creole. Vanessa was a community leader from New Orleans and gave a special report on Victory in Saving the Lower Ninth Ward. She thanked Wade Rathke for his support.

It was a moment I had looked forward to—meeting Wade Rathke the premier community organizer of his generation. I was anxious to meet him, and my palms sweat, Wade's reputation proceeded him within the ACORN community. I didn't know what to expect.

Wade Rathke, stood 6'o" tall, rugged and sinewy. He didn't appear to be a particularly imposing figure. Wade was shrewd, restrained and possessed an easy grace and quiet confidence. He was an organic genius on organizing and strategy, Wade was always calculating but slow to speak. He preferred to stand around the edges instead of commanding the center of the room. Unburdened by pretense, Wade made people comfortable because he was so comfortable with himself.

Wade was dressed in dungarees and cowboy boots, with monogrammed initials "WR" inscribed in the custom silver tips—a gift from former Governor Winthrop Rockefeller. With massive hair, Wade looked more like a throwback hippie, rather than the mastermind behind the most effective community organizing group in the country.

He said, "Living and working in New Orleans at ACORN's Headquarters, during the destruction wrought by Katrina, meant the entire ACORN family was intimately involved in the fight to rebuild the city, especially the lower-income areas like the 9th Ward where our members are concentrated.

"We couldn't leave the city, even if we wanted to, because fighting to come back from Katrina has made it home for everyone who's shared this experience no matter where they were born or how long they have been here."

Following the introduction and thanks, ACORN National Staff members made a series of reports to the Association Board. They were the key personnel in the ACORN universe and formed the brain trust for Wade Rathke.

POLITICAL REPORT

Zach Polett, the Political Director gave a report from the Political Committee and a special report on the recent Legislative and Political Conference in Washington, DC.

He described ACORN's Working Families Ballot Line Project and plans for Presidential Candidate Interviews at a mass meeting. "Our goal is for ACORN to host Candidate Interviews of Potential Prospects and Possibilities meetings between Presidential Candidates and ACORN members."

Zach said, "Maude has sent letters to the presidential candidates inviting them to participate in an ACORN Presidential Forum on ACORN's Working Families Agenda and to interview with leadership. After jockeying with the candidate's schedulers, we have proposed Monday, July 2, 2007 in Philadelphia for the candidates to be invited to a mass meeting with 1,000 to 1,500 ACORN members."

The Board approved the organization of a national presidential candidates forum for June 2007 in Las Vegas to be organized by the political staff on the program side and the field staff on the membership side. Las Vegas was chosen as the ideal location to garner the attendance of 1,000 members in a venue where plane fares and hotel rooms are inexpensive.

Marcel Reid listened intently, but remained leery of Zach and his remarks, since he was a master of political expediency. And like anyone who worshiped on the alter of expediency—Zach was willing to say or do anything.

I thought to myself, a political report? This was interesting. Since non-profit charitable groups can't engage in political activities, it would violate their 501(c)(3) tax exempt status. I need to see the organizational documents so I can understand how ACORN is setup.

NATIONAL OPERATIONS

Amy Schur, the National Campaign Director for ACORN, addressed the board and reported on National Operations. She announced ACORN recently joined Wade Henderson's Leadership Conference for Civil and Human Rights and reported on the Role of Organizers Forum.

Schur said, "In these discussions, we've found ourselves dealing with a range of issues: internal problems in a Cleveland chapter which wants to get rid of its organizer, a fund-raising fiasco in California, a massive voter registration drive in Chicago being delayed, and numerous complaints about under-representation of Black organizers in the association."

Finally, Schur reported on recent staffing changes and declared Steven Bradbury was taking over as Head Organizer for Illinois, replacing Madeline Talbot who had unexpectedly resigned her position. Wade seethed in anger, furious after Madeline Talbot shut down Chicago ACORN.

Steve Bradbury, stood 6'2" with an athletic build. Glib and confident at forty-one, he fashioned himself a protégé of Wade Rathke and Beth Butler. A Rathke loyalist, Steve didn't want any ACORN members who had ever seen a college campus, much less possessed a college degree.

Marcel whispered, "That's huge. Chicago is an ACORN stronghold, and Madeline was an excellent strategist. She was ACORN's strongest organizer."

"A woman?" I asked.

She looked square in my eyes, "Madeline was *The* strongest organizer in ACORN—including Wade."

The state Head Organizer for a long standing ACORN stronghold suddenly quits; I wonder why?

CAMPAIGN REPORTS

I listened as Liz Wolff delivered a summary report from the campaign committee beginning with the Sherwin-Williams Campaign. "The problem with lead paint is even if the paint was put down in 1920 and has been painted over six times, the 1920 paint is still there. If it chips off, the 1920 paint can chip off too.

"Federal guidelines say no amount of lead in the blood is considered safe. Children with even small amounts of lead in their blood can suffer learning disabilities, the guidelines say. Very high levels result in mental retardation, coma or even death."

Reverend Gloria declared, "We're fighting for the children in our communities. Lead paint was widely used because it was durable and pliable, so it would shrink and expand with buildings as they cooled and heated. But as useful as lead paint was, it could harm children who were exposed to even small amounts of lead chips or dust that had cracked or peeled off the walls."

Marcel said, "For years, paint manufacturers fended off lawsuits, which typically contended product liability laws had been violated. Product liability laws require plaintiffs to identify the maker of the defective product and to file the suit within a certain time frame.

"Those lawsuits were routinely dismissed before trial because the paint companies would argue they hadn't made lead paint in 40 or 50 years, and it was impossible to distinguish one company's paint from another's."

Wolff said, "Despite these long odds, Rhode Island filed a lawsuit against several paint manufacturers and the Lead Industries Association, an industry trade group. The suit contended the defendants marketed and sold lead-based paint knowing it was toxic.

"Besides arguing that the manufacturers had violated product liability laws, the lawsuit also included a new accusation—lead paint constituted a public nuisance."

"A public nuisance?" asked Vanessa.

"Legally defined, a public nuisance occurs if a defendant interferes in an unreasonable way with a public right. Practically speaking, if people play their music too loud late at night and disturb their neighbors, they could face public nuisance charges.

"The nuisance claim made it easier for Rhode Island to argue its case by not requiring the state to link any one company's paint to a particular house, and that approach would not allow companies to argue that too much time had elapsed, because lead was still a nuisance.

"We began our national campaign following the Rhode Island jury verdict. Sherwin-Williams is still being stubborn but we're getting their attention. Rhode Island's success, after decades of courtroom failures around the country, could encourage others to target the paint and coatings industry and result in a tidal-wave of litigation similar to the lawsuits which confronted the tobacco industry."

I stood and addressed the group. "I'm a new delegate, so this is all new to me, but how well are we doing against the paint manufactures?"

She smiled. "DuPont agreed to donate $12.5 million to several nonprofit organizations in June, 2005. So, the Attorney General dropped the company from the lawsuit. The judge also rejected a bid to throw out the case and ordered three paint manufacturing companies to clean up lead paint throughout the state.

"Judge Michael Silverstein also ordered the appointment of a special master to advise him on how to proceed with the cleanup and paint repairs, but the court didn't specify how much that might cost. Unfortunately, Sherwin-Williams, NL Industries and Millennium Holdings all said they will appeal."

INTERNATIONAL REPORT

Wade Rathke stood up before the board. "But if they appeal we will continue to fight." Wade went on to give a report on ACORN International Joint Projects and concepts, and announced recent invitations for Training and Assistance for India, Korea and Philippines.

He declared, "ACORN International is organizing unions of hawkers and waste-pickers in Delhi and Mumbai and Cartoneros in Buenos Aires. We're working in Canada, Mexico, Peru, Argentina, the Dominican Republic, India, and Kenya, and with partnerships in Indonesia, Korea, and the Philippines.

"We are working to assist in building membership-based organizations in the mega-slums of Dharavi, Mumbai; La Matanza, Buenos Aires;

NEZA, Mexico City and San Juan Laraguache, Lima which have arisen in some of the world's largest cities."

COMMUNICATIONS REPORT

Wade Rathke also gave a report highlighting e-mail communications, e-mail harvesting, radio stations: KNON and KABF, and ACORN United. As publisher and editor-in-chief of *Social Policy* magazine, Wade offered a forum for many voices from organizing, academia and on issues related to social change in America and abroad.

I thought to myself, an ACORN international report? I couldn't believe my ears. What kind of grassroots civil rights organization has an international division? How can they afford to operate internationally with only a few million dollars? Or, for that matter, own and operate radio stations and magazines? To my mind, each new status report actually raised more questions than they answered. I definitely need to see financial statements and organizational documents.

FINANCIAL JUSTICE CENTER

Following the ACORN International presentation, Jordan Ash gave a report on ACORN Financial Justice Centers, including the on-going Refund Anticipation Loan campaign and strategies, a report on EITC centers and expansion of the program, Predatory Lending Campaign, Sub-prime and Foreclosure Campaign and Banking work.

Jordan Ash said, "Over the last ten years, ACORN's Financial Justice Center has been able to focus on developing campaigns against the predatory practices of financial institutions, tax preparers, credit card companies, payday lenders, mortgage companies, and loan servicers."

WELLS FARGO

Jordan also gave a special report on settlement efforts with Wells Fargo. "Unfortunately, our efforts and actions against Wells Fargo found us confronting a deeply ideological opponent, a CEO who simply drew a line in the sand—unwilling to negotiate with ACORN under any circumstances.

"When business practices are trumped by personal animus, no one wins. The footprint of the Wells Fargo abuse was national, but the eventual settlement was limited to relief in the state of California only. Wells Fargo unilaterally conceded most of the best practices we demanded in order to deny ACORN the ability to expand on or even enjoy our victory.

"The best practices agreements ACORN negotiated would eliminate predatory loan abuses, increase disclosures and transparencies for the borrowers, enshrine the understandings in the operating and training manuals of the companies, provide hotlines for problems encountered by ACORN members, and mandate regular reviews of complaints and resolutions to enforce and implement the agreements.

"Unfortunately, the best practices they agreed to were decent, but they trickled out as part of the company's practices rather than being imprinted indelibly as part of an agreed and enforced reform."

HOUSING REPORT

Alton Bennett, stood and gave a report on ACORN Housing and Development Programs. He discussed new development activity in Houston, New Orleans and through East Coast Partnerships. Bennett said, "Ameriquest sprung from nowhere in Orange County, California, to become a leading mortgage lender, writing more mortgages than almost any other institution in the country. We kept hearing one complaint after another from our members and from other people who came through the housing counseling offices run by the ACORN Housing Corporation."

"What's the problem then?" I asked.

Bennett replied, "The heart of the problem centered on Ameriquest's mortgage broker distribution network and its outsourcing of the actual lending. This problem of outsourcing lending was epidemic throughout the subprime sector.

"Despite all the complaints, claims, and settlements, none of these companies, whether their intentions were honorable or not, ever did a good job of supervising their broker networks, thereby allowing them to be fertile fields for consumer abuse and deception."

Jordan added, "Ameriquest was one of the centerpiece actions at ACORN's 2002 National Convention in Philadelphia. We burst into an office complex downtown where Ameriquest had its offices and surprised Adam Bass, the Senior Vice President and General Counsel. Bass was smart and shrewd. He had seen the number of ACORN members in Philadelphia, and he agreed immediately to negotiations to try to resolve the issues."

Wade said, "He got the big picture, so he quickly tried to resolve the headache and came to an agreement on a set of best practices that would eliminate predatory conditions in Ameriquest's operations.

"Ameriquest also agreed to reduce its dependence on the broker network and to use its own people whom it would hire, train, and supervise to ensure fairer, more transparent lending operations. He initiated a ten-city trial program as part of the agreement with a small amount of multi-year support to implement the program.

"Ameriquest benefited by being an early responder in this campaign, realizing it was smarter, and much cheaper, to settle and deal with the problems rather than endure a protracted war in public, in the courts, and in the marketplace."

Jordan said, "Other lenders had to learn the lesson the hard way, particularly Household Finance. Household eventually understood an agreement with ACORN was essential to protect its international brand. In the end, the Household agreement was favorable to ACORN."

Wade boasted, "They settled with ACORN for $484 million, with most of the money going into a homebuyers assistance program which will be administered by ACORN Housing to refinance predatory loans and to provide assistance in getting homeowners back into affordable purchase programs.

"The agreement also includes $2 million per year each year for three years to increase our outreach efforts for home ownership, financial literacy, and membership and community benefits."

He complained, "At one point in the middle of the ACORN campaign. Household paid $1 million to Wade Henderson's Leadership Council for Civil and Human Rights, to have the council vouch for Household's so-called good record. If they were going to pay $1 million to have someone stand in our way, then they ought to pay at least double that amount every year for real work to be done, and so our lawyers and negotiators were able to deliver justice on many fronts."

The board cheered in approval.

During the discussions on Financial Justice and Predatory Lending, I thought to myself that this was a chance to raise Mortgage Fraud to the association board. I stood as a Delegate to ACORN National Board and explained the difference between predatory lending and mortgage fraud in such a way that the association board members could understand it.

I implored them, "The Winecoff Hotel case is not only a Georgia ACORN issue, but it is also a National ACORN concern because foreclosure fraud is a national epidemic. The Winecoff Hotel is on the national registry of historic places; it is a Georgia Landmark and a National Treasure.

"When crooked bankers and developer's can steal national landmarks and then finance it with public dollars intended for low to moderate income families, then ACORN has to get involved, both locally and nationally. Worse still, commercial mortgage and foreclosure fraud of this type leads to public corruption, due to the rush to re-develop inner cities like Atlanta."

I argued, "The Atlanta Police Richard Pennington and Paul Howard, Jr. the Fulton County District Attorney refuse to investigate low income or small business claims of mortgage fraud when the offenders are often large real estate developers or investment bankers with strong connections to the city."

I urged the national board to act. "We're not just fighting predatory lending, we're fighting Mortgage Fraud and we need your help. Georgia leads the country in Mortgage Fraud, and Texas, Florida and California are close behind.

"The Federal Government has already shut down one company, InterBank Funding Companies for illegally raising nearly $200 million to run a mortgage ponzie scheme, but the government didn't stop InterBank from conducting fraudulent mortgage foreclosures in ACORN communities. InterBank is a Wall Street Investment Advisor, which is stealing people's homes and businesses by using foreclosure fraud."

I asked, "Support Georgia ACORN's mortgage and foreclosure fraud action against InterBank Funding Companies."

The Association board overwhelmingly voted to support Georgia ACORN's Mortgage Fraud campaign, to stop the Mortgage and Foreclosure Fraud epidemic raging in Georgia, Florida, California and Texas.

Wade Rathke took the floor and announced, "ACORN is on the job concerning fraudulent foreclosure schemes, especially in sub-prime mortgage markets." He began to chant, *"Predatory Lenders"*... *"Criminal Offenders."* Mortgage Fraud will now be included in ACORN's Financial Justice Center Campaigns.

Black Labor

Saturday, April 14, 2007

I flipped through the board briefing books we were given, and noticed the association board was inundated with political briefings and local campaign reports. However, *no audited* financial statements were ever given to the board. ACORN Treasurer, Paul Satriano stood before the group and gave a brief financial report and presented the revised budgets for ACORN.

He noted the consolidated national organization's budget was not available and incomplete, but he promised to discuss its progress up to date. Satriano proposed a series of steps which would require monthly reporting by every ACORN chapter as a pre-condition to any distributions and all financial activity.

I scanned the financial overview being presented and whispered to Marcel, "There is *no way* ACORN is only worth a few million dollars, like this says. I'm easily looking at a $50 to $100 million, multi-national operation—at least."

Marcel rose to address the board. "One more thing, I'm a member of the By-Laws committee. Can you please provide the association board members with a complete organizational chart and audited financial records?"

A silent hush covered the room. Maude and the other ACORN staffer's looked surprised, but didn't know how to respond to Marcel's request.

"I agree with, Marcel." I stood and proclaimed, lowering my voice to baritone, "Georgia ACORN seconds DC ACORN's request. We also want to see the organizational chart, budget and audited financial records."

Maude Hurd and Wade Rathke both agreed to deliver copies of the financial and organizational records to Marcel and me, after the National Board Meeting. A master of effective communication, Wade understood that people have to believe they made their own decisions. No organizer can tell a community what to do, even when the organizer had a good idea of what they should be doing next. He would deftly suggest, maneuver, and persuade the national board toward action. Wade would never tell a community what to do. Instead, he led us through contrived situations and loaded questions—like a puppet master, pulling the right strings.

Marcel Reid thanked Maude and Wade and then addressed the association board. "When ACORN wins a congressional victory and gets millions of dollars in federal block grants for housing and social service programs, it's government whistleblowers who fight to make sure low-income communities actually get the money they are supposed to.

"The No FEAR Coalition is a DC based group which is introducing new civil rights and whistleblower legislation. ACORN fights the system from the bottom to the top. Whistleblower's fight the system from the inside to the outside." Marcel motioned the board, "ACORN should support increased whistleblower protections because no one should be afraid to stand up for what is right."

The National Board passed the DC ACORN resolution by majority vote. The Board also discussed a process for evaluating and developing a national campaign around education which would engage all school boards in the country with local ACORN offices.

FIELD OPERATIONS

Helene O'Brien gave a report on field operations staffing and locations, including new and re-opened offices, community expansion lists and timelines, and strategies for building a mass membership.

She also gave a report on special initiatives including United Way Support, CFC Support, Corporate Volunteer Programs, Insurance and Credit Cards and Leadership Business.

Dissatisfied, "I'm still confused by ACORN's service delivery model."

"What do you mean?" Marcel asked.

"This is not like any civil rights group or charitable organization I've ever seen," I said. "I mean, Maude Hurd is our President, right?"

"Yes—she is," replied Marcel.

"Steve Kest is our Executive Director?" I asked.

"Correct."

"Which is normal for any non-profit," I said. "And Paul Satriano is the Treasurer—but we don't have a Chief Financial Officer?"

"Humph," said Marcel.

I said, "So instead of having a CFO or a COO who reports to the board, we get our financial reports from—Citizen's Consulting Inc. a group which reports to management?"

"That's correct," she said.

"Well, if that's right," I stated, "then CCI must have a management contract with ACORN."

"Probably so, but so what?" asked Marcel. "CCI provides bookkeeping, accounting and other financial management services to ACORN and our affiliated entities."

"Which is fine, Marcel. I mean we can do that—but they disclosed the management contract."

"So what?" asked Marcel.

"Non-profit organizations only have to disclose management contracts if they charge fees over 30 percent," I said.

"They told us they charge less than five percent," replied Marcel.

"I know, but it doesn't add up. And another thing—ACORN titles look more like a political campaign, than a civil rights organization or charitable group. Look, here we've got Researchers, Political Directors and Field Directors. This looks more like a political campaign—rather than a civil rights group."

Marcel replied, "Yeah, it is. ACORN is a 501(c)(4)."

"It's not just that either, Marcel. "What is a Chief Organizer anyway?" I asked.

"He's in charge of all our campaigns."

"If Wade founded or co-founded ACORN, why isn't he the President or the Executive Director or something?" I asked.

It didn't make sense to me. Why just settle on organizing campaigns, when he could control the whole operation?

ORGANIZED LABOR

Wade Rathke was also the Chief Organizer of SEIU Local 100 in New Orleans, with members in Louisiana, Arkansas, and Texas, and SEIU Local 880 in Chicago, Illinois. He also directed the campaign to make Wal-Mart accountable to its workers and communities in Florida, California, and India.

He gave a report on labor organizing, "All of the evidence over the last fifty years indicates the dominant American labor-organizing model of NLRB representation, certification, and collective bargaining is not succeeding in increasing the membership and density of worker organization.

"Over the last three decades the greatest success story for organized labor in the United States was low-wage and service workers adding more than half a million members to unions during a period of massive union membership losses.

"ACORN Organizers developed strategies to leverage political clout in certain states where unions still had enough density and power with their deep and long-term organizational support from these workers to create solutions which solidified unions and delivered protections, wages, and benefits to their members."

He said, "This was achieved by patiently building member-based worker associations, creating strong community—labor alliances, and building sufficient strength to take advantage of eventual opportunities and leverage on the political side.

"There have been two successful strategies achieved by organizing low-wage workers and combining deep and extensive organization with political muscle and capacity. Over several years, SEIU Local 880 developed Executive Order and public-authority based organizational models in Illinois and California, which resulted in the largest union representation elections in the United States since the 1930s."

Wade concluded, "We need to begin thinking outside of the NLRA and collective bargaining, while there are still unions in the U.S. before they are obliterated completely. Workers don't have to be organized into traditional unions in order for workers to be organized."

I chuckled to myself, under my breath.

"What's so funny?" asked Marcel.

"It's ironic, but I guess I'm in the right place."

"How so?" she asked.

"I served on the advisory board for a national civil rights organization and I worked for the National Labor Relations Board. So I have both civil rights and organized labor experience."

"Is that right?" asked Vanessa.

I rubbed my chin in thought. "I worked on an advisory board for the A. Philip Randolph Institute, an AFL-CIO affiliate. Black Labor has always been an important part of organizing Black communities."

"How so?" asked Vanessa.

"Most people don't realize Black labor taught the civil rights movement how to organize."

"What do you mean?" asked Vanessa.

"People think civil rights leaders like Martin Luther King, Jr. or Malcolm X just emerged with huge followings. For instance, most people think it was Martin Luther King's March on Washington."

She agreed, "That's right, they do."

"People forget it was organized by Black labor, the March on Washington for Jobs and Freedom. Asa Philip Randolph a Black labor leader organized the march. Martin Luther King, Jr. was invited to speak. A. Philip Randolph was doing his part to reach back and support youth activists."

Marcel agreed, "That's right, Michael."

"You've got to remember the Martin Luther King back then was not the same Martin Luther King we know today. At least not until after he gave the *I Have a Dream* speech at the Lincoln Memorial."

"Oh, yeah?" said Vanessa.

"A. Philip Randolph successfully fought the Pullman Sleeping Car Company at the turn of the century by organizing the lowest poor Black workers."

"What was the big deal about the Pullman Company?" asked Vanessa.

"If you think about it, Randolph fought a major U.S. Corporation during the height of the railroad expansions, when the Pullman Sleeping Car Company was one of the most powerful companies in America.

"Pullman Sleeping Cars were the elite, first class accommodations for the Rail Roads. They provided opulent plush accoutrements, along with the exceptional service the Black porter's provided to wealthy passengers."

I said, "But the Black porters were underpaid, suffering from discriminatory practices, and lacked job security. The Black porters accepted these conditions as inevitable, a sign of the times. Demoralized, they thought—what's the use?

"They resented these circumstances, complained, talked about the futility of bucking the big shots and were generally frustrated, because they lacked an opportunity for effective action."

"That's true even today," said Vanessa.

"Then along comes A. Philip Randolph, a labor organizer and agitator. He starts making trouble by stirring up these angers, frustrations, and resentments. He highlights the specific issues and grievances that heighten controversy.

"He dramatizes their injustices by describing working conditions at other places where the workers are better off economically, and had better working conditions, job security, health benefits, and pensions, as well as other advantages the Black workers had never thought of.

"Finally, he convinces them to use their intelligence and energies to organize themselves into a power instrument called a trade union."

"But—a Porter's union?" I said. "Back then, service work was a great job, especially for African-Americans. They became educated through travel, visited with the wealthy and influential, and they drew great tips, if they had a good personality.

"In the days prior to integration, Blacks had limited employment opportunities. You could be successful, if you were either a teacher, barber, beautician, or a waiter.

"So Pullman Porters were on the high-end of the Negro employment scale. Anyway, it was the Pullman Porters who funded the movement and who paid the bail when the civil rights demonstrators were jailed."

Incredulously, "Railroad porters had the money?" inquired Vanessa.

I said, "They were the dues paying members for the NAACP and the SCLC, and Black labor taught the civil rights movement how to organize. When the civil rights leaders decided that they needed to organize the movement in the South, they went to the Black labor organizers.

"People like Bayard Rustin who worked with the A. Philip Randolph Institute traveled to Montgomery, Alabama to help the Montgomery Improvement Association maintain and expand the bus boycott, which is why A. Philip Randolph invited Martin Luther King Jr. to the March on Washington for Jobs and Equality.

"Consequently, the U.S. Department of Justice once called A. Philip Randolph the most dangerous Negro in America—because he was an organizer."

Vanessa asked, "So how do you know all this labor stuff anyway, Michael?"

"I'm an attorney with experience in labor organizing and worker's rights," I confided. "I know about labor unions, history and policy because I worked for the National Labor Relations Board in their Office of Advice.

"I learned about A. Philip Randolph when I served on the Advisory Board for the Recruitment and Training Program at the A. Philip Randolph Institute."

Surprised, "Oh you're a lawyer?" Vanessa asked.

"I'm a lawyer, MBA and CPA."

Marcel listened intently to this exchange and hastily pulled me aside. "Be careful. Don't let them know who you are!" she implored.

"Why not?" I asked.

"If they find out who you are, and what you know, they will get rid of you."

I stared at her in stunned silence.

"They don't let people like you on this board. It's almost like being on a slave plantation."

"A plantation?"

"A plantation mentality at least," Marcel said. "If one slave learned to read, they all had to hide him and protect him."

"That's right."

"If an overseer *–an organizer–* ever found out a slave could read, they would surely kill the slave. ACORN is just like that. If you want to stay on the association board, you can't let them know you can read, you can think, and more importantly count—the money."

I slowly began to realize just how backwards ACORN was, by design. The board members don't understand the law or realize their own power, and they are intimidated, even fearful of their own staff. The organizers were liberal whites with family money or political connections, people who could afford to write checks to the organization. Low-income minorities simply can't afford to be organizers; they didn't have the monetary resources or personal relationships to be successful; they were the volunteer demonstrators. The organizers were affluent and White, and they controlled the association *not* the membership. In reality, ACORN is a White, Power, Organization which masquerades in Blackface. Black Labor... White Power.

People's Platform

Saturday, April 14, 2007

Four diesel engines roared as char-
tered buses turned the corner at Third
and Center Street, for a Saturday
evening reception from 7:00-9:00 p.m.
I was eager to continue to meet with the local ACORN leaders from
across the country. Dave's Place was a proverbial hole in the wall, a small
restaurant and bar with a 70-seat capacity, which served traditional,
southern, and Cajun fried food—as well as stout drinks. The proprietor,
long-time friend and supporter of ACORN, hosted a reception during
the national board meeting, honoring the ACORN Board, Maude Hurd
and Wade Rathke.

Mike Sealy, fifty-seven, and the Head Organizer for Arkansas
ACORN, gave a brief introduction. "Arkansas Community Organizations
for Reform Now, started in 1970 with four little old ladies fighting for
fairness and welfare rights here in Little Rock. From these humble begin-
nings, this fledgling neighborhood organization became the most feared
and revered community organization in America."

He recited ACORN's nostalgic creed aloud: "We stand for a People's
Platform, as old as our country, and as young as our dreams. We come
before our nation, not to petition with hat in hand, but to rise as one
people and demand.

"We have waited and watched. We have hoped and helped. We
have sweated and suffered. We have often believed. We have frequently

followed. But we have nothing to show for the work of our hand, the tax of our labor. Our patience has been abused, our experience mis-used. Our silence has been seen as support. Our struggle has been ignored.

"Enough is enough. We will wait no longer for the crumbs at America's door. We will not be meek, but mighty. We will not starve on past promises, but feast on future dreams. We are an uncommon people. We are the majority, forged from all minorities. We are the masses of many, not the forces of few. We will continue our fight until the American way is just one way, until we have shared the wealth, until we have won our freedom.

"This is not a simple vision but a detailed plan. Our plan is to build an American reality from the American rhetoric, to deliver a piece of the present and the fruits of the future to every man, to every woman, to every family. We demand our birthright: the chance to be rich, the right to be free.

"Our riches shall be the blooming of our communities, the bounty of a sure livelihood, the beauty of homes for our families with sickness driven from the door, the benefit of our taxes rather than their burden, and the best of our energy, land, and natural resources for all people.

"Our freedom is the force of democracy, not the farce of federal fat and personal profit. In our freedom, only the people shall rule. Corporations shall have their role: producing jobs, providing products, paying taxes. No more, no less. They shall obey our wishes, respond to our needs, serve our communities. Our country shall be the citizen's wealth and our wealth shall build our country.

"Government shall have its role: public servant to our good, fast follower to our sure steps. No more, no less. Our government shall shout with the public voice and no longer the private whisper. In our government, the common concerns shall be the collective cause.

"We represent the people's platform, not a politician's promise. We demand the changes outlined in our platform and plan. We will work to win. We will have our birthright. We will live in richness and freedom. We will live in one country as one people."

Sealy finished the creed to rousing applause.

Hearing that, it slowly dawned on me that marching and demonstrations are things the NAACP and SCLC do in the course of serving their congregations or membership. ACORN is different. ACORN is unapologetically confrontational. Direct action, fearless advocacy, in your face protests, street demonstrations and demands is what ACORN does. I felt a sense of pride swelling in my chest as I listened to those words. I began to understand what ACORN was all about.

I'd been a member of traditional church and religious-based civil rights organizations. "So that's why ACORN is so much more effective and successful at community organizing than NAACP, SCLC or other civil rights organizations?" I asked Marcel.

She sipped from her glass of wine. "Traditional civil rights groups are single-issue charitable organizations. ACORN is far broader than civil rights. It is a multi-issue political organization."

"Wait a minute, Marcel. You're saying civil rights groups are limited because they focus on civil rights?"

"Focusing on a single issue drastically limits your appeal. Organizations are built on issues which are specific, immediate, and realizable, but they must be based on many issues. Multiple issues can attract many potential members necessary to build a broad, community-based organization."

"Why?"

"Because organizations need actions to stay relevant, it's impossible to maintain constant action based on a single issue. Many issues means many members."

I reflected. "So that's the problem with the civil rights movement—single issue groups and Black leaders couldn't cross over and organize White people?"

She said, "Besides, ACORN is not really, or rather not only—a civil rights organization."

"What do you mean?" I asked.

"Civil Rights groups are charitable 501(c)(3) organizations. ACORN is not charitable; it's more political—it is a 501(c)(4). ACORN is a cross between a civil rights group which operates like a labor union."

Sealy continued his introduction, "Financial Justice, dealing with income and assets are constant themes of Wade's organizing, no matter what the venue or vehicle. For 40 years Wade Rathke has been recognized as perhaps the premier organizer of his generation. During these hard-fought efforts, ACORN found not only that change is possible, but it is possible to create a different and better world.

"The common themes of all these decades of hard fought welfare rights organizing, community organizing, and labor organizing are how to unite people at the bottom income levels around their issues to build sufficient power to impact their lives, improve their communities, and change the direction of our country."

The crowd of supporters, ACORN Board members and local community residents, joined in a tremendous round of applause given in recognition and appreciation of Wade Rathke, ACORN National President Maude Hurd and the National Board of Directors.

Following the heart-felt introduction, Wade Rathke stood before the group and cleared his throat. "We traveled a long road to the place where we stand together in our fight for both social justice and economic justice. What we started right here, in Little Rock, Arkansas with four courageous women fighting for welfare rights, became a national organization with more than 100 offices and 400,000 member families.

"Back in the late 1960s, when I organized for the National Welfare Rights Organization in Boston and Springfield, our primary slogan on every sign and banner was ADEQUATE INCOME NOW!" He said, "Women on welfare didn't win then and they are certainly not winning now. But, in some ways this unrecognized issue remains at the center of the campaign for economic justice.

"Over three decades, we fought pitched battles in the mid-1970s against the banks which were exploiting our neighborhoods. We've not only seen the passage of programs which make a difference, but we've also seen some of our opponents in these campaigns gradually changing course and becoming partners.

"I also think we learned important lessons from thousands of campaigns which were created to fight government and some of the world's most prominent corporations both on the streets and at the bargaining tables—in engaging, shaping and changing their operational models and persuading them to change their political position to advance economic justice. When you build an organization, it ceases to be about the organizer and becomes about the many who make it live and grow and win.

"None of this was possible without the sacrifice and struggle of thousands of grassroots leaders and members who swelled the ranks of the organizations which I've been honored to serve over the last thirty-five years."

The audience cheered and applauded.

"Specifically, let me single out the presidents of the ACORN board during my tenure as chief organizer. They are my personal heroes and in a thousand ways led the organization for the last dozen years: Steve McDonald, Larry Rodgers, Elena Hanggi Giddings of Little Rock, and especially Maude Hurd of Boston. They wrote new definitions for the meaning of community leadership.

"I would say the same for the presidents of SEIU Local 100, where I also served as Chief Organizer: Mildred Edmond and then Rebecca Hart of New Orleans and Sedric Crawford and Vernon Bolden of Baton Rouge. They are all warriors for workers!

"Let me honor a couple of other people who took chances with me and made a difference. George Wiley, now long deceased, founded and directed the National Welfare Rights Organization, and recognized the potential in a young, redheaded kid. He backed me all the way on my crazy vision for building ACORN, as long as he could."

The audience gave a wild applause.

"And John Sweeney, president of the AFL-CIO, and Andy Stern, first as organizing director of SEIU and then as president of SEIU, who let me build Local 100 as the premier union of lower-income workers in the South and organize hotel workers in New Orleans and Wal-Mart workers in Florida using different ways and means others would never have allowed.

"Thanks to the directors of the ACORN Financial Justice Center, Lisa Donner and Jordan Ash—particularly for their work with me on the campaigns around predatory practices with subprime mortgages and tax preparers.

"Thanks to Mike Shea with ACORN Housing, my partner in many tough negotiations with some of these banks—and I can't leave Helene O'Brien out. She made the trains run on time as ACORN's field director during the last decade of my work with ACORN."

Wade concluded, "I cannot thank all of the organizers by name who worked with me over the years; all of you were great. I just wish I could have been even better to lead you further, but every win in the past and victory in the future is also yours to savor for the time you spent and the work you did."

Following Wade Rathke's remarks, I walked over to Wade. "Congratulations, it's an honor to work with you. Let me buy you a drink."

Wade dropped his eyes and shook his head. "Thanks for the offer, but I don't drink."

Surprised, "You don't drink—ever?" I asked. This seemed strange to me, since so much bonding and negotiating actually occurs over cocktails and meals.

"At least not publicly. ACORN is too important. I've got too many powerful enemies to mess around and risk a DUI."

I laughed nervously, as Wade rejected my hospitality.

He smiled, "But go ahead, enjoy yourself. It's a party."

"This is all so new to me. I've been working on the local level." I confided, "And so, I never realized how broad ACORN actually is."

"I know what you mean," said Wade.

"So how did you get involved in all of this?" I asked.

"I started organizing more than forty years ago when I dropped out of college to organize students against the Vietnam War."

"Is that right?"

"I was an anti-war student organizer, after which, I organized welfare recipients in Massachusetts for the National Welfare Rights Organization."

"What about you?" he asked.

"I grew up in a low-income community in Pine Bluff, Arkansas."

"I know that area well. Maxine Nelson our Secretary is from Pine Bluff. We did a lot of organizing down there."

I smiled. "Raised in that environment, I developed my burning desire to improve the living and working conditions of other people living in communities just like mine."

"Oh, that's good."

"So, I'm looking forward to serving on ACORN's national board with you."

"I'm sure you will do fine." Wade turned slowly and walked away, with a twisted smile on his face.

Wade was affable, and seemed so devoid of color constructs he absorbed the ethnicity of those around him. Wade possessed an easy, off-handed, self-deprecating humor and quiet confidence. In one word—unflappable.

I walked back towards the rear of the bar and rejoined Marcel Reid, Fannie Brown, John Jones, and Reverend Gloria Swerginia, along with Kevin from Minnesota, the only Caucasian in the group.

Fannie the Chair of California ACORN was always strong and proud. A former member of the California Black Panther Party, Fannie won't back down or bite her quick lip. California was an ACORN stronghold due to their prior success in organizing statewide worker's unions and associations.

John walked slowly back to the table holding a warm cognac snifter as he balanced a full four finger pour of Hennessy.

A white male from Minnesota, Kevin was an outsider to the community and curious about the Black experience. Kevin asked "Do you actually believe the FBI targeted Black Power groups and organizations?"

"We know they did," said Fannie.

"How so?"

"We were there; we are members of Black Power groups which were targeted. I was a member of the California Black Panther Party."

"And I studied under Dr. Ron Karenga the founder of US Organization," said Marcel.

Puzzled, Kevin asked, "I know about the Black Panthers—but who is Karenga and who or what is -*US*- Marcel?"

"He is an author, political activist, and college professor. I stood out as a teenage prodigy in his classes filled with liberal white students. His lectures were always upbeat, lively and entertaining, but he is best known for inventing Kwanza, a Pan-African holiday celebrated in the U.S., and the Caribbean.

"Your teacher created Kwanza?"

"He also founded the US Organization, an outspoken Cultural Black Nationalist group in 1965. He was inspired by the Pan-Africanism transformation of Malcolm X. His US Organization was a rival of the Black Panther Party in California."

Kevin asked, "So what was the difference between the Black Panthers and US?"

Fannie laughed. "for one thing the Panthers had a *Ten Point Plan* a which offered bread and green, and they referred to the US organization as the United Slaves, which was often mistaken for the group's official name."

Marcel said, "Professor Karenga believed Black people should strive to define and understand themselves as a people who speak truth, do justice, respect our ancestors and elders, support and challenge our children, care for the vulnerable, relate rightfully to the environment, struggle for what is right, honor our past, engage our present and plan for and welcome our future."

Fannie said, "The Panthers and -*US*- had different aims and tactics but often found themselves competing for young recruits. But J. Edgar Hoover and the FBI used the competition to create friction between the Black Panther Party and the US Organization."

Kevin laughed. "So Fannie you were a Black Panther and Marcel you were a rival member of -*US*-?"

Marcel smiled. "I was 16 years old, draped in Black Power rhetoric and black velvet dashikis. I occasionally attended *US* meetings with Professor Karenga, but I never actually joined the militant group.

"They called me little Angela (Davis). Tall, skinny legs too long, eyes too big with too much hair, I smiled a lot and looked far too serious for my age."

Fannie said, "We wouldn't have been rivals if it hadn't been for Hoover. The FBI destroyed the Black Panthers and *US,* not to mention Malcolm X and Martin Luther King."

"How did they do it?" asked Kevin.

"Counter intelligence," Fannie replied. "The FBI sent spurious letters to the Los Angeles Black Panther Party supposedly from a member of *US* claiming the youth group was aware of a Black Panther 'contract' to kill Ron Karenga, and *US* planned to ambush the leaders of the Black Panthers in Los Angeles."

"That is so low down," I mumbled under my breath.

Fannie said, "So the FBI used counterintelligence measures to stoke a *US* versus Black Panther vendetta, which caused a power struggle to take place between the Black Panther Party and the US Organization. It took on the aura of gang warfare with threats of murder and reprisals."

"What happened?" I asked.

Fannie continued, "The rivalry ultimately erupted when the Black Panthers and the US Organization disagreed over who should lead the new Afro-American Studies Center at UCLA. Professor Karenga and his supporters backed one candidate, the Panthers another.

"The Black Student Union set up a coalition to try to broker peace between the groups, but ended when two members of the Black Panthers were shot dead in a violent clash on the UCLA campus."

Marcel frowned. "Ultimately, the COINTELPRO was so low down—but devastatingly effective."

An uneasy hush covered the table.

"That's incredible. Nobody can beat the government, but what about the church?" asked Kevin.

"What do you mean?"

"If the government was the problem, then why not use the churches to organize around them? I mean use the constitution, the separation of church and state, to deflect the government." asked Kevin.

Reverend Gloria replied, "For religious reasons, the Black Church usually avoids economic or political actions. They believe politics and money are sins."

I replied, "I think politics and money are the answer."

Marcel said, "Professor Karenga believed we must continue and expand political education process through literature, forums and social practice which defines and clarifies issues, reinforces community, and teaches and increases political participation and political action.

Reverend Gloria said, "But Church leaders are loathe to participate in economic justice because it directly involves wealth—and money is the root of all evil. Many Christian ministers preach it's easier for a camel to fit through the eye of a needle than for a rich man to get to heaven."

"The love of money is the root of all evil," replied Marcel.

"That's exactly right," I said. "In the minority neighborhoods I visit, it is the lack of money which is the root of all the evil I see."

They all laughed aloud.

Reverend Gloria said, "And that's a problem. You can't go to church leaders and complain about a business loan, a government contract, a franchise opportunity, or anything like that. If you get tazered by the police—no problem, but you can't get Black churches to support economic justice."

Marcel said, "They think because they are charitable non-profit institutions, they can't advocate for your right to acquire wealth."

I said, "With enough economic justice—you can purchase social justice in America.

"What do you mean by that?"

I said, "Think about it, Kevin. Church groups in the south often marched to protest when the Sheriff lynched Black folks—that's social justice. But what if the Black folks had enough money and influence to elect their own Sheriff, or at least one who wouldn't lynch them?

"So with enough economic justice, they could solve their own problems through capitalism and political participation."

Kevin hesitated. "Okay, I see what you mean. You might have a point."

"What I want to know is," I asked the group, "how did a middle-class white guy from Wyoming learn to organize Black neighborhoods and create ACORN?"

"That's a good question," said Fannie. "He takes the credit but it wasn't just Wade."

She said, "Four Black women on welfare here in Little Rock, hired Wade Rathke and Gary Delgado to help them fight to empower low and moderate income families in Arkansas."

Fannie said, "Wade used to work for the Black guy, George Wiley, in the National Welfare Rights Organization."

"Eventually, the low-income Black members in the NWRO started to resist being organized by middle class white folks, like Wade. So Wiley sent Wade to Little Rock to help build an organization that would organize middle class working people in addition to low-income minorities."

John chimed in, "It was four women members and a brother. George Wiley sponsored ACORN to expand the fight for welfare rights to the middle-class."

"So Wade was a paid organizer?" I asked.

"That's right." Fannie replied, "Wade Rathke and Gary Delgado—another organizer."

Marcel added, "But Wade was shrewd. Over time he wound up forcing the others out."

"That's right." John said, "After the brother died."

"He died?" I stammered. "Did anyone suspect foul play?"

"They say it was an accident," replied John. "Dr. George Wiley was reported missing and presumed drowned, while sailing in the Chesapeake Bay."

A nervous silence covered the group.

"I hate to play into racial stereotypes, but poor black folks don't swim or sail. And George Wiley, a strong Black activist, mysteriously disappears in a boating accident? It seems suspicious to me."

Fannie said, "As for foul play, you never know for sure. Plus he was on Nixon's master list of political opponents, right before he disappeared."

"Was he?" I asked.

John said, "Whether it was fratricide by ACORN, or homicide by the government, George Wiley was a militant Black leader who would have easily been a target of the FBI's Counter Intelligence Programs."

Naively, "Counter Intelligence?" asked Kevin.

"The FBI used a series of counterintelligence programs to neutralize political dissidents and targeted radical political organizations. COINTELPRO was initiated to expose, disrupt, misdirect, discredit, or otherwise neutralize Black Nationalist organizations and groups, their leadership, spokesmen and supporters." Fannie said.

Kevin asked, "But those were radical communist front-organizations. You don't believe that the FBI targeted ordinary people and civil rights groups do you?"

Fannie said, "Over the years, similar programs were created to neutralize civil rights, anti-war, and many other groups, many of which were accused of being communist front organizations."

Marcel added, "J. Edgar Hoover believed Communists had been trained in deceit and secretly worked toward the day when they hoped to replace our American way of life with a Communist dictatorship. They utilized cleverly camouflaged movements, such as peace groups and civil rights groups to achieve their sinister purposes."

Fannie said, "George Wiley was eventually forced out of NWRO because he wanted to organize the middle class, not just poor people. Wiley still believed welfare was a good issue around which to organize the poor, but recognized that a multi-issue organization would have a greater chance for long-term success.

"Wiley believed the poor and Black in America could not win further significant improvements in their status, unless they became a part of a new majority movement to change society which he called the Movement for Economic Justice, which sponsored more than a hundred tax clinics for the poor before he mysteriously disappeared in 1973."

Marcel surmised, "COINTELPRO was designed to *neutralize* those who could not be prosecuted in order to prevent the rise of a black messiah, and to prevent the long-range growth of militant Black Nationalist organizations, especially among the youth."

"But I do know this." She said, "Once George Wiley was out of the way, Wade Rathke took over ACORN."

"That's why ACORN serves low and moderate income families. It's not just a Black thing."

"Which is also why, there aren't any Blacks in Wade's inner circle," said Fannie. "Wade gets rid of Black folks before they develop any real power in ACORN."

"Well, what about Maude?" I asked.

"She's the President, but she's no match for Wade," said John.

"They're long-time friends from Massachusetts, I guess," replied Fannie. "He keeps her around because she is controllable and the public black face of ACORN."

"So is ACORN a civil rights group, like Rainbow Push or the National Action Network?" I asked.

"It is—but it isn't," said Marcel. "Wade is smart, but he doesn't want fame. Wade wants power."

I reiterated, "So ACORN doesn't use a national spokesmen like Jesse Jackson or Al Sharpton?"

Marcel said, "ACORN uses ordinary people, especially women, little old ladies from any neighborhood or community, as its public face."

She said, "You never see strong Black men within the association—at least not for long."

"The face of ACORN is always the face of the local community," said Fannie. "Wade stays behind the scenes and under the radar, but he's always in control."

Marcel said, "He controls the organizers, the paid staff. They have to raise twice their salary in the first month just to keep the job. If they fail to meet the fundraising goals by the second month they are placed on probation; after the third month they are fired."

Deep in thought, I decided the membership quotas and fundraising goals insured low-income people would never become successful organizers at ACORN. The members volunteered for the organization; they paid dues and provided the bodies for mass demonstrations and protests. The organizers controlled the membership and the organization. To the working poor, ACORN was a highly effective civil rights organization. For the organizers, ACORN became a training ground for liberal causes and Democratic political operations.

Banana Republic

At 3:00 p.m., Wade Rathke introduced a special guest from organized
labor, during the closing session.
He facilitated a discussion about
ACORN's Position on Immigration
and Temporary Labor with Ana Avendano from AFL-CIO and Ben
Monterroso, from the SEIU Change to Win Campaign.

Monterroso sought board approval from ACORN to support immigration reform legislation. He gave an impromptu demonstration, "I want
everyone in this room, who aren't immigrants, to stand up."

Slowly, reluctantly, and pensively Marcel Reid stood, followed one-by-
one with Fannie Brown, Yvonne Stafford, John Jones and me, along with
another handful of African-Americans in the room.

Startled, "What are you all doing?" asked Monterroso. "If you're not
a Native American, you shouldn't be standing right now. We're all immigrants; we're a nation of immigrants."

Everyone remained standing; none sat down.

"What are you all doing?" asked a petite woman with a Caribbean
accent. Tamecka Pierce, thirty-three, the Chair from Florida ACORN,
sat near Beverly Campbell and Eddy Weatherspoon. With family from
the islands, Tamecka was both sexy and exotic. A true believer, she was a
long-time Rathke loyalist.

Marcel explained, "We're standing because we aren't immigrants.

Black people didn't ask to come here. We support you, and liberal immigration policies, but we are not *All* immigrants.

"Slavery was not immigration!" argued Fannie.

"We're all immigrants; we're all the same," insisted Monterroso.

"You're trying to act like you think you are better than us," replied Tamecka. "I'm standing up. I'm speaking out and I've got more to lose than anyone else on this board."

"What do you mean, Tamecka?"

"I've got a criminal record—a felony. So I'm at risk every time I speak out, but we've got to support immigration reform now! My family, immigrated from the Caribbean, and they're trying to make a living and live a better life."

Surprised, I whispered to Marcel. "She's not serious about the felony, is she?"

"I don't know for sure, Michael, but why would she say that if it wasn't true?"

Monterroso continued his plea. "We are all the same. There is no legal or illegal; we're all immigrants."

"No, that's not it at all." Marcel said, "We're with you. We do not have to be immigrants to support liberal immigration. However, you're disrespecting African-Americans. Slavery and the middle-passage was the greatest holocaust in history. WE are not immigrants; we're abductees."

Kevin, the retired VA scientist, moved to table Wade's motion, by making it depend upon conditional language. "I think our Black members want to support immigration reform so long as they are not displaced by a rush of new immigrants."

However, as a result of the contentious discussion about what was and was not immigration, the association board rejected the resolution pushed and supported by Wade Rathke.

Visibly exacerbated and embarrassed, Wade withdrew the SEIU resolution for ACORN participation in comprehensive immigration reform from the floor. Kevin was a research scientist for the Veteran's

Administration, but by opposing Wade Rathke, Kevin had served on his first, and *last* association board meeting.

Sunday, April 15, 2007

I listened to delta-blues on KABF, ACORN's local radio station, while I drove Marcel Reid to the Little Rock National Airport for her return flight. Excited and relieved, I had finished my first National Association Board Meeting. However, the meeting ended prior to the election of new officers.

I was pleased and overwhelmed with our success during my first national board meeting. By convincing ACORN to take up Mortgage Fraud as a national campaign, I had saved Georgia ACORN and started a new national campaign to reclaim the Historic Winecoff Hotel.

Incredulously, I asked, "So wait a minute Marcel, you're telling me Maude has remained President of ACORN for decades but there has never been an actual election?"

"That's right, Michael. At least I've never seen one."

"And does that hold true for the Treasurer and Secretary, also?"

"It does," she replied.

I paused and reflected, "How can that be, Marcel?"

"They're slick," quipped Marcel. "The staff sets the meeting agenda, and they always place National Elections last on the agenda."

"Okay, so what?" I asked.

"They schedule a four day agenda for a three day board meeting. They know we'll never get to the actual election, and the old guard stays in power."

"That's fucked up, Marcel," I replied. "So ACORN's so-called *democratic leadership* is more like a Banana Republic. I'd heard rumors about Maude stepping down ever since I joined ACORN. Now I see it was just a ruse."

"What's worse," said Marcel. "Ron told Maude -*He*- wanted to run for President after she stepped down."

"What? Ron Sykes, our Ron?"

"Yep, big mistake!" said Marcel. "That's why they took his fellowship away—too much ambition."

"Yeah, that wasn't smart at all," I said.

Marcel replied, "I wondered what he was thinking myself, I guess he was getting too friendly and comfortable with management."

I asked, "Anyway, Marcel, since the board supported our Mortgage Fraud action, what do we do now?"

"I don't know Michael," she replied. "Wade is pulling it in under the Financial Justice Centers."

I asked, "That's a good thing. Right?"

"In a way," she said. "But you've got to make sure Georgia ACORN continues to lead the initiative."

I looked pensive and confused.

"Otherwise, ACORN will push the issue nationally, but *you* and Georgia ACORN won't get any credit."

"You mean ACORN will take our issue but still won't help us?" I asked.

I dialed Ronald Sykes, placed him on speakerphone and told him what happened.

"Oh, hell no!" Ron replied, "We can't let that happen. We need to put out a press release immediately and claim Mortgage Fraud as the signature Georgia ACORN issue. Michael, you put the Mortgage Fraud press release out, and I'll get it posted on the ACORN website."

Marcel laughed and handed me a tattered copy of an opposition research report before she left the car for her plane. The caption read: *Rotten ACORN*. I chuckled at the cover, which displayed a cracked acorn.

I read aloud. "After ACORN employees delivered a petition demanding union recognition, Wade Rathke called a meeting of ACORN's inner circle, which included his common-law wife, Beth Butler, the Head Organizer of Louisiana ACORN, and his brother Dale Rathke, the financial guru of the outfit.

"They used classic union-busting tactics, which could be expected from any major corporation, to divide and destroy the worker's solidarity.

By 2003, the National Labor Relations Board found ACORN management guilty of using union-busting tactics against its own employees."

"Oh?" Marcel said.

I quickly leafed through the document and skimmed the section on governance. I read aloud, "On September 3, 1987, the *Arkansas Democrat-Gazette* reported: "Dorothy Perkins contended all funds received by ACORN were controlled at New Orleans by Wade Rathke. Dorothy Perkins, thirty-two, Arkansas ACORN chair complained the group was *run like a Jim Jones cult* where all the money ended up under Wade Rathke's control and was *never seen* by the low-income individuals the organization claimed to represent. Dorothy also said that Wade Rathke told disgruntled Arkansas ACORN members they 'could pull out of ACORN if they wanted to but the money is staying with me,' Wade boasted. He had the votes by a margin of 44-to-1 to do whatever he wants."

The report continued: "Gary Delgado, thirty-seven, a co-founding ACORN organizer described allegations that when member leadership was at odds with organizers, it was the members who were always forced out—never the staff. In a front-page story headlined 'ACORN Official Barred from Meeting; Leader Resigns' in the *Arkansas Democrat* dating back to April 22, 1979, Nevada ACORN chairman William Brookerd, forty-five, having resigned his position, charged, 'If the leadership at any level insists on pursuing their priorities over staff priorities, they are *democratically exorcised* from the leadership." I realized then, the power structure of the association leads to public confusion. The group described *community leaders* who consisted of dues-paying members, while organizers were paid staff controlled by Wade Rathke, his family and his supporters.

Marcel replied, "ACORN's culture was designed to create dependency on the organizers and produce members who were loyal to ACORN staff, but not their own elected leaders. The organizers were in charge, they had all the resources, they knew all the answers; the organizers developed the tactics and strategy for ACORN campaigns.

"Local organizers were taught to hand-pick the so-called leaders within local ACORN chapters, but even more importantly to identify and eliminate free thinking members who might become troublemakers for ACORN management. ACORN preferred local leaders who acquiesced to being ceremonial. Consequently, the organizers sought out and promoted members who weren't intellectually curious and didn't ask follow-up questions.

"Ultimately, the organizers controlled the membership by controlling the information, financial resources, local and national officers, meeting agenda and board minutes. The local organizers reported to state Head Organizers. The Head Organizers reported to Wade Rathke, the Chief Organizer. In ACORN, the members were pawns, the organizers were Generals and the Chief Organizer—was GOD."

Friday, April 20, 2007

The following day, Georgia ACORN Chair Deacon Dana Williams and Ronald Sykes issued a press release and posted pictures of the Winecoff Hotel and the Juneteenth Mortgage Fraud March and Rally on the ACORN website.

The release read: "During the April 14, 2007 board meeting for the Association for Community Organizations for Reform Now held in Little Rock, Arkansas, founder and Chief Organizer Wade Rathke announced, "ACORN is on the job concerning fraudulent foreclosure schemes, especially in sub-prime mortgage markets.

"This statement came in response to concerns raised by Michael McCray, Georgia ACORN Delegate about the Mortgage Fraud epidemic currently raging in Georgia, Florida, California and Texas—while chanting *Predatory Lenders . . . Criminal Offenders.*"

The release continued: "Also, this week on, Wednesday, April 18, 2007, right before ACORN's grassroots campaign kick-off, national staff from ACORN and ACORN Housing discussed proposals to stem the tide of foreclosures at a *Housing Preservation Summit* meeting convened by

Senator Christopher Dodd, Chairman of the Senate Banking, Housing, and Urban Affairs Committee.

"ACORN members have been engaged in a major effort since 1999 to protect neighborhoods from predatory lending. The campaign has included working to shine a spotlight on and reform the practices of individual lenders, playing a leading role in passing city and state legislation against predatory lending, and winning reform from federal regulators.

"The case of the Historic Winecoff Hotel was cited as a prime example of how extreme mortgage and foreclosure fraud is in the state of Georgia, and how out-of-state developers and investment bankers actually prey on innocent Georgia residents and small business owners due to Georgia's lax and un-enforced foreclosure laws.

"So lax in fact, Atlanta and Fulton County Officials refuse to investigate the true ownership of the Winecoff Hotel despite giving over $1.2 million in taxpayer funds to Jay Furman and the Ellis Hotel Company, the co-conspirators in the InterBank Funding mortgage and fraudulent foreclosure scheme.

"InterBank Funding Companies, an unlicensed Wall Street Investment Firm which defrauded small business owners and real estate holders, and a Georgia ACORN member by conducting the alleged "fraudulent foreclosure" was shut down by the U.S. Securities and Exchange Commission in 2002 for raising over $180 million through securities fraud and mortgage *ponzie schemes,* which realized quick profits.

"Amazingly, the City of Atlanta recently issued over $1.2 million in taxpayer bonds, and approved construction and building permits for this property, which is currently under litigation in Fulton County Superior Court.

"The Ellis Hotel, the *straw purchasers,* have never produced any proof of purchase, clear title records or a receipt proving they ever purchased the property at all—neither to the City of Atlanta nor in Fulton County Superior Court.

"Chicago Title Insurance Company actually conducted the *paper closing* for the Ellis Hotel, a.k.a. Kelco/FB Winecoff. Chicago Title had a long history of conducting fraudulent settlements in residential and commercial mortgage transactions and signed a $6.2 million settlement with the Department of Treasury and HUD for closing fraudulent mortgage loans in 2005. Worse still, commercial mortgage and foreclosure fraud of this type leads to public corruption, due to the rush to re-develop cities like Atlanta.

"The Atlanta Police Department and Fulton County District Attorney's Office refuse to investigate low income or small business claims of mortgage fraud when the offenders are often large real estate developers or investment bankers with strong political connections to city officials.

"Atlanta Police Chief Richard Pennington, Fulton County District Attorney Paul Howard Jr., and Mayor Shirley Franklin were all notified about the allegations of commercial mortgage fraud and theft concerning the Winecoff Hotel beginning back in 2003.

"Unfortunately, the District Attorney's office and Atlanta Police Department have refused to assign a detective to investigate Dillard-Winecoff's criminal complaint after receiving pressure from the Mayor's Office. Despite her so-called *Open Door* policy, Mayor Shirley Franklin refused to meet with Georgia ACORN members Courtney Dillard and Michael McCray to discuss this or other Georgia ACORN issues."

The pace of engagement after joining the ACORN national board had been a mind-boggling experience both in terms of the sheer number of community activists from around the country I was privileged to meet and the amount of information I received. I had learned about a myriad of organizations, initiatives and partnerships—local, state and international. Now it was time to turn my attention elsewhere and return to the real world of presidential politics.

I knocked on the door of a two-story, Victorian home near Little Rock Central High School. Carol Willis answered the door, wearing his trademark Black fedora with 10th Calvary crossbars and gold tasseled rope cords. "C'm o n. . . in, McCRAY," he said, in a long southern drawl.

My visit was to discuss the African-American outreach, and the Hillary Clinton Campaign. An avid baseball fan and civil war buff, Carol Willis often wore Negro League baseball paraphernalia, and his home displayed civil war memorabilia, recognizing the contributions of African-Americans in baseball and the civil war.

Willis often donned Ninth and Tenth Calvary insignia, during campaign seasons. Those were the two Black divisions of the Union Army who fought with such courage and tenacity that Native Americans called them Buffalo Soldiers, which became a moniker for the Politicos Carol Willis worked with.

As their General, Willis was serious about baseball and considered politics, civil war. Overworked and under funded, this rag-tag group of Black politicos were seasoned political operatives and talented outreach specialists. These political organizers devised strategies and door-to-door maneuvers in minority neighborhoods and communities where other political operatives refused to campaign. Their efforts in grassroots organizing and outreach often resulted in a 3 to 6 percent boost from African-American voter turnout on Election Day.

Perplexed, I asked, "What are we waiting for Willis? We need to hurry up and get out in the field. We have to start strong *if* Hillary is going to pull this thing out."

"They don't think they need us," replied Willis.

"Why not?" I asked.

"The Hillary Clinton campaign is a juggernaut. She is 30 points ahead in the polls with $45 million cash in the bank, while Obama maybe has $3 million cash on hand."

"I see what you mean, Willis, but don't forget, he is a community organizer."

Willis paused, and asked, "When do you think we need to start moving out?"

"I'm ready now, but we definitely need to be on the ground six to nine months out. They always wait to the last minute and then send us out a day-late and a dollar-short, and then they want miracles."

"If it was easy, McCray, they wouldn't call us." He told me. "But keep your bags packed. I'll let you know when we hear back from the campaign."

Carol Willis flew into Reagan National Airport to meet with Senator Clinton, Bob Nash and other senior campaign officials, in order to discuss African-American Outreach and Political Strategies. "Remember, where the black vote is concerned, the bar was set so high under President Clinton. He didn't just tap blacks for his Cabinet and staff," touted Willis. "In 1996, we had more than 45 Black professionals on the campaign staff, nearly 30 percent of the total. In addition to volunteers, some 300 Blacks worked in campaign posts throughout the country. We've already got a dedicated team of seasoned political operatives ready and willing to work for you, Hillary, all you have to do is give us the word to get started."

Willis had worked under then Arkansas Governor Bill Clinton for more than 13 years and was the key strategist who developed support among Blacks during the 1992 campaign. As the Senior Advisor to the DNC Chairman and Director of Community Outreach Services, Willis had also served at the Democratic National Committee. Willis had once been scrutinized by Whitewater Independent Counsel, Kenneth Starr as a coordinator of the *Get Out The Vote* effort in Clinton's Arkansas campaigns, and the 1992 Clinton-Gore presidential race.

Bill Clinton engendered overwhelming, unwavering support from black voters, due in part to his record in Arkansas and his credentials within the civil rights community. As governor, Bill Clinton attended all the civil rights meetings, and he would invite all the leaders to brief and talk to him. His intimacy with the Black community allowed Bill Clinton to pursue policies others would never have dared. He exhibited mutual respect, even when people disagreed with him on something like welfare reform or the three-strikes laws; we knew that President Clinton was on our side. Consequently, Hillary Clinton enjoyed substantial support from the Black community, due to name identification and her husband's long-time support from Blacks and the civil rights community. Senator Clinton maintained solid leads in most national polls, and the polls in early-voting states, like Iowa and New Hampshire, showed her holding her own.

As the primaries neared, internal polling showed Hillary Clinton winning more than 60 percent of black voters, and the 42 House members in the Congressional Black Caucus, split down the middle between Senator Obama and the former First Lady. In response, Congressman Jesse Jackson, Jr., warned his colleagues in the black caucus about the risks of shunning Senator Obama's candidacy, reminding them of the political aftermath of his fathers' campaigns in the 1980s.

Most black Congressional Democrats sided with the white presidential candidates, back then too, and Jesse Jackson carried many of their districts in 1984, and virtually all of them in 1988, driving up voter registration in the process. As a result, over the next few election cycles, a flurry of primary challenges and the retirement or defeat of several incumbents ushered the arrival of a new class of black congressmen in Washington. Jackson's message was crystal clear; even if Senator Obama loses, there will be a price to pay from the Black community for opposing him.

Private Equity

Sunday, May 13, 2007

The air pressure in my ears popped as my flight descended in to Reagan National Airport. I flew to Washington in order to attend Washington Whistleblower Week, which consisted of a series of events from May 13-19, 2007 organized to raise awareness about whistleblowing and First Amendment activism. This historic event was organized by Adam Miles and Tom Devine of the Government Accountability Project and was timed to coincide with the fifth anniversary of the enactment of the Notification and Federal Employee Anti-discrimination and Retaliation Act of May 15, 2002. The federal *No FEAR Act* was the first civil rights legislation of the 21st century.

The week was promoted by the Make It Safe Coalition, a cadre of fifty organizations and included a diverse group of participants recruiting followers, from a United States Senator, to 9-11 conspiracy theorists. The individual member organizations came together to host a series of events on various aspects of whistleblowing. During the week-long event, whistleblowers and their allies gathered for awards ceremonies, speeches, panel discussions, and training sessions, including testimonies from courageous whistleblowers.

Jeffrey Wigand, a former tobacco executive reported the industry's manipulation of nicotine levels in cigarettes and was featured in the movie *The Insider*.

Bunnatine Greenhouse, of the Army Corps of Engineers opposed the process which awarded no-bid government contracts to Halliburton, Inc. and could have slowed the U.S. march to the Iraq War.

Stephen Kohn hosted a series of workshops to aid whistleblowers and their lawyers. Kohn refers to his law office as the "National Whistleblower Center" and reminded participants that they stood to gain monetarily from whistleblowing activities.

Coleen Rowley, blew the whistle on the FBI's negligence preceding the September 11 terrorist attack. Ms. Rowley was named as one of *Time Magazine*'s Persons of the Year, along with Enron whistleblower Sherron Watkins. The FBI oversight panel was led by former FBI Special Agents Rowley and Mike German.

Other distinguished attendees included Congresswoman Sheila Jackson Lee of Texas, Congressman Albert Wynn of Maryland and Reverend Walter Fauntroy, former Congressman and Civil Rights icon who chaired the Citizen's Tribunal on Capitol Hill. Marcel Reid, chair of DC ACORN, participated on the citizen's panel.

Janet Howard, Joyce E. Megginson and Tanya Ward Jordan were members of the No FEAR Coalition and class agents who blew the whistle on race discrimination at the Department of Commerce.

Dr. Marsha Coleman-Adebayo, an EPA employee won a racial and gender discrimination lawsuit after alleging a United States company was exposing South African miners and their families to toxic levels of vanadium.

Finally, I represented the No FEAR Coalition and U.S. Department of Agriculture whistleblowers, and passionately testified before the Citizen's Forum in support of Judicial Reform and enhanced No FEAR II—Legislation.

It was a remarkably successful event. It was featured in the *New York Times* and announced in the Congressional Record by Republican Senator Charles Grassley of Iowa, who received a lifetime achievement award for his fight against waste, fraud and corruption in government.

Following the Citizen's Tribunal on Capitol Hill, I returned to Arkansas, grabbed a cup of coffee and turned on the television to watch national news coverage of the Presidential election. Through most of 2007, front-runner status shifted depending on the reporting news agency, but the consensus listed three candidates as leading the pack after several debate performances. I was intrigued. Even after it was clear Al Gore would not run, he and John Edwards each hovered between the third and fourth place in the polls behind Senators Clinton and Obama.

"I think they've run a great campaign," Obama adviser, David Axelrod, fifty-two, declared. "She's been a very disciplined candidate. They've been deft in trying to get ahead of this tidal wave of people out there who want change. They are doing the best they can with it."

Axelrod, pointed out Senator Clinton's foremost vulnerability. "The question is ultimately, is she credible? Will people buy her as an agent of change in Washington? If they do, she'll do well."

Joe Trippi, fifty-one, a senior adviser to John Edwards, opined, "You used to be able to say the front-runners, Hillary and Obama, but I don't think that's the case anymore. It's clear she has pulled away."

Senator Obama and John Edwards faced tough decisions. They saw the same path to victory, which included turning the contest into a two-person race with Senator Clinton. Senator Obama moved to deal directly with his weakest flank, concerns about his lack of experience, through television ads. He decided to address the issue of experience head-on, despite his staff's concerns about inviting new attention to a weakness.

John Edwards tried to shake up the race when most of the attention was being focused on Clinton and Obama, by escalating a series of attacks on Senator Clinton. Edward's decision to tackle Senator Clinton could backfire and help Senator Obama in states like Iowa, where caucus voters often recoiled against two-candidate spats.

Tuesday, June 12, 2007

The states which held early primaries and caucuses were, chronologically, Iowa, New Hampshire, Nevada, and South Carolina. But Florida and Michigan moved their primaries into January against the Democratic Party's official rules.

Harold Gist, Kevin McGraw, Darrin Peters and I drafted a memo for Carol Willis. It was an urgent call to Senator Hillary Clinton, regarding Democratic Presidential Primary Election Campaign Strategy, which read:

"With less than 200 days until the 2008 Democratic Presidential caucuses and primaries begin, you are leading in most state polls and national polls but have yet to galvanize the solid support of African-Americans which Bill Clinton and Al Gore enjoyed.

"Arguably, most African-American support in the early voting states is now split among several candidates. Polling data seems to affirm my assessment which is—your support in the African-American community is vacillating and, in some instances, evaporating.

"Black Democrats are internally conflicted with whether to support your candidacy or Barack Obama, with John Edwards also getting support in the early caucus and primary states. Obama has secured commitment from many of our key Democratic activists and a number of key ministers. We should not underestimate Obama or take anything for granted. And if former Vice President Al Gore enters the race, dynamics change even more regarding African-American voters.

"Most voters are holding your campaign to a different standard. Expectations for you are high coming out the gate, unlike the other candidates. There are a number of intangibles we must address, such as staffing, message development, campaign surrogates, etc. that will arrest the hemorrhaging in African-American support. We must capture the support of those individuals still holding out and neutralize those leaning toward other campaigns.

"The window of opportunity to secure this support is narrowing. Personnel with winning presidential campaign experience must be assembled. Many key activists connected to the Clinton organization have made commitments to other campaigns, and they are continuing to take sides. We can stop (and reverse) this slippage by hitting the ground hard and expeditiously. The right organization, proper resources and key personnel, will allow us to make a major positive shift in the attitudes of African-Americans toward your candidacy.

"Your campaign should have a much stronger and more aggressive operation than both WJC and Gore, in part, because many African-Americans view Obama's candidacy as a different opportunity than what Reverend Jackson offered in each of his runs. Additionally, certain Clinton detractors will attack your campaign with examples of mis-steps during the WJC administration (i.e., Lani Guinier, Welfare Reform, Crime Bill, etc.)

"Action should be taken now to more effectively reach out to African-Americans. In securing the 2008 Democratic nomination, a comprehensive strategy targeting African-American voters in the early primary/caucus states must be developed. This strategy will compliment and enhance the overall campaign strategy. This strategy is not to be separate and apart from your general campaign strategy, but is to be an integrated and seamless approach.

"What is paramount to fully developing and executing this strategy is to engage key personnel immediately. Please know my team is, and has been, reaching out to supporters and potential supporters in your behalf. This allows an informal assessment in our designated states. Yes, we look to expand and expound upon the Clinton legacy, but we have to demonstrate a Hillary Clinton presidency is a fresh, new and progressive approach for the country.

"It is estimated that in specific designated early states, African-Americans may represent up to nearly half of Democrats voting, depending on the state. Outlined below is a synopsis of the strategy that should be employed in the following states: Iowa, Florida, South Carolina, Nevada, Michigan, New Jersey, California, and Arkansas. Also, we should consider early voting states like Tennessee and Ohio that begin voting in mid-January, 2008. We do not want Senator Obama to be viewed as the *-comeback kid-* after January 29, 2008.

"We have a daunting, but not insurmountable challenge before us. I cannot overemphasize the need for your campaign to engage key consultants/personnel. These individuals are experienced and adept at developing and implementing a voter contact plan with activities that culturally connect with our targeted voter. A communication (paid/earned) and field strategy which leverages and maximizes our national network is much needed.

"It is proven that generic campaign messages do not effectively motivate African-American voters. Message development for this targeted voter is important. Part of our success hinges on developing and delivering the right message and underlying themes for these voters. The message is not only verbalized by you and the campaign surrogates, but includes every aspect of the campaign's content, context, and style that is projected.

"In addition to a specific message, intangibles such as who is supporting your candidacy, who are your advisors/consultants, business done with African-American vendors, all contribute to a message portrayal in the African-American community. We want to touch and move African-American voters to your candidacy. Some of the items that should have action include:

"Mid-June 2007: Engage key consultants and personnel at HQ; Present Strategy targeting African-American voters. July–August 2007: Engage and deploy key consultants and political operatives in designated states; Begin State and Regional Leadership Roundup Strategy meetings; Develop State-specific outreach plans.

"July–November 2007: Continue State and Regional Leadership Roundup Strategy meetings; Attend various national and state conferences; Begin implementing state-specific plans; Conduct on-going outreach activities in designated states; Begin Voter Contact programs.

"September–January 2008: Continue on-going outreach activities in designated states; Execute Voter Contact programs; Continue State and Regional Leadership Roundup Strategy meetings.

"January 2008: Continue on-going outreach activities in designated states; Execute Voter Contact programs for Primary and Caucus Elections; Schedule GOTV/Early Vote activities.

"February 2008: Continue on-going outreach activities in designated states; Continue Voter Contact programs for Primary and Caucus
Elections; Schedule GOTV activities.

"BUDGET (TBD) - Budgets are about priorities. Costs in any
campaign depends on many variables, for example, staff experience level,
opposition's strength, soliciting and maintaining supporters, etc. The
budget is the strategy expressed in dollars and cents. Our budget strategy
is based upon a plan that will provide ultimate coverage in designated
states."

Internally, Clinton's strategists set a goal of receiving half the black
vote in the southern primaries, although they estimated they needed as
little as 30 percent in order to defeat Senator Obama. As the primaries
neared, internal polls showed Hillary Clinton winning more than 60
percent of black voters.

Independent counsel, Kenneth Starr had once subpoenaed the
personal financial records of Carol Willis, a longtime friend and political
aide to President Clinton. Starr accused Willis of paying off Black ministers to support Bill Clinton by distributing tens of thousands of dollars to
influential ministers and political figures in Arkansas' Black community
during Clinton's 1990 reelection campaign for Governor.

Wednesday, June 27, 2007

Marcel Reid closed and locked the doors on her Silver Cadillac, and
walked into the DC ACORN office. She was immediately confronted
by Belinda Ferrell. "Do you have a minute, Marcel? You should talk to
Anita."

"Talk to her about what?" Marcel asked.

"People are complaining about her. She's mooching off members,
borrowing money from staff. She may even be using fake addresses to
apply for government assistance."

"That's a serious accusation, Belinda. Do you know that for sure?"
asked Marcel.

"I don't know for sure, but that's what they're saying around the office, and its starting to become a problem."

A young single mother, Anita MonCrief experienced severe money troubles during her employment at Project Vote. She earned a meager income during this period and borrowed a total of $1,500 from her employer.

She took the loan in two cash advances on her salary which was to be repaid by payroll deductions, but only $500.00 of the advances was ever repaid.

Consequently, Anita applied for a Pitney Bowes Purchase Power Visa card issued in Project Vote's name. She listed herself as the *authorized user* of the card, activated the on-line Internet access privileges for the account, and used the on-line access features.

Anita continued to use the Pitney Bowes Purchase Power Visa card but sent the front pages of monthly invoices, which did not include her itemized charges, to Project Vote's accounts payable operation in Little Rock, Arkansas.

Project Vote began paying the credit card balance. Mistakenly believing the cover pages of Pitney Bowes Purchase Power Visa invoices were business-related Pitney Bowes invoices, Project Vote's accounts payable staff paid a total of $1,741.43 on the Pitney Bowes Purchase Power Visa.

Wednesday, September 19, 2007

"White financiers are all flooding up to the Waldorf Astoria this morning for the opening of today's Dow Jones Private Equity Analyst conference!" a shrill voice cried out. Bertha Lewis, fifty-six, stood defiant wearing a Dashiki, braided hair, and sea shell earrings. She was the Head Organizer for ACORN in Brooklyn, and co-chaired the New York's Working Families Party.

Bertha came to New York as an education activist. After a protracted battle with the city and a notorious landlord, Bertha became a tenant and housing rights leader, and then a tenant and community organizer. She helped organize a city-wide coalition of labor, religious, community and political groups which passed a new Living Wage law in City Council, covering over 50,000 New Yorkers, in 2002.

The Waldorf-Astoria was the quintessential New York destination accessed through a discreet separate entrance located on 50th Street, between Park and Lexington Avenues. The Waldorf Astoria enjoyed a storied reputation of unparalleled hospitality and service. As one of the first grand hotels to combine elegance with luxurious amenities and services, the Art Deco landmark has been world-renowned for over a century. The Waldorf-Astoria was home to celebrities, corporate moguls, royalties and every American president since Herbert Hoover. Today it hosted a private equity conference and the local community groups which protested it.

Angered by the trillion-dollar buyout, the industry's treatment of workers, and inequitable tax breaks corporate takeover giants receive, two-dozen protestors from the Working Families Party and the New York chapter of ACORN burst into the third floor ballroom of the Waldorf-Astoria. More than 1,000 analysts and investors gathered await-ing remarks from David Rubenstein, fifty-eight, the co-founder of the Carlyle Group, a global private equity investment firm headquartered in Washington, D.C.

The firm managed more than $84.5 billion from 28 offices around the world. Their focus was on leveraged buyouts, growth capital, real estate and leveraged finance investments; but amid the frenetic politicking, which occupied the higher reaches of that world, few had paid it much attention. Elsewhere, few had even heard of the secretive group—which was exactly how Carlyle liked it.

Armed with signs picturing a hotel doorman asking, "Why does Carlyle Group founder David Rubenstein pay taxes at a lower rate than this guy?" and, "Why do New York state pensioners see risk while David Rubenstein sees profits?"

The protestors demanded the buyout industry, and key players like

Carlyle's Rubinstein, to change their business practices and pay their fair share.

"It's Not Fair."

"Pay Your Share."

"It's Not Fair."

"Pay Your Share."

Chanting protestors stormed the ballroom floor, while two protest leaders dropped a banner from the balcony above the ballroom, which read: "Why does David Rubenstein pay taxes at a lower rate than an NYPD officer?"

Organizing poor communities always took finesse and some political theater. But from the beginning of the Carlyle campaign, when the SEIU failed to muster up the required public outrage, they switched tactics. They called in ACORN.

ACORN spun the fight against the Carlyle Group as rich whites versus poor blacks. The demonstration was a new campaign to raise awareness about the little known world of private equity and the effect it had on the lives of average New Yorkers.

Hotel security guards quickly hustled the ACORN protesters off the Mezzanine level, but the banner remained tied to the balcony above the audience, in clear view of the crowd and media below. "The Carlyle Group is the poster child for an industry which has made billions by fleecing taxpayers and loading up companies with unsustainable levels of debt," declared Dan Cantor, a fifty-two, Executive Director of the Working Families Party.

"David Rubenstein made $260 million last year; yet, he paid taxes at a lower rate than the doorman at this hotel. Not only that, companies like Carlyle don't pay their fair share in corporate taxes," declared Pat Boone, sixty, and the President of NY ACORN.

"What does this mean to your average New Yorker?" asked Boone. "Plenty. The takeover industry's tax cheats increase the tax burden on the rest of us while undercutting vital public services like schools, healthcare and affordable housing."

The action followed an earlier announcement of a new coalition of New York labor and community organizations who were angry with buyout industry executives for saddling regular New Yorkers with an unfair tax burden, while engaging in risky debt-fueled investments which put New Yorkers' retirement funds at risk. The SEIU, which represented 1.9 million janitors, security guards, health care workers and others, had already marshaled a significant portion of its membership and their resources.

Field First

Thursday, July 27, 2007

Kevin McGraw, thirty-six, short, 5'6" and stocky with brown eyes and a muscular build closed the Blackhawk County phonebook. "I think I've found a couple of prospects. It seems like Mount Carmel and Antioch Baptist are the largest churches in the Black community."

"That's good Kevin, who are the Pastors? Maybe we can set up an appointment?" asked Harold Gist, a forty-six year-old, Deputy Director of the African-American Strategy Team. A hardy man, sporting a salt-and-pepper goatee and Malcolm X glasses, Gist spoke in a booming baritone voice, "Get It Done!" This was his personal motto.

"It looks like a couple of young guys—Frantz Whitefield and Michael Coleman. I'll make a few calls to the church offices and see what happens."

Harold Gist and Kevin McGraw had flown to Waterloo to scout the local conditions in the Black community for Carol Willis and the African-American Strategies Team. The Buffalo Soldiers typically engaged in the South Carolina Primaries, the first in the South and the first Democratic Primaries with any significant African-American population. This year, they started in the mid-west because the Iowa polls were tightening.

Kevin and Gist, were longtime Clinton aids and Carol Willis loyalists. During their visit, they also met Frieda Weems, forty-four, an attractive slender women and local Democratic Activist. She was fond of Democrats and roughnecks. The daughter of a local civil rights leader, Frieda was a politically savvy, petite Black woman, with short, close-cropped hair and a feisty attitude.

Frieda escorted Harold Gist and Kevin McGraw to the state's Commission on the Status of African-Americans announcement of a new initiative to organize the black community in the state's largest cities, including Waterloo.

Waterloo was the county seat of Black Hawk County, Iowa. Located near Cedar Falls, Waterloo was the larger of the two cities by population, although its growth had declined since 2000. Waterloo had the highest concentration of African-Americans in the state. Blacks constituted 13.9 percent of the city's 67,054 population, and Black Hawk County held 4.68 percent of the caucus weight in 2008.

The group of 30 community members included several pastors, Representative Deborah Berry and Michael Blackwell, sixty-three, director of the University of Northern Iowa Center for Multicultural Education.

Gist said, "Frieda, tell me something about the Black community here in Waterloo."

Frieda replied, "During the late 1800s, thousands of German, Greek, and Bosnian immigrants came to Waterloo to farm or take jobs in the local factories. African-Americans were first drawn to Waterloo by Illinois Central Railroad's repair shop at the rail yard on East Fourth Street.

"In 1910, fewer than 20 African-Americans lived in Waterloo, but by 1920, nearly 1,000 residents were African-American. The biggest migration of African-American people occurred when a railroad strike shut down the repair shop, and Illinois Central Railroad recruited Black workers from Mississippi. Blacks settled on the East side, while Whites lived everywhere. Over time, the East side stagnated while the West side became more prosperous and affluent."

The community meeting began. The state initiative, called the Ongoing Covenant with Black Iowa, was also active in Burlington, Cedar

Rapids, Davenport, Des Moines, Dubuque, Fort Dodge, Iowa City and Sioux City.

"With newfound political influence and funding, now is the time to act as a unified force to improve the lives of black Iowans," declared Michael Blackwell, who also led the African-American Leadership Coalition in Waterloo, which the group agreed would oversee the initiative. The $200,000 funding for the effort was due to the efforts of a group of legislators, including Representative Deborah Berry, (D-Waterloo), who flexed their political muscle on behalf of Black Iowans.

"That amount of money the commission received surprised people in Des Moines," declared Reverend Abraham Funchess, Jr., thirty-nine, of Waterloo, the commission's top administrator. "They're not thinking about Black folks at the state capitol. They don't expect us to get this kind of money. It's unprecedented."

The effort was still in its infancy, but ideas included forming a communications task force to involve the entire community in the effort and bringing back a summer work program for youth. "If you could put 700 kids to work in the summer, what kind of difference would that make?" asked Walter Reed, Jr., fifty-three, of Waterloo, and director of the Iowa Commission of Human Rights. "Program ideas from across the state were consolidated into a legislative action plan to secure state funding. Increasing test scores for black students by 15 percent, issuing annual legislative priorities to state legislators and reducing the crime rate by 5 percent with the help of public safety officials are goals we hope to achieve by 2010."

"The biggest challenge for the black community in the Cedar Valley will be to come together by putting past differences aside," argued Nation of Islam minister Michael Muhammad, thirty-six, a slender man from Waterloo who was president and CEO of radio station KBOL. "We get caught up in talking about our failures and our problems, and we don't come together."

Reverend Funchess said, "Part of the reasoning behind forming the new effort was to give black Iowans across the state a neutral organization everyone can join and approach legislators with a unified voice to advocate for themselves."

Following the state commission meeting, Harold Gist and Kevin McGraw met two prominent ministers in the African-American community, Reverend Michael Coleman, forty-nine, an energetic and engaging minister who maintained a professional demeanor as the Pastor of Antioch Baptist Church and Reverend Frantz Whitfield, twenty-six, a fair-skinned hefty man with a deep baritone preaching voice, and the interim Pastor of Mt. Carmel Baptist Church.

Thursday, October 4, 2007

Senator Obama addressed an enthusiastic crowd of onlookers at the University of Northern Iowa, "This team understands strong organizations are built from the bottom up and is committed to running a campaign designed to challenge the way we do politics in this country. I look forward to working to build grassroots support in Iowa the old fashioned way, by reaching out to caucus-goers, one Iowan at a time."

The area was home to U.S. Representative Bruce Braley, and U.S. Senator Charles "Chuck" Grassley from nearby New Hartford. Waterloo's sister city was Cedar Falls, which had a population of 36,345 and was home to the University of Northern Iowa.

The Obama campaign philosophy was *field first,* which contradicted most traditional campaign operations. By doing so, the Obama campaign utilized the principles of community organizing—even if they didn't use the term overtly. In the political campaign world, Field Operations referred to building a campaign organization which was capable of turning out large numbers of people on an election day or caucus night.

The Air referred to broadcast media, television and radio advertising. Traditional political consultants preferred this approach due to the ability to reach thousands, if not millions, of potential voters with a controlled and consistent message, not to mention the fees they earned from large campaign ad-buys.

Some states like California were so large they could only be won through the air. Other states, like Iowa, were small and compact enough to be won on *The Ground,* which referred to personal contacts, retail politics and local networking. Developing an effective ground game was much more effective but far more labor intensive and difficult.

Michael Blake, twenty-five, Deputy Political Director, had the unenviable but all-important job of bringing in new Iowa voters to caucus for the Illinois Senator. In years past, the candidates who had bet on getting new faces to sacrifice an hour and a half of their time to argue politics with their neighbors had more often than not seen their campaign hopes completely dashed by morning.

And while Jimmy Carter and Gary Hart both brought in significant numbers of new faces, many more candidates, like Howard Dean, had failed in spectacular fashion. The former Vermont governor bet the farm that more college and high school students, inspired by his insurgent candidacy, would turn out to caucus for him. Instead, he ended up coming in third behind John Kerry and former North Carolina Senator John Edwards.

Other campaigns focused most of their efforts on one or two constituencies, the way John Kerry successfully courted military veterans in 2004. Senator Obama spent an unprecedented amount of money and effort to turn out a wide cross section of new caucus-goers.

"This is the most extensive effort to reach out to new constituencies in the Iowa caucuses—ever," declared Michael Blake. The mahogany skinned local activist from the Bronx had graduated from a program Senator Obama started to train minorities to effectively use the political system.

"Campaigns here have gotten attention for going after one or two groups. We're applying the same principle and I hope we will enjoy similar success with multiple groups," touted Blake. Over the last eight months, Michael Blake, and his two-dozen staff members, had been developing peer-to-peer contacts. Veterans called veterans, high school students called high school students, and so on.

Seven staffers reached out to Black voters, led by Rick Wade, forty-four, who stood 6'0" with a stocky build, a Senior Advisor and the Director of African-American Outreach, and three others handled Latino voters who made up only 3 percent of Iowa's population of three million and the 67,000 blacks in the entire state.

Wednesday, October, 31, 2007

On Halloween, Service Employee's International Union members paraded in front of Carlyle's offices wearing rubber David Rubenstein face masks and passed out Sugar Daddy suckers. These unorthodox protests were a part of a campaign by the SEIU and ACORN to position themselves as a check on a new economic order dominated by big private buyout firms.

Andy Stern and Stephen Lerner, fifty-two, had been meeting with the heads of private-equity firms asking them to be more generous with health care, salaries and other employee benefits. The Carlyle Group was one of the five biggest buyout firms in the nation.

Carlyle was founded in 1987 by David Rubenstein, a policy assistant in the Carter administration, and William Conway, its managing director, along with Daniel D'Aniello. For decades, with almost no publicity, the Carlyle Group had signed up an impressive roster of former politicians, including President George H.W. Bush and his secretary of state, James Baker, III. Former British Prime Minister John Major, one-time World Bank treasurer Afsaneh Masheyekhi Beschloss and several southeast Asian power-brokers used their contacts and influence to promote the group.

The Firm employed more than 890 employees, including 495 investment professionals in 20 countries with several offices in the Americas, Europe, Asia and Australia. The Firm's portfolio companies employed more than 415,000 people worldwide. Like most areas of its work, Carlyle, a Global Private Equity Firm, was not obliged to reveal details and David Rubenstein preferred not to do so.

Lerner, the tough and wiry SEIU director, stated, "You are now employers and you have a responsibility to make life better for employees—but when we didn't get the response we wanted, we turned up the heat."

Stern said, "We targeted Carlyle and its co-founder because David Rubenstein often speaks publicly on private-equity issues." The SEIU set up a web site called "Behind the Buyouts" and issued a 42-page pamphlet criticizing the big profits at buyout firms.

Forget the marches and strikes which once defined the union movement. Big labor was relying more on guile and theatrics than blunt force to attack a new form of corporate ownership—private equity. With ACORN, the tactics often got personal.

Carlyle spokesman Chris Ullman argued, "SEIU's goal is less about global economics and more about recruiting new union members and enhancing its ability to organize workers. SEIU is conducting several similar campaigns designed to embarrass companies like Wackenhut and HCA. Wal-Mart is going through a similar hazing from the United Food and Commercial Workers union."

Ullman blamed Service Employees International Union's recent attention to the union's desire to organize 60,000 workers at Manor Care, the Ohio-based nursing-home company which Carlyle had recently acquired. SEIU sought a slice of the $6.3 billion on the table from the sale of Manor Care.

Monday, November 19, 2007

A Silver Cadillac pulled up in front of the DC ACORN offices. Marcel Reid hurried into the DC ACORN storefront office as Thanksgiving Holidays approached.

"Hi Belinda. Are you doing anything special for Thanksgiving?"

"We're going to my grandmother's house to eat, Marcel, like we always do."

Belinda leafed through her papers and notes. "Did you see this, Marcel?"

"Did I see what?"

"Rhode Island just asked for $2.4 billion for lead abatement."

Surprised, "Let me see that."

Belinda handed her a faxed copy of Providence Journal-Bulletin from September 14, 2007. The clipped article read, "Attorney General Patrick Lynch proposed that three former manufacturers of lead paint, convicted by a jury in 2006 of creating a public nuisance with their product, pay $2.4 billion for lead abatement in 240,000 homes.

"Judge Michael Silverstein still had to approve the plan. The three companies involved, Sherwin-Williams, NL Industries and Millennium Holdings, had appealed the 2006 ruling. Consequently, the court decreed the abatement plan would not be put into effect while the appeal was pending."

Elsewhere in the second story office, the robust Anita MonCrief borrowed an additional $500 from her employer—which was never repaid. In total, Anita had borrowed a total of $1,500 from Project Vote but only repaid $500 of the sum.

A heated discussion erupted in the second floor conference room of Project Vote between Zach Polet and Karyn Gillette, in December 2007.

Zach announced, "I need to talk to you about Anita MonCrief."

"What's going on?" asked Karyn Gillette.

"Something has come up. There may be trouble. Tell me how Anita MonCrief has been doing?"

Gillette hesitated, "Anita was hired to perform various research and writing tasks including writing fundraising materials."

"So what happened?"

"Unfortunately, her written work product turned out to be unsatisfactory. So we had to limit her to research tasks and providing technical assistance on PowerPoint presentations."

"Was that all?"

"She once had some responsibilities related to grant administration and donor research—but ultimately her duties were limited to opening mail, receiving and recording donations, forwarding office mail to the accounting office, and other administrative tasks."

Zach lowered his eyebrows. "Did you know she has personal charges on a Project Vote Credit Card?"

Her eyes widened. "Personal charges? I didn't know Anita *-Had-* a credit card!"

"Oh yeah. She took out a Purchase Power Visa credit card—in her name!" said Zach.

Gillette stood silent and stunned.

He said, "I'm looking at a $343.53 charge to a Bad Check Restitution Program. What's that got to do with Project Vote?"

Shocked, "I have no idea."

"You are her supervisor—right?" Zach asked, "You didn't authorize her to get one?"

"She had some money problems in the past because she asked for cash advances. But I don't know anything about a credit card—or personal charges on it!"

"Is that right?"

"Absolutely not, but I will definitely get to the bottom of this. I can assure you of that!"

Surrounded in plush leather seats and cherry-wood appointments, Marcel Reid thought to herself, *"I can't believe her Anita MonCrief is going to screw up her career and disrupt the whole DC ACORN office along with it—over petty money problems."*

The suspension roared on her Silver Cadillac as Marcel rounded the corner down Pennsylvania Avenue. The on-star phone feature decreased the volume on the radio, as the car phone suddenly activated.

Surprised, Marcel had never used this feature before. Who on earth could be calling? "Hello?"

A soft-sweet voice—smooth like honey on velvet answered, "Hello, is this Marcel Reid?"

"Yes it is. Who's calling?" Marcel wondered how they got this number?

"Hello Ms. Reid. I'm calling on behalf of Mr. David Rubenstein.

"Mr. who?"

"David Rubenstein, of the Carlyle Group." The voice said, "We're a private equity firm here in Washington."

Still perplexed, Marcel repeated. "The Carlyle Group?"

The voice asked, "Is this Marcel Reid the head of DC ACORN?"

"Ah yes—yes it is."

Sternly, "Mr. Rubenstein wants to wish you a Happy Thanksgiving."

Unnerved, Marcel pondered. *What on earth is this—Happy Thanksgiving?* She didn't know whether to be pleasantly surprised or dreadfully afraid.

The voice repeated, "Mr. Rubenstein wants you to have a Happy Thanksgiving Ms. Reid, and he also wanted to find out if we have a problem?"

Confused, "What do you mean? a problem?"

"We have just received a disturbing letter from you."

Startled, "You received a letter, from me?"

"We received a very threatening letter from you in fact," the voice explained. "Mr. Rubenstein wanted to ask you *personally* if we have a problem with you or your organization."

"I don't know what you are talking about. I can assure you that I am not aware of any problem which I have, or which DC ACORN has, with the Carlyle Group."

"I am very happy to hear that, Ms. Reid." Relieved the voice asked, "What should I expect you to do about this letter?"

"I will double check as soon as I get back to my office," Marcel replied. "I will get to the bottom of this."

She disconnected the phone and fumed in disgust. Who do these people think they are? They can't use my name to threaten a major well-connected, international corporation—for no reason whatsoever.

White-walled tires screeched to a halt at the corner of Eighth and H Street as Marcel Reid careened back to the DC ACORN Offices. The Cadillac door slammed shut, and Marcel stormed through the ground floor offices.

"Belinda!" Marcel asked, "Did you sign my name on a letter to the Carlyle Group?"

Caught off guard, Belinda Ferrell stammered an unintelligible response.

"I'll ask you again," Marcel said. "What do you know about a DC ACORN action against the Carlyle Group?"

Sheepishly, "They told me to do it."

"*Who* told you to do *what,* exactly?"

"Craig Robbins said we had to do this," replied Belinda.

"If it is a national action, why did they use my name instead of Maude Hurd?" asked Marcel.

"I just did what Craig told me to do, Marcel."

"How could there be a national action in the District of Columbia if DC ACORN did not vote on it?"

"I don't know, Marcel."

"I'll tell you what. You tell WHOEVER told you to do this—that DC ACORN has not authorized or voted for an action against the Carlyle Group!"

Meekly, "Ok, Marcel."

"Hell, most of our members don't know who, or what the Carlyle Group is!" Marcel said, "More importantly, you write the Carlyle Group back and you tell them this was a big misunderstanding. DC ACORN has not started an action against them!"

Belinda nodded, "Uh-huh."

Sternly, "You do understand me—don't you?"

Reluctantly, "I hear you Marcel."

"No! Let me be crystal clear." Marcel stared Belinda in the eyes. "Whatever you decide to do, *Do Not* contact the Carlyle Group under my name, or on behalf of DC ACORN... ever again!"

Marcel Reid sped back to Mount Vernon. Tired and exhausted, she stormed into her kitchen, a quiet tranquil place which served dual purposes, a peaceful respite away from the frantic pace of Washington life, and her own personal War Room. Marcel preheated the oven to 425 degrees and started to prepare the ingredients.

10 tablespoons (1 1/4 stick) unsalted butter
1 1/2 cups confectioners' sugar
2 (1-ounce) squares semisweet chocolate
6 (1-ounce) squares bittersweet chocolate
3 large eggs
3 egg yolks
1 teaspoon vanilla extract
2 tablespoons orange liqueur
1/2 cup all-purpose flour

Marcel cradled a cordless telephone under her chin and whisked together egg yolk and sugar in a small bowl. Her flour-dusted fingers trembled and dialed.

Ring, ring, ring... "Hello?" I answered.

"Hello Michael," her voice trembled. "Do you know who the Carlyle Group is?"

"Yeah, Carlyle is probably the world's largest private equity firm. It's the world leaders' investment fund, with something like a $100 billion under management."

"Oh, wow!" Marcel gasped.

"If you're a conspiracy theory buff, Marcel, they are the *New World Order*."

She nervously greased six 6-ounce custard cups, and dusted them with powered sugar. She placed the butter and chocolate on a stovetop double boiler stirring each until melted.

"The firm employs political figures and notable investors, former U.S. President George H. W. Bush, former British Prime Minister John Major, former U.S. Secretary of State James A. Baker, III, even international financier George Soros," I said.

"Oh boy!" her trembling fingers peeled the security band from the signature red cap as Marcel uncorked the distinctive amber bottle of Grand Marnier.

The aroma of sweet orange liqueur filled the air. She didn't normally drink alcohol, one half glass of wine—only, but if there ever was a day that Marcel could use a stiff drink, this was it.

"The world of private equity is a inherently secretive, especially when you add the Bushes."

"The Bushes?" she asked.

"It's rumored, President George W. Bush was appointed to the board of an airline food business called Caterair, one of Carlyle's first purchases, which they sold at a loss."

Marcel laughed aloud. "George Bush bankrupted everything he ever touched—including the economy." She added the vanilla to the mixture and stirred in the orange liqueur and whisked the combined batter.

"That's right. When George W. Bush left the board in 1992 to become Governor of Texas, he appointed several members to the board, which controlled the investments of Texas teachers' pension funds. A few years later, the board invested $100 million of public money in the firm. Hey, it sounds like you're in the kitchen, Marcel. What are you making?" I asked.

"I'm trying out a new recipe for Chocolate Molten Lava Cake." Marcel added flour and continued to whisk the mixture until the ingredients were well-blended.

"You've got good ears," she said.

Surprised, "A homemade Chocolate Molten Lava Cake— you're good," I replied. "Anyway, the firm became the largest private equity firm in the world by topping a 34 percent rate of return on investments, mostly due to its political connections."

She thought to herself, which is what attracted ACORN to them in the first place. Marcel divided the mixture among the custard ramekins, and carefully poured the batter into the cups. Marcel placed them into the oven and baked the mixture for 12 to 14 minutes—careful not to over bake the mixture.

"Why do you want to know?" I asked.

"ACORN launched an action against them—under my name."

"They did what?"

"You heard me. Belinda launched an action against the Carlyle Group under my signature, without my knowledge—and without our authorization."

Astonished, I asked, "Can they do that?"

"Hell No! DC ACORN never voted for it. I don't think most DC ACORN members know what the Carlyle Group is."

"Maybe it's ACORN National, not DC ACORN."

"I'm still on the national board," Marcel said. "They never voted on an action against Carlyle either. I think somebody looked up a list of profitable finance companies, and then -They- decided to launch an action against the top firm."

"They can't do that, Marcel," I replied. "If the members didn't vote on it, that's not a protest. That's extortion!"

"I don't know how they got the number—to my car. I never use the car phone for anything. Nobody has that number!" Marcel carefully inserted a toothpick 1/2 inch from the edge of custard cups; it came out clean.

I said, "That's some big brother shit, Marcel. The phone call was a warning for you. That was the iron fist inside the velvet glove."

Marcel stuck a second toothpick in the center of the custard ramekin; this one came out wet. Perfect, the edges are firm but the centers were runny.

I said, "You don't need to have your name anywhere near this. They are corrupt and arrogant. You shouldn't contact the Carlyle Group again."

"I told Belinda to straighten it out, and to withdraw my name from the letter."

"Do you think she'll do it?" I asked.

"I'll find out tomorrow," Marcel said. She allowed the individual cakes to cool for ten minutes on a wire rack, and ran a sharp knife around the inside edges of the custard cups to loosen them. She flipped the cakes onto serving plates.

"I'll tell you what, Marcel. If ACORN staff really did attack the Carlyle Group, they're in for a big surprise."

"I know. They screwed this one up real bad." Marcel said.

"ACORN can fight major corporations, and maybe they can even take on a whole industry, but that's entirely different from fighting the Carlyle Group.

"Carlyle is the billionaire boys club for political leaders across the globe. ACORN just made a big mistake. Carlyle is definitely the wrong company to fuck with."

Marcel dusted the tops with powdered sugar and tasted the orange flavored treats. The warm orange-laced chocolate ganache filled her mouth. "They won't even know what hit them," she said aloud. And then thought to herself, *Someone has got to do something about this. ACORN management is out of control. They are flaunting the law, ignoring the members and making bad decisions. This madness has got to stop!*

Buffalo Soldiers

Monday, December 1, 2007

Dozens of eager protestors donned iridescent HAZMAT suits and lined the streets along Pennsylvania Avenue. The Service Employees International Union had bused dozens of demonstrators to the Carlyle Group's Washington, DC headquarters, where they stood outside chanting:

"Better staffing."
"Better staffing."
"Better care."
"Better care."
"No more money…"
"For billionaires."

There is no address closer to the heart of American power than Pennsylvania Avenue. The offices of the Carlyle Group, located on Pennsylvania Avenue, lay midway between the White House and the Capitol building, amid numerous government departments.

Carlyle Partners included James Baker and the firm's chairman, Frank Carlucci, Ronald Reagan's defense secretary and a former deputy director of the CIA. At fifty-nine, Carlucci arrived with a phalanx of former subordinates from the CIA and the Pentagon. But what set Carlyle apart was how it exploited its political contacts; the firm dispatched an array of former world leaders on a series of strategic networking trips.

The protest outside the headquarters of the Carlyle Group was part of the union's bid to organize Manor Care—the Toledo-based nursing home giant Carlyle purchased for $6.3 billion. Stephen Lerner, the Director and SEIU Private Equity Project, still sought the local support of DC ACORN to continue the SEIU campaign against Carlyle's Washington interests. However, DC ACORN Chair Marcel Reid adamantly refused to budge.

"We shouldn't allow the unchecked greed of buyout billionaires like David Rubenstein to put our communities at risk," declared Lerner. "With billions of taxpayer dollars at stake in these contracts, accountability and transparency is a primary concern since the Carlyle Group operates behind a veil of secrecy."

SEIU held a demonstration outside Carlyle's Washington, DC offices with protestors dressed in HAZMAT suits to highlight the health risks that could go undetected if Carlyle refused to disclose information about its sewer sludge business.

Meanwhile, the SEIU released a press statement warning of the possible health risks posed by the Carlyle Group: "This week, SEIU began contacting environmental groups and state and municipal governments that contract with Synagro to raise concerns about Carlyle's lack of transparency and encouraged these groups to join the call for Carlyle to disclose potential risks of its sewer sludge business."

The focus on Carlyle's sewer sludge business was part of a larger national effort by SEIU to hold Carlyle accountable for the impact of its actions on taxpayers, workers, and communities. After several staged demonstrations across the country and even more tactical changes, SEIU "hired" the Association of Community Organizations for Reform Now as *consultants* to protest the Carlyle Group.

Craig Robbins, the Northeast Regional Director of ACORN, eagerly accepted the SEIU money without prior board knowledge or approval, but he had one problem – how to make ACORN's low-income membership actually understand, and care about this issue. Craig faced the ultimate dilemma of how to get these people to care about the issues and concerns associated with a global private equity firm.

Marcel Reid refused to sign the SEIU/ACORN contract on behalf of DC ACORN without a formal vote of approval from DC ACORN membership, especially since most ACORN members didn't know who Carlyle is—or what private equity was. Undeterred, Belinda Ferrell and Craig Robbins continued to push against Carlyle.

A few days later, Marcel received a confirmation email which acknowledged that Mary Spencer, Vice-Chair of DC ACORN, had in fact signed a protest-for-hire contract with Stephen Lerner's office between SEIU and ACORN for direct action demonstrations against the Carlyle Group—without notice, authorization, or a formal membership vote.

Saturday, December 8, 2007

My ice-covered plane landed at the International Airport in Des Moines, Iowa. Excited and raring to go, I thought to myself, *"We are finally going to get on the ground and get to work electing Hillary Clinton."* On this frightfully cold and freezing night, I used the GPS system in a rented PT Cruiser to negotiate my way over ice-covered streets to the downtown Comfort Inn and Suites in Des Moines.

Dozens of new campaign workers flooded the cities and counties of Iowa, to work on the Clinton Campaign—including the Buffalo Soldiers working as African-American Political Strategists in a last-ditch push for Senator Clinton. Meanwhile, Democratic presidential candidate, Senator Barack Obama, addressed a campaign rally in the state capital. Senator Obama spoke convincingly to black voters, and his half-sister Maya Soetoro-Ng, thirty-seven, half-white and half-Indonesian, campaigned for him among Asian-Americans.

The Obama campaign pursued a comprehensive caucus strategy, while his chief rivals, who benefited from the vast majority of union endorsements, took more targeted approaches. John Edwards, the only Democrat who had been to all 99 of Iowa's counties, focused on turning out rural caucus-goers. Senator Clinton focused her efforts on women, a natural constituency for the former First Lady.

However, Senator Obama didn't cede the female vote to Hillary Clinton. He appealed for the women's vote through Oprah Winfrey and also attempted to appeal across party lines. Senator Obama even reached out to Republican and independent voters, who could change their registration at caucus sites by signing a letter of intent.

The caucus format was the perfect expression of confrontational organizing and direct political action. No privacy, no voting booth or secret ballots—you had to stand up for your candidate publicly, in front of your family, friends, neighbors, preachers, and employers.

Elsewhere, African-American Strategists gathered in a downtown Des Moines hotel room as they prepared to deploy across the state. "Brother McCray!" I was warmly greeted in the small suite, by a group of Black political operatives.

Harold Gist, the Deputy Director of the African-American Strategy Team, Reverend William Smart and Kevin McGraw were longtime Clinton aides and Carol Willis loyalists. The new faces—Jamie Scott, sweet with girl-next-door good-looks; Charla Bailey, light-skinned and shapely; Ricky Broadway, tall and tan with sporting waves; and Tramon Arnold, brown-skinned with curly hair, were all from North Little Rock: and Arron Harris, from Memphis—all vibrant and young, around twenty-six.

I dusted snow and ice off of my hat and coat, exasperated. "There's only a handful of African-Americans across this whole state. So why are we here?" I asked. "We don't usually get involved until South Carolina."

Gist confided, "This is an unusual race. By Democrats splitting the vote between a half-dozen candidates, the small, concentrated African-American vote could actually determine the outcome of this race."

Arron said, "If that's the case, they should have called us weeks ago—if not months."

"Well, we're here now," replied Gist. "And we're the Buffalo Soldiers. They wouldn't have called on us if it was going to be easy."

Sardonic laughter filled the room.

"Okay, so how are we going to break this down?" asked Kevin McGraw, a former Clinton White House staffer.

"We need to cover Des Moines, Waterloo, Davenport, Cedar Rapids and Iowa City. That appears to be where most of the Black people are."

Gist said, "Kevin, you're the state lead. You coordinate all our efforts from here at Headquarters and work Des Moines, with Jamie and Charla."

He said, "Arron, I want you to take the lead for Davenport."

"Will do!" said Arron.

Gist said, "We'll get you some help down there, but you're in charge."

Gist turned toward me and said, "McCray, Broadway and Arnold, you guys go to Waterloo! You've got the biggest job. Outside Des Moines, Waterloo has the largest concentration of Black people in the state. McCray you're the Team Lead. You already know the drill. You guys work Waterloo and Cedar Rapids."

I pulled Gist into the hallway for a sidebar conversation before loading the car for the drive to Waterloo.

"I don't know why they always wait until the last minute to call us in—damn!" I said, "We should have been on the ground months ago."

"Why so much earlier?" asked Gist.

"We shouldn't underestimate Senator Obama," I replied. "Don't forget; he's a trained community organizer. He does what we do."

Gist laughed. "Barack is just the candidate; he's not the campaign manager. That's David Axelrod and David Plouffe; we're fighting those guys."

Gist pondered aloud, "We've probably got more to worry about from Rick Wade, his Director for African-American Outreach, rather than Barack."

"What do you mean by that?" I asked.

Gist said, "Rick Wade ran for Secretary of State in South Carolina and the Buffalo Soldiers worked his race. So he knows our program and how we operate. He's seen *our* playbook in action."

"Sure you're right, but vision starts from the top." I clarified, "All I'm saying, is we need to be careful since Barack understands community organizing. This is the first time we'll face a campaign that knows what we know, or one that actually does what we do. So we shouldn't let them get too much of a head start on us."

Exasperated, Harold Gist lamented, "I'm getting sick and tired of all this Obama mess."

"What do you mean?"

"The whole Obama campaign is all smoke and mirrors. They send out all these press releases touting how many people are involved, naming folks on his steering committees."

"That's right."

Gist said, "But when we check behind them, and talk to people on their lists, half of them didn't agree to anything. They may have helped out in some way or been asked their opinion about something. Then all of a sudden, they are named on an Obama steering committee or something in the newspapers. It's all flash—no substance."

I knew that was the first rule of community organizing. Power isn't what you have, but what people think you have. I was getting concerned because there seemed to be arrogance, if not complete dismissiveness, in the Clinton campaign against Obama—that he's a lightweight and couldn't get black support.

Gist said, "A lot of the black leaders don't know him, don't think he's black enough, and don't think he's close enough with the civil rights movement."

I agreed with Gist, "Yeah, I see what you mean."   Black enough referred to the perception among some black leaders that not only had Senator Obama not shared their generational experience, but also that he hadn't shared the African-American experience, period. Barack Obama's father was a Kenyan academic. His family came to America on scholarship, instead of in chains.

Elsewhere, Andi Smith, a born-again independent, hosted a house party for a dozen undecided friends and neighbors in a warm cozy living room in Ames, Iowa. She believed a lot of independents and Republicans would support Barack Obama on caucus day. "Barack is probably the only candidate that could bridge the party gap. It's important to him; he knows it's central to what he wants to accomplish," boasted Smith. She had voted for President Bush—twice, but switched her registration to support Obama.

Obama's co-chairman, for Story County, attended her party. While Senator Obama could suffer a surprising defeat like Howard Dean, his supporters believed that Obama's operation was different.

"What's the difference? Organization!" Tom Harrington laughed while cajoling the group of residents over wine and cheese to support Obama. Harrington had supported Howard Dean in 2004. "Dean never asked me to do anything but show up and caucus," Harrington said. "This is my fourth house party for Obama, and I've got another two this weekend."

Small, regular contributions of time, money and social relationships bonded Iowa volunteers to the Obama campaign. The caucus format allowed the participants to argue, cajole and even intimidate other caucus goers to support their side. Even voters supporting other Democrats were seen as fair game by the Obama camp.

"The Obama campaign is extremely aggressive in asking folks if we're not people's first choice," declared Gordon Fischer, a former Iowa Democratic Party state chairman who endorsed Senator Obama months before. "The campaign follows up and asks if we can be their second choice."

Two visitors who were already committed to other candidates, New Mexico Governor Bill Richardson and Senator Joe Biden, also attended the Ames house party. They were shopping for a second choice, in case their candidates didn't reach the viability threshold. When any Democratic candidate failed to get 15 percent, their supporters would go to whoever was second on their lists.

Later that night, the Buffalo Soldiers fanned out across the state, driving through the sleet and freezing rain. The Buffalo Soldiers specialized in grassroots political organizing. Community organizing converges with political operations because they both derive, and ultimately rely on establishing a mass power base.

Tuesday, December 11, 2007

Adorning a trademark black fedora, Gold Arm Crossbars with the Ninth Infantry insignia, and long black duster coat, I arrived through the snow and freezing rain-covered streets of Waterloo to lead African-American Strategies for Senator Clinton.

Being a Buffalo Solider was almost like a military operation behind enemy lines. Take any experienced operative and drop them into an urban core neighborhood in any major metropolitan city, with nothing more than a cell phone and two phone numbers, and in thirty days or less, they will assemble an army, or an election day field organization to get out the vote in minority communities.

Bone chilling did not begin to describe the hypothermic cold of a Midwest winter. I thought to myself, that the sub-zero temperatures felt like death had reached into my body and was ripping out my soul, through every inch of exposed flesh. Winter in Iowa was cold enough for you to die.

I was the Lead Strategist for African-American outreach in Waterloo. Ricky Broadway, twenty-six, a jovial young man was my college outreach coordinator, and Tramon Arnold, twenty-six, an engaging son of a prominent Baptist Minister was my faith outreach coordinator.

We launched the outreach program by identifying 25 to 30 local community leaders for targeted African-American outreach efforts. As this initial list continued to grow, we contacted various community leaders and arranged face-to-face meetings with key community leaders to solicit their support for Senator Clinton.

I began by identifying a current African-American baseline and organized priority targets and strategic goals for door-to-door canvasses and outreach.

Arnold accessed the Democratic vote builder database and tabulated the current situation, which read—VAN-1 (108); VAN-2 (280); VAN-3

(580); VAN-4 (37) and VAN-5 (108). Thus, Senators Clinton and Obama were tied, with strong support— both had (108) — but HRC had a huge advantage with (280) leaning HRC versus only (37) leaning BHO. But the real number was the undecided, which totaled (580).

The Buffalo Soldiers often manned 24-hour shifts, because Willis and Gist would spot check the operations at 3:00 or 4:00 a.m. Campaign days, long and intense, often started before 6:00 a.m., on the east coast and ended after the last mid-night campaign call on the west coast. The blistering pace of campaign life was fueled by soda pop and grease. Sit down meals became a distant memory. On the fast-paced campaign trail, you ate what was there, instead of what was healthy.

We ran a disciplined operation. The mornings were for planning, the afternoons for canvassing and phone banks, the evenings for neighborhood and community meetings, leaving the nights for analysis and reporting.

I ordered Broadway and Arnold to develop a list of organizations and community gatherings in order to develop a local community events calendar. This community calendar would be used to schedule visibility activities, target persuasion activities and as a basis to build out events for surrogate operations.

Rickey Broadway and Tramon Arnold slid back to the sleet and salt covered Jeep Cherokee, clutching greasy brown paper bags filled with fried chicken gizzards and french fries. The meal was a feast for the day.

Broadway was assigned to college outreach, and he drove to Cedar Rapids to recruit college students for Hillary Clinton. Black Hawk County was home to the University of Northern Iowa, with 14,000 students. The college was originally founded as a teaching college in Cedar Falls.

Broadway was at a disadvantage because Senator Obama's rock star status helped him recruit high school and college kids. But no one knew if they would actually turn out to caucus. Caitlin Harrington, a freshman at the University of Iowa, organized 47 of her classmates to caucus at home through *Rock the Caucus* on Facebook. She worked to find them precincts in areas near their homes to caucus during vacation.

While all of her classmates were Iowans, the Obama campaign was criticized for its zeal to rally the college vote. Campaign workers passed out some 50,000 fliers encouraging students from out of state to return to campus early to participate in the Iowa caucuses. Although strictly legal, they were technically residents of Iowa. It went against the spirit of the caucuses—and Senator Obama was roundly chastised in Iowa papers for doing so.

Wednesday, December 12, 2007

My cell phone rang a Muddy Waters, jazz/blues piano riff at 2:49 a.m. A distinct but familiar voice called out in a slow southern drawl, "McCRAY, what's going on out there. I need a report."

I said, "They were running a glorified phone bank. There wasn't any outreach going on here, Willis."

Willis asked, "What do you mean?"

"The folks here are not going out into the community at all—white or black," I replied. "They sit around the office and make phone calls all day. It's all phone based voter identification."

"That's what's wrong with high-tech campaigns," said Willis. "Computers are fooling people out of outreach."

"You're exactly right. These people forget an election is not a computer game. Technology helps, but it can't replace old-fashioned campaigning. The African-American staff here is burnt out and demoralized, and nobody knows anyone in the neighborhoods." I said, "We've got another problem, Willis. Black people are acting paternalistic towards Barack."

"What do you mean?" he asked.

"A lot of older Blacks are so proud of Barack and his campaign... They're not looking at him as just another candidate. They identify with him as family—like a son or grandson."

"Meaning what?" asked Willis.

"The folks I'm talking to like Hillary, but they're protective of Barack,"

I said. "They realize politics is rough and tumble, and the Clintons play to win."

"That's right," said Willis.

I said, "It's going to be a fight, but they want it to be a fair fight. Your child might lose, but you don't want them to get cheated."

"I see what you mean," said Willis.

I said, "It's a long-shot. They think the Clintons will probably win, but if we turn too negative, we'll lose the Black vote for sure."

A running debate continued within the Clinton campaign about how aggressively to attack Obama.

"I hear what you're saying. Anything else to report?" asked Willis.

"Obama has set up college outreach, peer-to-peer networks and a proprietary database of African-Americans."

"Which means you've got a lot of catching up to do," said Willis. "Obama has a lot of natural talent. He's a stallion, so we can't let him get out of the barn! Get in the streets and catch up with the preachers."

"I'm on it, Willis, but they've been on the ground for at least six months—having regular prayer breakfasts and luncheons with Black ministers, twice a week."

I was pleased because Hillary Clinton was leading in the polls. Broadway and Arnold conducted street canvases in the Waterloo 404 precinct and visited 75 homes. Arnold had been given full access to the VAN system and entered the data from that day's activities in the VAN database. Broadway needed additional training on the system.

We continued our African-American outreach program by identifying an additional 10 to 15 local community leaders for targeted outreach and met with four religious leaders in the African-American community, including Reverend Jay Burt, forty-eight, a stocky man with long processed hair and President of Eastside Ministerial Alliance, and Elders Randolph Dean and Fredrick Hill, two Senior Deacons at Mount Carmel Baptist Church.

I also met with Gary Montgomery, forty-three, who stood 5'9" with a slight build. He was the station manager and program director at KBOL. I sought to establish a positive relationship with this community radio station, to combat KBBG which heavily favored Senator Obama. I decided that a positive relationship with KBOL could result in referrals of community events and *on-air* interviews for visiting Clinton surrogates.

Thursday, December 13, 2007

Broadway and Arnold conducted targeted canvases in the Waterloo 405 precinct—hitting 62 doors. The Buffalo Soldiers generated great visibility by posting three large billboard signs in high visibility locations. The first was directly across from Payne Missionary AME church one of the largest African-American churches in Waterloo whose leadership had been leaning towards Obama. The second was placed near a major business intersection in a targeted precinct, and the third was posted near the parsonage of the Antioch Baptist Church, an influential African-American ministry located in a targeted precinct.

I continued to build a positive relationship with KBOL. In a follow-up meeting, the station manager and program director assisted the Clinton outreach program by identifying 23 additional African-American local business and community leaders for targeted outreach.

Famed author and activist, Dr. Cornell West, appeared at East Side High School for the Obama campaign. I led Broadway and Arnold on an opposition, lit-drop at this celebrity event in the Black community. The literature drop was designed to increase the visibility of the Clinton campaign in the Black community. I believed undecided voters or soft Obama supporters might attend the East Side High School event, since Dr. West was an intellectual celebrity within the African-American community.

Heated cell phone conversations rippled through the Obama field offices. Our defiant action infuriated the Obama campaign staff. But Hillary Clinton was here; the ground game was on. The Buffalo Soldiers had arrived!

POTUS MAGIC

Thursday, December 13, 2007

My cell phone rang. "McCRAY, what's going on out there?" Willis inquired. "We've got the President ready to come to Iowa. I need a report."

"We need him here—bad, Willis." I replied. "We're planning an event at the local Boys' Club."

Perplexed, "Boys' Club? Will that reach our folks?" Willis asked. "Tell me about the preachers."

"Yes and no. It's the Blackhawk County Boys and Girls Club, which will pull everyone from around the county. But it's located on the East Side of Waterloo, so it gives us a chance to put together a small gathering for our people before or after the event."

"Ok, sounds good. Who do you have in mind?"

"We're still putting the complete list together but we definitely want to start with Reverend Frantz Whitfield."

"Who's he?"

"Reverend Whitfield is the Interim Pastor of Mount Carmel Missionary Baptist Church. He's 26 years old and grew up in Des Moines, and he leads the second largest Black church in Waterloo with well over 450 members."

"Oh, he's a young guy."

"Yeah, but he's our main guy—right now. Reverend Whitfield

attempted to meet Hillary Clinton at the Dr. Walter Cunningham School for Excellence Event but wasn't able to meet her."

"That's too bad, a missed opportunity."

"Exactly. What's worse, other campaigns have actively recruited Reverend Whitfield and his name appeared on Obama's Iowa Faith Steering Committee."

"So, is he with us or not?" asked Willis.

"I don't know for sure, Willis. Reverend Whitfield says it's a mistake, and he's still undecided, but he's concerned because Senator Obama, his surrogates and celebrities, have been actively recruiting clergy in Iowa."

Willis agreed, "He's right; it is a problem."

"Reverend Whitfield believes we must get African-American surrogates for Bill Clinton and Hillary Clinton to Waterloo as soon as possible."

"We're working on that right now," said Willis.

"A call from Bill Clinton or Senator Hillary Clinton is crucial to ensure his support." I hung up the phone and typed a call sheet and prepared to brief former President Clinton for his upcoming visit.

Saturday, December 15, 2007

Senator Obama visited Waterloo, followed by four celebrity surrogates the next day. Cheryl Lee Ralph, Jasmine Guy, Alfre Woodard, and Hill Harper hosted a prayer breakfast and visited churches the following Sunday.

The Buffalo Soldiers made a visible presence by visiting barbershops and local restaurants in the community and increased campaign visibility in some of the main neighborhoods and local businesses in the area.

We began to target outreach to minority owned businesses and executed literature drops in two cornerstone businesses. They discovered that much of the high visibility and apparent Obama support was actually soft support.

Simply by walking in and talking to people, we turned an "Obama-1" into a Senator Clinton supporter, with signed support cards. We convinced minority business owners to remove Obama store signs and replace them with Clinton campaign signs, or got minority business owners who supported Barack Obama to also place Hillary Clinton signs next to the Obama signage.

In a follow up meeting, I visited former councilwoman Willie Mae Wright, seventy-five, to solicit her support for Senator Clinton. A former Councilwoman, this frail but respected and opinionated woman maintained significant influence in the African-American community. I discovered she greatly respected Reverend Wilson Rideout, an Arkansas native and staunch Clinton supporter.

Broadway and Arnold canvassed precinct 402 during which they knocked on 47 doors in the freezing cold and posted six yard signs, before we attended Payne AME Church and fellowshipped at their Annual Church Christmas dinner.

The team met and engaged with congregational leadership and local officials. Unfortunately, Senator Clinton had no national African-American surrogates confirmed for Waterloo this weekend.

Sunday, December 16, 2007

I retrieved Reverend Marcia Dyson, fifty-five, from the Dubuque Air Port and provided surrogate speaking opportunities at large religious events on the east side, including Antioch Baptist Church and a major pastor's appreciation service at Corinthian Baptist Church.

An ordained minister, devout feminist and a staunch Hillary Clinton supporter, Marcia was married to Michael Eric Dyson, an author, motivational speaker and ordained minister who taught African-American studies at Georgetown University. Michael was an early supporter of Barack Obama. Since they were two intelligent, articulate, and strong-willed community activists, the dinner table at the Dyson household must have been a site to behold.

Celebrity surrogate Hill Harper, forty-one, gave a rousing testimony at Antioch Baptist Church supporting his Harvard classmate Barack Obama, after which Marcia eviscerated Harper's statements with her own political remarks. Reverend Dyson and I provided increased visibility in the African-American community by attending various Sunday morning and evening worship services including the Ambassador's for Christ, Pilgrim Rest Baptist Church, Antioch Baptist Church, Mount Carmel Missionary Baptist Church and we fellow-shipped at a Pastor's Appreciation Service at Corinthian Baptist Church.

Broadway and Arnold canvassed precinct 401 through the sleet and freezing rain. They knocked on 22 doors and posted two yard signs. They made a visible presence by visiting four religious services in the community. They also promoted the upcoming Bill Clinton and Earvin "Magic" Johnson, Boys' Club event.

Later that evening, Tramon Arnold and I visited Reverend Lovie Caldwell, fifty-five, Pastor of Pilgrim Rest Baptist Church. Reverend Caldwell was leaning towards Senator Obama; however, Reverend Caldwell, an Arkansas native, greatly respected Bill Clinton and was open to support Senator Hillary Clinton.

Monday, December 17, 2007

Hillary Clinton was leading in the polls. Broadway and Arnold canvassed precincts 404 and 403 through the ice and snow, during which they knocked on 45 doors. However, while going door-to-door, they were confronted by aggressive Obama canvassers who used profanity and approached them in a dangerous and threatening manner. "Hey cuz, who you wit!" challenged one Obama supporter. "You better not be passing out no Clinton shit around here—partner. This here's Obama country!"

They approached Broadway and Arnold with hostility and aggression, more like gang-bangers rather than seasoned political operatives. "Y'all fools better recognize!" exclaimed another Obama supporter.

Political campaigns are not supposed to be a gang thing, like holding down a street corner to protect drug sales. It was merely knocking on doors and handing out campaign literature—but when you are out in the streets, it's wise to concede a certain degree of respect, even to ignorance.

National Surrogate, Reverend Marcia Dyson also participated in the neighborhood canvassing. We visited KBBG and garnered a morning drive-time announcement for the Bill Clinton and Earvin Johnson event. Reverend Dyson was booked for an -on-air- interview during the afternoon drive time radio. This was significant because KBBG had almost exclusively promoted the Obama campaign. The morning drive time interview was with Rick Wade, a Senior Campaign Official for the Obama campaign. If not for Reverend Dyson, then Senator Clinton's positions would not have been heard on the radio in Waterloo.

Broadway and Arnold also visited two locally-owned businesses and posted literature and delivered campaign paraphernalia to two local minority businesses.

I engaged in crowd building for the upcoming Bill Clinton and Earvin "Magic" Johnson event. In building for this event, Broadway, Arnold and I aggressively targeted the African-American community in East Waterloo.

I attended the swearing-in of Quentin Hart, thirty-six, to the office of City Councilman for Ward 4. Brown-skinned, with a slight build, Councilman Hart wore a short-Afro and was the founder and director of the From the Heart: Waterloo Home Enhancement Project. Hart brought youth volunteers to the city this year to help low-income, elderly and disabled residents improve their homes and he also sponsored the Multicultural Business Expo to showcase local businesses. To his credit, Councilman Hart did not retreat from public service after narrowly losing a bid for the Waterloo, Ward 4 City Council seat in 2003, by 58 votes.

The ceremony was held at City Hall, and I met with Councilman Hart and introduced myself to Reverend Joseph Barring, Pastor of Payne AME Church. Noticing his Obama button, I extended my hand respectfully, "Hello Reverend. I'm the opposition."

He eyed my Clinton button and we laughed together.

Reverend Barring shook my hand and looked me in the eye. "You seem like a bright young man. Why aren't you supporting Barack?"

"We don't really know him and I don't think he can win," I said.

"Why do you say that?" Reverend Barring asked. "Do you mean white folks won't vote for him?"

I replied, "I've been involved in Presidential politics since 1992. And one thing I've learned about the electoral map is, Democrats don't win if they can't carry a southern state."

Surprised, "Really?"

"Think about it," I said. "Carter won because he was from the south and he carried southern states including his home state Georgia."

Reverend Barring conceded, "That's right."

I said, "Clinton won because he was from the south and he carried southern states and his home state Arkansas. Gore would have won if he had carried his home state of Tennessee."

"Gore got robbed," replied Reverend Barring.

I agreed, "You're right, but understand my point." Guys like Mike Dukakis and John Kerry, a war veteran, actually lost during a time of war. He was from Massachusetts and he couldn't carry a southern state."

Reverend Barring conceded. "I never thought of it that way before."

I replied, "So I'll ask you again Reverend, which southern state do you think Barack Obama can win?"

Reverend Barring stood silent with nothing to say.

After the ceremony, I congratulated the new councilman and reversed the question, "Why Barack?"

He looked me in the eye, "Honestly, the Clinton campaign never reached out or contacted me," said Hart. "The Obama Campaign was all over me, encouraging me and asking if they could help with the projects I'm working on."

I confided, "I certainty can't argue with that."

Hart said, "Hillary is an impressive candidate, but she's running a terrible campaign. As far as I can tell, she's nowhere in the Black community."

"That's why we're here—now," I said.

"I appreciate you coming, and I'll check you guys out," promised Hart. "But I think it might be too little, too late, for Clinton."

Tuesday, December 18, 2007

Former President Bill Clinton and Earvin "Magic" Johnson, forty-eight, visited an enthusiastic crowd of 500 at the Waterloo Boys and Girls Club. It was a special day for the Clinton Campaign, including poll watchers, precinct captains and volunteers from throughout Black Hawk County.

As Team Leader for Waterloo, I was responsible for coordinating the community meeting with our special guests, and to brief President Bill Clinton who asked, "Any major development projects?"

I replied, "There's a proposed coal plant in northeast Waterloo which has generated much debate. A group of concerned citizens has formed an organization, called The Clean Air for Waterloo Campaign. The campaign is concerned about the environmental and economic impact of the plant on the community."

"How is it being received in the Black community?" asked President Clinton.

"The plant was scheduled to be built five miles northeast of downtown Waterloo. Black people are concerned because East Waterloo is so close to the plant, which is the largest predominantly African-American community in the state. The plant is controversial. Most of the community is strongly opposed to the plant. In fact, 82% percent voted against the proposal in recent polls, but the plant will create about 100 new jobs in Waterloo." I said.

"Anything else I should know?"

I thought for a moment. "Construction began this past summer on a $159 million ethanol plant near New Hampton. Homeland Energy Solutions will build and operate the 100 million-gallon-a-year plant. The ethanol plant, a dry mill corn-processing plant, will employ about 50 people and construction will take 14 to 16 months, start to finish."

The Black Hawk County Boys and Girls Club provided a place in the community for recreation and companionship as an alternative to the streets. Magic Johnson was a member and avid supporter of the Boys and Girls Club.

Magic Johnson was a professional athlete; a NBA All Star and international brand. While *Earvin Johnson* was a businessman; a Real Estate Developer who ran a $500 million development fund which targeted inner city and urban core neighborhoods.

You could smell the wax from the pine wood floors and bleachers while Magic described how progressive Bill Clinton and Hillary Clinton had been in the areas of equal access and economic development. Subsequently, the Waterloo Outreach Team hosted a private meeting with President Clinton and Earvin Johnson with a dozen influential ministers and community leaders to garner their support for Senator Clinton.

Enraged Obama supporters conducted a retaliation, lit-drop on the Clinton campaign office with African-American campaign literature early that morning. The Buffalo Soldiers were making inroads.

In response, Tommy Vietor, the Obama Iowa campaign spokesman, criticized the influx of new Clinton campaign staff. "This is exactly why it's a problem for the Clinton campaign to bring in 100 new staffers in the last month. We've been working and developing personal relationships and a network of Iowans for months."

"I do think Obama's got a more legitimate claim to bringing in new people: younger voters, college voters, bringing in a new audiences," observed Iowa State Senate majority leader, Michael Gronstal. "Senator Obama made the single biggest bet on reaching out to different groups of voters. If he brings in enough, that's the advantage; if not, then Senator Clinton's old line of establishment Democrats becomes telling."

This set up the classic campaign scenario, a local community organizer versus the statewide political establishment.

Saturday, December 22, 2007

Broadway and Arnold canvassed precincts 402 and 404, during which time they visited 143 homes and received ten supporter cards. They posted a large 8x4 billboard, and seven yard signs. Broadway and Arnold also visited two local eateries and anchor businesses and left campaign literature to be viewed by neighborhood patrons. Hillary Clinton was still leading in the polls.

I retrieved Wellington Webb, sixty-four, the former Denver Mayor, from the Cedar Rapids Airport. I provided surrogate speaking support at a Women's Forum at Allen College and retail political opportunities within targeted African-American precincts on the Eastside.

I introduced Mayor Webb to the community when we visited the Annual Christmas Party at the Eastside Ministerial Alliance. Their mission was to "establish, conduct, and maintain educational, social, charitable, economic, and recreational programs and endeavors as may assist in the advancement of its members and aid in the general welfare of a population in the community which is underserved or has otherwise fallen through the social service, economical, and educational cracks."

Following the holiday meeting, Mayor Webb and I met with Quentin Hart at the Southern Soul Café, a downtown local watering hole for drinks. The affable Mayor was a delegate for Bill Clinton in 1992 and believed the former first lady had shown a depth of understanding of what cities like Denver faced. Quentin Hart whispered, "If you don't mind me asking, why aren't you supporting the Brother?"

Mayor Webb said, "I sat down with both Bill and Hillary Clinton after she announced she was running and quizzed them both about urban issues like housing, education and transportation. Race never entered my thinking. I never asked anybody to support me because I was black. I asked people to be for me because I was the best candidate when I ran for City Council and then for Mayor."

He boasted, "I'm proud of the votes I received. I'm proud I received the votes of the majority of the African-American community and the majority of the vote from the white community. I never asked anybody to give me anything because I was black. I asked people to give me a chance because I was the best."

"My bad. I didn't mean to insult you."

"It's not an insult; it's presumptuous. It demonstrates the notion that the African-American community, unlike any other, is completely monolithic, as if, everyone in the African-American community does the same thing in lockstep—unlike any other ethnic group."

He was puzzled by the notion that he should support a candidate simply because they both had dark skin. "I mean, I don't remember seeing John Kerry on TV and anybody saying to him, I can't believe you're not supporting Hillary Clinton. Why not?" asked Mayor Webb.

"That's a good point," said Hart.

"I understand the prospect of a black president after hundreds of years of discrimination is powerful motivation for many African-Americans. Quentin, as a City Councilman, you have another responsibility to the residents of Waterloo, which is to help run this City to the best of your ability. In the context of what we do for a living, I've never figured out a black way, or a white way, to fill a pothole."

Hart was struck by his openness and candidness, he asked, "Mayor Webb can I call on you sometimes for advice. This being my first term and everything?"

For most African-Americans, Senator Obama's candidacy represented a racial milestone, the natural next phase of a 50-year movement. The reverse was also true -Not- supporting Obama's candidacy marked racial progress, too. The movement was about the freedom to choose your own candidate, white or black.

Wet heavy flakes of snow pelted the ice-covered windshield, while Kevin strained to see black-ice on the snow covered highways. Topping speeds of 90 miles per hour, the SUV's halogen headlamps darted through snowdrifts and flurries.

Tired and sleepy, Kevin McGraw was surprised when his SUV slowly slid off the snow capped highway shoulder. The fuel gauge was well below "E," and the heat immediately dissipated from the passenger compartment after the engine stalled.

"Fuck!" He panted. His frosty breath was thick and visible, almost like cigar smoke, in the cold night air. This was a hell of a time to run out of gas. Anywhere else, or at any other time, this might be funny. Not here, not now. Running out of gas on a winter night in Iowa could be deadly.

Kevin pulled off his leather gloves with his teeth and frantically retrieved his cell phone. He already felt the warmth leaving his face, and his fingers becoming numb from hypothermia. "McCray! I need you brother. I just ran out of gas outside of Des Moines."

Surprised, "You did what?" I said.

"You heard me, I ran out of gas on the highway! I got started late and was rushing to make it your way for the President Clinton event in the morning, but I forgot to check my gas."

It would have been funny, if the situation was not so serious. "Hold tight, Kevin. Exactly where you are," I asked. "We'll get somebody to pick you up."

Kevin replied, "I'm not sure, it's hard to tell in this blinding snow. I'm about an hour outside Des Moines—-near the turn off from I-35 North and US-20 East."

I hung up the phone and immediately called the State Police/Highway Patrol to notify them of a stranded motorist outside Des Moines. And sent Broadway and Arnold to go find Kevin. "We have to look out for our team. Don't come back without him."

It was well past mid-night on a deserted highway, well-below freezing in the blinding snow. Kevin couldn't risk standing outside to try to flag down a passing car, even if he saw one. All he could do now was wrap up in layers of campaign tee-shirts from the back of the SUV, bundle himself into a ball—and pray. Icicles covered the dimming headlights as the battery power began to slowly drain.

Ricky Broadway and Tramon Arnold hopped in the Jeep Cherokee and rushed from Waterloo, desperate to find Kevin stranded in the snow. Time was of the essence.

Watch Night

Sunday, December 23, 2007

I woke early—giddy with excitement.
Black churches were not a mainstay of
Iowa politics, but with 11 days left before
the caucuses, Hillary Rodham Clinton
and former President Bill Clinton appealed to one of the state's largest
minority populations. Five precincts in Waterloo, with a total of 40 delegates, had significant African-American populations, and the Clintons
considered this pocket of the state important enough to brave stormy
weather for one final visit, less than two days before Christmas.

Kevin McGraw joined the Waterloo Outreach Team and provided
logistical support for religious services and a prayer luncheon for Senator
Clinton and President Clinton when they visited an enthusiastic crowd
of 85 people at Mount Caramel Missionary Baptist Church. City
Councilman Quentin Hart, Reverend J.J. Moses of Lakewood Church,
and Reverend Marcia Dyson, along with other local and national religious and community dignitaries, filled the Mount Caramel Missionary
Baptist Church Sanctuary.

Reverend Samuel Mingo, Reverend Joseph Curry and Mother Ella
Thomas, the former First Lady of Mount Caramel, along with Reverend
Willie Campbell, Pastor of Cathedral of Faith Baptist and Reverend Ed
Loggins of Christian Fellowship Baptist Church, were also in attendance.
They were joined by Peggy Morgan, a local Community Activist, Joyce
Marshall a community leader and radio announcer, and Susan Kincaid, a

local radio announcer, along with Ana Mae Weems a veteran civil rights activist and her daughter Frieda Weems a local Democratic activist.

The Clintons arrived shortly after noon, flying in from their home in Chappaqua, New York shortly after the religious services had already begun. The young Reverend Frantz Whitfield introduced the former President Bill Clinton. "I once saw a television episode of Truth or Dare," Reverend Whitfield began, as nervous whispers emitted from the half-filled pews, including myself. Reality TV shows can be raunchy. Just where was Reverend Whitfield going with this story?

"The contestant had to risk his most prized possession—as a dare." Reverend Whitfield laughed. "When asked, the winning contestant said his most prized possessions was a neck-tie he received from Bill Clinton."

Following an audible sigh of relief, the congregation erupted in laughter, including former Iowa Governor and his wife, Tom and Christie Vilsack, Denver Mayor Wellington Webb, and Bob Nash a former Clinton White House senior advisor and current campaign official who joined them in the church service.

Hailing Christmas as "the birth of the God of second chances," Bill Clinton introduced his wife as a -giver- and encouraged congregants to vote. He cited Romans, saying the Bible instructs people to "be good citizens as well as good followers of the Lord."

"For as long as I have known Hillary, she has been giving of herself to benefit others. I think we want that sort of giver to lead our country," said Bill Clinton. "In this Christmas season, I think the thing I would like to say most, after 36 years of knowing her and 32 years of marriage—we are all supposed to be givers. Day after tomorrow, we will give. But every day for 36 years she has given, and I believe if you will make her the next president, she will be a giver to America and the world and we will all be proud."

Hillary Clinton took the podium and declared, "This is the day the Lord has made." She delivered an abbreviated, softer version of her standard stump speech to rousing responses from the congregation. "This is a time, not just for those of us who run to be president but for all of us, to resolve that in this Christmas season we will be instruments of peace and change," declared Hillary Clinton.

"And as we think about the choices which face us, let us remember all of those for whom we speak. Because when you go, as I hope all of you will, to participate in the caucuses January 3, 2008, you will be there not just for yourselves and your families but for so many others who cannot."

As she closed, Hillary Clinton said, "We are going to give the people of Iowa a well-deserved timeout from politics" over the Christmas holiday. But she promised, "I will always do my very best to make the kind of changes that will give people not just hope—but results."

In a classic southern close, Bill Clinton loosened the knot on his bright orange necktie and removed it from his neck. He rose, with a natural smile, and draped it around Pastor Whitfield's shoulders, to a rousing round of applause from the congregation.

After the benediction, Reverend Whitfield hosted a private meeting with Senator Clinton and National Surrogates after the morning service for a dozen influential ministers and community leaders to garner their support. We subsequently gathered 18 signed HRC supporter cards.

Friday, December 28, 2007

I woke early and started a treacherous snow-covered drive to Cedar Rapids to pick up Congresswomen Stephanie Tubbs-Jones, fifty-eight, from the Eastern Iowa Regional Airport, and had a slow drive back to Waterloo.

After missing the 10:15 a.m., drop-by at the Eastside Ministerial Alliance, due to inclement weather, we arrived at 11:00 a.m., at a local senior center, and met up with the rest of the Waterloo Outreach Team. Ricky Broadway and I provided surrogate support for the Congresswomen in her second visit to Waterloo.

Two-dozen people ultimately came down to meet Congresswoman Tubbs-Jones. One woman declared she was definitely going to caucus for Senator Clinton and was going to drive people from the center to the caucus location. After enjoying cookies and ice cream, the group watched a "Caucusing is Easy" instructional video.

I was particularly gratified because this was the first time the property manager had allowed any political campaign to address its seniors—and this was our third attempt. This was a low-to-moderate income senior facility located next to a prime caucus site in targeted African-American precincts.

The Renaissance Park Senior Living Facility consisted of mobile seniors who were willing and able to caucus. Many of the seniors who supported Senator Clinton would vote absentee in November, but they were not physically able to caucus on January 3, 2008.

Following the senior meeting, Congresswomen Tubbs-Jones was interviewed by both KBBG and KBOL in Waterloo, and she prepared a public service announcement for Des Moines. The Congresswoman was interviewed in-studio by Iowa State Representative Deborah Berry and Scharron Clayton. The ladies fell in love with her. Jovial and fun, they talked about education and "Why Hillary Clinton?"

Congresswoman Tubbs-Jones participated in a call-in interview with KBOL which focused on the importance of caucusing. After the radio interviews, we visited Morg's Diner, right before closing, and ate lunch with four patrons and the kitchen staff of three, one of which was a Clinton precinct captain. We also visited Sookies, a neighborhood landmark in the Black community, the only sit-down soul food restaurant on the East Side of Waterloo.

I had rescheduled the meeting previously set for 10:00 a.m. to 4:00 p.m. Congresswoman Tubbs-Jones visited the Eastside Ministerial Alliance and met with two pastors and six other African-American community leaders and representatives about Hillary Clinton.

The religious and community leaders included Ashley Caldwell, twenty-four, the daughter of Reverend Lovie Caldwell, Pastor for Pilgrim Rest Baptist Church; Sharon Goodson, fifty-eight, the President of the local NAACP Chapter; Reverend Jay Burt, President of the Eastside

Ministerial Alliance; and Reverend Marvin Jenkins, fifty-five, Pastor of Union Missionary Baptist Church.

Finally, we visited the Waterloo public library to attend a local women's meeting. Five people showed up; one was undecided but left as a Senator Clinton supporter. They questioned her about unfair sentencing in the black community, taxes after retirement, religion, gay marriage, rehabilitation after incarceration and other issues. Congresswoman Tubbs-Jones fielded them all diplomatically.

Sunday, December 30, 2007

Yet again, I braved a treacherous early morning drive to the Cedar Rapids Airport. This was my second attempt, due to a prior flight cancellation, to pick-up Reverend Floyd Flake, sixty-two, in time for Sunday morning church service in Waterloo.

After being recognized during church service at Antioch Baptist Church, Broadway and Arnold, canvassed precinct 403 in the frozen snow, during which time they visited 27 homes. Tramon Arnold and I participated in surrogate support for the former Congressmen and Reverend, Floyd Flake in his visit to Payne AME Church.

After a brief introduction and strong recitation of his support for Senator Clinton, Reverend Floyd Flake gave a rousing sermon as a guest speaker at Payne AME Church. With a growing membership approaching 400, Payne was the third largest church on the East Side. However, only 65 worshipers including Reverend Wilson Rideout, eighty-eight, were present and received Reverend Flake's rousing message.

Reverend Rideout was the retired pastor of Payne AME Church and a past recipient of the Dr. Martin Luther King, Jr. Award from the Iowa Commission on the Status of African-Americans. Reverend Rideout was an Arkansas native and was an outspoken supporter of Senator Clinton. He was also a board member on the Eastside Ministerial Alliance.

After church service, Reverend Flake and I visited Carpenter's Restaurant and ate lunch. Eight patrons filled the restaurant, four of whom were union members and the kitchen staff of three. Reverend Flake greeted the patrons and staff on behalf of Senator Clinton. After lunch at Carpenter's, Reverend Flake was interviewed on KBBG, in-studio, by Dr. Scharron Clayton, his college classmate. They talked about education, economic development and the importance of caucusing.

After the interview, Reverend Flake attended a meeting of African-American clergy, hosted at Mount Carmel Missionary Baptist Church. It was a special meeting which allowed Reverend Flake to speak to several religious leaders as a peer, and on a pastor-to-pastor basis. Reverend Flake discussed community and economic development, and the importance of wise political participation to the development of minority communities. He discussed viable strategies to finance affordable housing development and his personal history, and the role Bill and Hillary Clinton played in helping him develop Allen Cathedral AME Church—his mega-church in Jamaica, Queens. By the end of this meeting, we collected three additional Clergy Endorsement Forms, pledging support for Senator Clinton.

Monday, December 31, 2007

I woke early to meet Rodney Slater, fifty-two, a distinguished look-ing gentleman with salt-and-pepper hair in the Marriott hotel lobby. I greeted him cordially. "Long time—the Empowerment Zones, right?"

Rodney Slater was the former Transportation Secretary and a former student and long-time friend of Bill and Hillary Clinton from their days teaching Law and Politics at the University of Arkansas in Fayetteville.

"That was a long time ago, but I remember the good old days," Secretary Slater smiled. "So how are we looking?"

"It's still uphill right now. A lot of our folks still like the Clintons, but they've been inspired by Obama."

"He's an appealing candidate, but even if we just get half of the black vote—we'll do fine."

I confided, "Mr. Secretary, an even split would be outstanding. But with what we're seeing out here—I hope we get one third of the black vote."

After breakfast, I gave former Secretary Slater a windshield tour of the

East Side and described the history of the African-American community in Waterloo, which remained segregated, while Cedar Falls was primarily Caucasian. "The Black community literally resides across the railroad tracks from the broader community."

We drove by local landmarks including a railroad boxcar monument dedicated to the troubled history blacks endured during the great migration as railroad strike-breakers. Afterwards, we made an unscheduled visit to Antioch Baptist Church in order to introduce Secretary Slater to Reverend Michael Coleman, prior to Watch Night Service.

Reverend Coleman was the senior pastor of the Antioch Baptist Church and Secretary of the Eastside Ministerial Alliance. Antioch Baptist Church was the largest church on the Eastside with a current membership of 600. Reverend Coleman had served the congregation for 12 years.

We visited him in the Pastor's Study. "Racial diversity works generally well, but Waterloo experienced its share of racial tension and hostility. The Black community always had a strained history here in Waterloo," Reverend Coleman explained.

"At the turn of the century, there was a huge railroad strike and Blacks were brought in from the south as strike breakers against the Illinois Central Railroad Company. That's why so many families from the south are here—Arkansas, Alabama and Mississippi." Reverend Coleman looked at me. "Some of the people you have already met."

"That's right." I replied.

"Hallelujah! Black folks saved the railroad," scoffed Reverend Coleman. "But we weren't welcomed with open arms—oh, no! The landlords wouldn't rent to African-Americans, and property owners refused to sell to Blacks. In the end, Black families migrated all the way from the deep south, but had no place to live."

"So what happened?"

"Since the railroad company still needed Black workers, they allowed their workers to live in old rusted boxcars."

"Is that right?" asked Secretary Slater.

"Absolutely!" Reverend Coleman boasted, "The Eastside Ministerial Alliance maintains a replica of one of the boxcar houses Black families lived in, which is why the Black community literally developed around the railroad yards—and grew around the east side of the railroad tracks."

Secretary Slater said, "This is definitely a community which should apply for economic development funds from the Department of Transportation."

Reverend Coleman paused, and looked us in the eyes. "Explain one thing to me. As two proud Black men, why aren't you supporting the Black candidate?"

I said, "The way I see it Reverend Coleman, it's not about him; it's about us."

"What do you mean?" he asked.

I confided, "I'm a legal and community development professional. In the real world, I work for non-profit organizations, faith-based groups and disadvantaged small businesses. So let me start by saying, my heart and my passion are with the community."

"Okay," replied Reverend Coleman.

I said, "So the question for me is, which electable candidate will best protect and promote our interests?"

He said, "So you don't think he can win."

"First, I don't know him, and I don't think the Black community really knows him either."

"What do you mean?" asked Reverend Coleman.

"Two words—Clarence Thomas."

They all laughed out loud together.

Reverend Coleman asked, "You're not calling Barack an Uncle Tom, are you?"

I smiled. "He's no Thurgood Marshall; that's for sure! I don't think so, but I have another fear."

"What's that?" asked Reverend Coleman.

"Sometimes a new Black manager will go so far out of the way to prove he's not favoring Black workers that he actually holds them back. Right?"

"Yeah."

"I'm afraid Barack might do the same thing to us. Think about it. He hasn't made a single public promise to the Black community."

Reverend Coleman said, "Come on Brother; he can't do that and still win white support."

"I know, but we're giving him a pass. With a wink and a nod, thinking that he's just saying what he has to say. We all *Hope* he will do the right thing—if he gets elected."

"Yeah, you're right," said Reverend Coleman. "That's exactly what we are doing."

"We don't know what he's actually going to do. Worse, he hasn't promised to do anything for us. We just hope."

"Is Hillary any better?"

"Economically, the Black community was in the best shape it ever was under the Clinton Administration. And the Clinton's have been true friends to our community for decades."

"That's right," conceded Reverend Coleman.

"We know the Clintons, good and bad; and what to expect from Clinton policies. I'm not naïve. They're not perfect, but at least we know them."

Reverend Coleman nodded. "Better the devil you know, so to speak."

"Don't get me wrong, Reverend," I said. "As a Black man, like yourself, I'm not anti-Obama. We're just pro-Clinton."

Rising to leave, he said, "Well, Brother, I'm glad you guys finally got here. Senator Obama has been here for months."

Reverend Coleman escorted us to the door. "And I'll give some serious thought to what you've shared with me today."

We turned to leave the Pastor's study. "Thank you Reverend. What do we have to do to get your support?"

He laughed. "I'm not making any promises like that my Brother, but I'll tell you this—I will give you guys equal time. That's the best I can do."

Emancipation Day

Monday, December 31, 2007

Braving the bitter cold, Rodney Slater and I met with Reverend Michael Coleman prior the Watch Night service, and engaged in a lively discussion 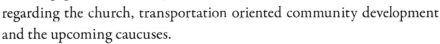 regarding the church, transportation oriented community development and the upcoming caucuses.

Reverend Coleman gave Secretary Slater a personal tour of the Eastside Ministerial Alliance Community Center and its Head Start Program. Impressed by the history of the organization and the community services it provided, Secretary Slater offered to assist the group in seeking funding for an African-American museum through Department of Transportation related funding.

Excited about the upcoming caucuses, Reverend Coleman emphasized the importance of providing information to his parishioners—without choosing sides. He invited Secretary Slater to participate in tonight's church service.

President Abraham Lincoln signed the emancipation proclamation on January 1, 1893. *Freedom's Eve* was celebrated by many African-Americans in *Watch Night* services on New Year's Eve, followed by church services the next day. These time-honored traditions were practiced by the African-American religious community in Waterloo. Reverend Coleman acknowledged he was allowing other campaign surrogates to participate in the service as well, but promised equal time for the Clinton campaign.

Following the community tour, Secretary Slater was interviewed on black radio in Waterloo. He was interviewed in-studio by Dr. Scharron Clayton who was impressed, if not enamored, with the former Secretary. She was affable and flirty as they talked about the history of blacks in Waterloo, education, economic development, and the importance of caucusing.

Secretary Slater found the historical perspective useful in his radio interview, private meetings and public speaking forums. After the interview, Secretary Slater and I met with Reverend Marvin Jenkins while canvassing at Morg's Diner, prior to attending Watch Night service.

Reverend Jenkins was an old friend of Secretary Slater and Pastor of Union Missionary Baptist Church which had a current membership of 200. Reverend Jenkins had served Union Missionary Baptist Church for the last seven years.

Monday, December 31, 2007

Broadway and Arnold knocked on 104 doors, collected eight supporter cards and posted four yard signs. Later that day, Harold Gist joined the Waterloo Outreach Team and brought food to share at the "pot-luck" gala on a cold winter night.

Broadway and Arnold provided high visibility at the service by placing prominent Clinton signage and banners at a large exhibit table and placed prominent decals on the donated food, beverages and beverage containers.

The local churches attending this community service included Antioch Baptist Church, Mount Carmel Baptist Church, Payne Memorial AME Church, Union Missionary Baptist Church and Christian Fellowship Baptist Church. Four hundred and fifty souls attended the banquet and Watch Night Service, which began at 8:00 p.m., and continued past 1:30 a.m., a tremendous turn out for this event.

During the service, Reverend Marvin Jenkins acknowledged former Secretary Slater and myself from the pulpit, which was a let down. We had hoped for something more. Reverend Jenkins welcomed us in the beginning of service and asked us to stand and be recognized, along with other visitors and visiting campaigns.

Later in the service, Reverend Coleman specifically identified Secretary Slater, and noted his historic service in the Clinton Administration and allowed him to formally address the congregation.

Tuesday, January 1, 2008

We started to feel real pressure. Senator Clinton held the lead in nearly all nationwide opinion polling, until January 2008. By the start of the year, support for Senator Obama began rising in the polls, surpassing Hillary Clinton for first place for the first time in Iowa.

I advanced and provided surrogate support for New York Lieutenant Governor David Patterson and former Secretary Rodney Slater for Emancipation Day services, while Broadway and Arnold knocked on 56 doors in inclement weather, collected two supporter cards and posted a yard sign.

Lieutenant Governor Patterson and Secretary Slater met with Reverend Frantz Whitfield and senior church leaders prior to service. They engaged in a lively discussion regarding the caucuses, and the prospects of the first Black candidate who might enjoy mainstream support.

Lieutenant Governor Patterson said, "People forget. The first mainstream Black Presidential campaign was Virginia, Governor Doug Wilder's presidential bid in 1992. The short-lived campaign offered a compelling model for black elected politicians who worked within the system. They could take a larger role in national politics."

Secretary Slater replied, "The majority of viable presidential contenders are either senators and governors, but there isn't a single black senator or governor in the south. This is partly because many of the party's most talented black politicians hail from the South, where any Democratic candidates, especially minorities, face uphill battles to win statewide office."

Lieutenant Governor Patterson argued, "Unfortunately, while racial gerrymandering to establish political advantage for congressional districts in the south can guarantee minority representation in Congress, it can also hurt a minority representative's chances for higher office.

"The political center is so different in a majority-minority district. But to win statewide office, you'd have to turn around and reinvent yourself. What's worse, even talented black candidates get overlooked when money and resources are distributed by the party."

Secretary Slater asked, "So if Black candidates can't win statewide offices in southern states, how can Barack hope to carry a southern state?"

"Humph... I don't know the answer," answered Reverend Frantz Whitfield. "But I see your point."

Reverend Whitfield emerged from his study and escorted the two dignitaries into the sanctuary for Emancipation Day Service. They were joined by other representatives from the Obama Campaign—who were introduced first.

The worship services began at 12:00 noon and continued until 1:30 p.m., before a modest turn out with 65 parishioners present. The participants dressed in period attire, flowing dresses and overalls for service, and were served wild game including venison, rabbit, and duck at the luncheon. Reverend Whitfield acknowledged all of the campaigns in attendance which included Rick Wade an Obama Senior Advisor, in addition to Lieutenant Governor Patterson and former Secretary Slater.

Illinois State Senator Emile Jones declared, "Black people don't owe Bill Clinton or Hillary Clinton a damn thing. We voted for him. That's it!" He continued making incendiary and inappropriate political remarks from the pulpit, encouraging Black people to caucus for Obama.

Lieutenant Governor Patterson and former Secretary Slater were both given time to address the congregation and provided strong but appropriate remarks. They fellowshipped with the congregation during a period themed lunch served after Emancipation Day Service.

Wednesday, January 2, 2008

I advanced and provided surrogate support for Congresswoman Sheila Jackson Lee, fifty-eight, and Secretary Rodney Slater for a final rally with

Bill Clinton in Waterloo, Iowa. Broadway and Arnold canvassed across seven targeted precincts and knocked on 176 doors, received 14 supporter cards and posted ten yard signs.

Prior to caucus night, through the frigid conditions, the Buffalo Soldiers had attended 19 community events, identified 18 community leaders, posted 189 yard signs, knocked on over 1,433 doors and visited numerous community meetings and venues.

I accessed the Democratic Votebuilder database for a final tabulation. The final pre-caucus standings, read—VAN-1 (84); VAN-2 (75); VAN-3 (133); VAN-4 (58) and VAN-5 (87). This meant that Senator Obama possessed a slight advantage in strong support with HRC (84) and BHO (87), while Clinton held the advantage among leaning HRC (75) versus leaning BHO (58). The big number, the undecided, totaled (133).

Thursday, January 3, 2008

The moment of truth arrived and I prepared for caucus night at East Side High School. The frigid night air was filled with both possibility and anxiety. No matter what, it was a historic night, one which might catapult the first female or African-American candidate towards the presidential nomination of a major political party.

Secretary Slater and I manned the East Side High School site, where multiple precincts were co-located in the expansive East Side High School complex—the largest caucus site in the African-American community. Ricky Broadway and Tramond Arnold chaperoned Representative Sheila Jackson-Lee to the next largest location.

Dozens of Obama caucus goers entered the building. A loud cry echoed through the cold night air:

"Rock your."

"Tee-shirts."

"Rock your."

"Tee-shirts"

On cue, hundreds of Obama supporters waved baseball caps, towels and tee-shirts in the air. Caucus night in Waterloo looked more like an ACORN national demonstration, rather than a presidential selection process.

An endless torrent of eager caucus goers overwhelmed the internal management infrastructure and aging poll workers; it was unmitigated chaos. The extreme number of young, eager caucus participants flooded the facility and prevented any meaningful identification, or checking in by the elderly caucus workers and staff. People roamed freely throughout the building.

A demoralizing experience for the Buffalo Soldiers and Clinton campaign staff, we didn't have to wait for election returns to come in. Tonight's results were obvious and plain. The inevitable candidate had been completely overrun.

I called Ricky Broadway to check on the results at his caucus site.

"Brother, McCray, this shit is crazy. How is it looking where you are?" asked Broadway.

Secretary Slater was standing next to a local news reporter and myself when the phone call came through. Putting my best foot forward while in earshot of the reporter, I replied, "It's been a challenging night here at Eastside. Barack Obama was the clear winner, but Hillary Clinton maintained viability and earned some delegates."

Exasperated, "Man you're being all politically correct and shit. Over here—we got SMASHED!" Broadway exclaimed.

Waterloo was a harbinger for things to come across the state. Whether by design or happenstance, the Obama campaign exemplified all the characteristics of successful community organizing, which was evidenced by the caucus night turnout. Senator Obama won the Iowa caucus handily, with John Edwards coming in second and Hillary Clinton in a distant third.

Obama's win was fueled by first time caucus-goers and independents, which proved Iowa voters viewed him as the candidate of change. They controlled the message, mastered communications, and ran an issue-based campaign on inspirational values of "hope" and "change", rather than a caustic or personality-based one of expediency or inevitability.

The Buffalo Soldiers regrouped in a suite at the downtown Marriott; the Obama victory party was held downstairs.

"We got out organized," declared Gist.

Organizing is hard work. I knew from ACORN that people who organize their local communities were sometimes incapable of going elsewhere to design and execute new structures in a different community. Some people could organize ethnic constituencies and minority groups. Others learned to be outstanding organizers in particular kinds of communities with specific ethnic groups, but in different communities with different ethnic groups, they couldn't organize their way out of a paper bag.

During the sixties, student organizers and the campus activists could organize a substantial number of students to fight the draft; but they couldn't relate to or organize lower or middle-class workers.

Labor organizers organized around the NLRA collective bargaining units but couldn't organize broad-based community coalitions. Some studied sociology or were trained in schools of social work to become community organizers. They took classes like Community Organizations and even acquired a specialized vocabulary. They meant well but oftentimes were unwilling or incapable of transforming their community organizing and activism into political clout.

"Okay guys, keep your heads up. This doesn't mean anything. Ya'll know the Clintons, and we're not going to quit. We didn't quit back then, and we're not going to quit now. All it means is we're going to have to do this the hard way," Harold Gist said.

I asked, "So Gist, where are we really?"

"Look, they won the state, but we're still ahead in terms of total delegates," said Gist.

"How so?" I asked.

Gist said, "It's not being reported in the news, but we started off with a big lead in super-delegates from the start." The "super-delegates" consisted of DNC members, Democratic Congress members and Governors, and other prominent Democrats.

He said, "They're not going to cover it in the news. Barack taking the lead is a better story, but we're still ahead. We wanted to win this one early. Now it's a knife fight. Pack you're bags; let's take this show on the road. McCray, Broadway, Arnold and Harris you are going to South Carolina with Willis."

"I'm going to Vegas, along with McGraw and Jamie."

"What about New Hampshire?" I asked.

Kevin McGraw said, "There's not a large enough minority presence for us to make a difference in New Hampshire. So we'll have to pray for them, but work the hell out of Nevada and South Carolina."

Within hours of Senator Obama's victory in Iowa, Hillary Clinton's Black support began to fade.

Black voters, young and old, simply hadn't believed a black man could win in white states. Once he did, a wave of pride swept through African-American neighborhoods in the South. Internal polling from both campaigns after Iowa showed Obama suddenly garnering closer to 75% or 80% of the black vote in primary states.

These voters did not have the deep affection for Hillary Clinton which many of their ministers and local politicians had for Bill Clinton. "I always heard people say, I know *Bill Clinton*. I don't know Hillary. So I'll give Barack Obama a closer look," said Carol Willis, a Clinton aide who had led the campaign's outreach to Black voters.

Joe Biden and Christopher Dodd withdrew from the nomination contest immediately following the Iowa caucus. Barack Obama became the new front-runner in New Hampshire overnight, after his poll numbers skyrocketed following his victory in Iowa.

Ironically, senior Hillary Clinton's strategists made a similar miscalculation during the Gore Presidential race, after Al Gore finally decided to accept Bill Clinton's assistance and the full support of the Clinton Team. The mistake was over-reliance on an established political candidate to deliver a victory in a critical state. The Clinton Team coordinated nationally through the DNC, but relied on Gore's operations for his home state Tennessee, one he had never lost—until then.

In this case, Clinton Strategists over-relied on the former Governor for Iowa as a Hillary Clinton supporter. We assumed Tom Vilsack had a political operation which could actually deliver his state for Clinton. We thought Governor Vilsack had an Iowa machine; we were wrong.

Tuesday, January 8, 2008

I anxiously monitored the New Hampshire returns with South Carolina Hillary Clinton Staff members: Kelly Adams, thirty, the State Director, an attractive and petite, cinnamon skinned woman; Glenn Rushing, forty-three, the Political Director, an affable skinny man with curly brown hair; and Reverend William Smart, the Director of Faith Outreach at the HRC Campaign Headquarters in Columbia, South Carolina. The New Hampshire primary results could affect the race in South Carolina.

Following her loss in Iowa, Mark Penn, fifty-four, Hillary Clinton's Campaign Manager insisted on doing televised interviews in which he repeatedly referred to Obama's use of cocaine. Barack Obama had admitted to recreational drug use during his college days in his memoirs.

But in what may have been the turning point for her campaign, Hillary Clinton gave a strong performance at the Saint Anselm College, ABC and Facebook debates, followed by an emotional interview, live on national TV.

By the end of the day, Senator Clinton won the New Hampshire primary by 2% of the vote, contrary to the predictions of pollsters who consistently had her trailing Senator Obama for days leading up to the primary date.

Barack Obama took the stage to theme music by Stevie Wonder and prepared to give his concession speech. I exclaimed, "We're still in. We're still alive."

The South Carolina staff cheered.

We had finally found a way to reach Democratic voters, "The

Presidency is too important to risk, Barack is a great candidate but he simply can't win."

Barack Obama echoed a defiant refrain, "It was whispered by slaves and abolitionist as they blazed a trail toward freedom—*Yes We Can*." It was if he was answering me directly through the television set.

Sarcastically, Reverend William Smart declared, "I can't believe they came out to *Signed, Sealed, Delivered*. They thought this race was going to be over—tonight!"

Reverend Smart recited the Buffalo Soldiers creed, "We are the dedicated few who against insurmountable odds have accomplished so much, when given so little for so long, we have convinced the whole world that armed with nothing—we can achieve the impossible."

"That's what I'm talking about," said Glenn Rushing. "We're going to do it right here in South Carolina next!"

"I wonder when the media is going to pick up on his pastor—Jeremiah Wright?" asked Smart.

"Who?" I asked.

"Reverend Wright is a Black Liberation Theologian and an icon in Chicago's black community, but he's a firebrand. He's built a large and loyal following at his church with his mesmerizing sermons, mixing traditional spiritual content and his views on contemporary issues.

"Reverend Wright is considered one of the country's 10 most influential black pastors. He's on Obama's faith-steering committee and Barack has praised at least one aspect of Reverend Wright's approach, referring to his *social gospel* and his focus on Africa."

A few weeks later I discussed Election Day GOTV with Heyward Bannister, fifty-five, South Carolina Field Director, as the first in the south primary approached.

I inquired, "I don't get this Heyward. Why is HQ pulling our resources out of South Carolina?"

He said, "We're down in the polls, so it makes perfect sense to me."

"What do you mean?"

"The campaign is focused on winning Super Tuesday. If we need to shut down South Carolina in order to save resources, then so be it."

"But Heyward!" I argued, "Even though we are down in the polls for South Carolina, that doesn't mean we should pull all our resources out of the state."

"Why not?" he asked.

"Because the nomination is based on total delegates. South Carolina has proportional representation."

"And?" asked Heyward.

"If we pull out of the state entirely and don't have any GOTV, then we might save some money, but we could lose the state entirely."

"That's right."

"But if we don't give up and actually have Election Day operations we might lose the state, but still win some delegates."

Heyward acquiesced "Uh-huh."

"The goal should be to win delegates, not states. If this was a GOP Primary that would make sense, because Republicans are winner take all. The Democrats are not."

Heyward said, "Either way, it's not our call, but I think we should save our money now, and focus on winning Super Tuesday."

Thursday, January 10, 2008

David Rubenstein gave a speech at the University of Pennsylvania, when angry labor activists shouted him down with signs and bullhorns. It was a testy exchange between Rubenstein and SEIU activists who amassed and clashed.

Rubenstein complained. "These campaigns are three-dimensional, negative political campaigns waged against the reputation of the target. The SEIU's true goal is to inflict as much pain as possible so the employer gives the union what they want."

The SEIU's chief target had been the Carlyle Group after David Rubenstein bought a copy of the Magna Carta for $21 million which he gave to the National Archives. The SEIU instantly prepared a *Top Ten* list of reasons why Rubenstein donated the Magna Carta, and labeled him a medieval baron.

Marcel Reid entered the DC ACORN office and was greeted by Belinda Ferrell.

Belinda asked, "Guess what? Anita got fired."

"Fired? for what?" Marcel asked.

"I don't know for sure, but she cleaned out her desk, and a computer is missing."

"Missing computer? What?"

Belinda said, "For real, girl. I'm not accusing her of stealing or anything. I'm just saying."

Project Vote conducted an internal investigation into the acquisition and usage of the Pitney Bowes Purchase Power Visa credit card which totaled $1,741.43 in unauthorized and unpaid charges.

The unauthorized card was issued to Anita MonCrief and she was summarily fired, with good cause. Bitter, worried and scared, Anita seethed anger and vowed to get even with Project Vote for terminating her—whatever the cost. After she was escorted from the building, a Project Vote laptop computer mysteriously disappeared from the Washington, D.C. offices.

Saturday, January 19, 2008

I sipped from a hot cup of coffee and opened the USA Today. I looked for the results from the Nevada primaries and slammed the paper down in disgust. "I can't believe this shit—man! We come back and win Nevada, but the media touts Obama because they won more delegates."

I quickly dialed Harold Gist from my cell phone.

Gist said, "Yeah, brother, I know what you mean. We focused on organizing Las Vegas, the most populated area in the state, and we won. But they earned more delegates because they carried the rural districts across the state."

I said, "So when we have more delegates, the news reported Obama won the state, and when we won the state, the news reports Obama won more delegates. What the fuck!"

Democratic rules stated delegates were awarded through proportional representation with a minimum threshold of 15% of votes in a state or congressional district to receive delegates.

The pledged delegates were allocated according to two main criteria: first, the proportion of votes each state gave the candidate in the last three Presidential elections, and second, the percentage of votes each state has in the Electoral College. The delegate population must reflect the state's ethnic distribution, and at least 50% of the delegates must be women.

Still angry at the slanted coverage of the Nevada primaries, I was even more distraught seven days later when Senator Obama won the South Carolina primary on January 26, 2008. The South Carolina Primary was the first primary with any significant African-American population. Senator Obama swept the state and earned more than twice the vote his rival Senator Clinton did, 55% to 27%. Former Senator John Edwards was third with 18% of the vote. John Edwards suspended his campaign after placing third in the New Hampshire and South Carolina primaries, but he did not immediately endorse any remaining candidate.

The most damaging moment for Bill Clinton and the campaign's outreach to the Black community came after the South Carolina primary ended when Bill Clinton waved away Senator Obama's victory by comparing it with Jesse Jackson's wins in South Carolina in 1984 and 1988. From then on, the Democratic nomination fight became racially contentious, with every word parsed for ethnic undertones and emotions rising to the surface. Was it just an accident Clinton used the word *spadework* to deride her opponent's record?

Democratic Whip James Clyburn and Bill Clinton had long and tense phone conversations because of several comments the former president made. Clyburn said, "There was something about the condescension on his face and the dismissiveness in his voice. It was a verbal pat on the head."

Bill Clinton's long-time appeal in the Black community was grounded less in his civil rights background or ties to black leaders, but more because of his deep personal comfort with Black America. Clinton had exhibited such comfort and identity with the Black community that Toni Morrison once called him *"our first Black President."* After South Carolina, that bond had been breached. As predicted, Senator Clinton immediately lost all of the remaining support from the Black community.

Decapitation

Over the next six months, I traveled across the country fervently working on African-American strategies and outreach for Hillary Clinton with the Buffalo Soldiers. Ironically, Barack Obama ran the kind of community organizing campaign the Buffalo Soldiers had always dreamed of, but Democratic candidates never fully supported. Hillary Clinton boasted the best campaign professionals money could buy, but we faced a grassroots movement, which couldn't be purchased with money.

I witnessed first-hand the epic political clash, beginning in Iowa, through South Carolina, Ohio, Pennsylvania, Oklahoma and Arkansas. The major Democratic candidates had agreed not to campaign in Florida or Michigan, since the Democratic leadership said it would strip all delegates from Florida and Michigan. John Edwards and Senator Obama even removed their names from the Michigan ballot. Senator Clinton ultimately won a majority of delegates and popular votes from both states, although 40% of the vote was uncommitted in Michigan.

She subsequently led a fight to seat all the Florida and Michigan delegates. While self-serving, Senator Clinton's action was a pragmatic attempt to forestall Florida or Michigan voters from becoming so disaffected they wouldn't vote for Democrats in the general election. It fueled speculation that the fight over the delegates could last until the DNC convention in August.

Tuesday, January 29, 2008

I drove my Chrysler Le Baron to Tulsa, Oklahoma to meet Larry Freeman, forty-one, an intimidating man, tall and forceful, to prepare for the upcoming Oklahoma Primaries. Freeman was a high school classmate of mine who had worked the South Carolina Primaries with me before. Steeped in history, we set up in a cheap hotel near the historic *Black Wall Street* neighborhood of Tulsa.

Flipping through the news channels, I stopped on CNN. Maxine Waters was talking about the state of the country. She declared, "At a time when the economy continues to worsen and so many of my constituents are losing their homes and their jobs, we need someone with the leadership and experience who can step in on day one to tackle the economic challenges our country is facing."

"Hey, Freeman, check this out. Maxine Waters just endorsed Senator Clinton."

Larry Freeman walked back into the stale hotel room.

Surprised, "That's huge for us. It's a boost and it's national support. It should make big waves." Freeman said.

This endorsement came on the heels of Senator Ted Kennedy's endorsement of Barack Obama. As a Congressional Representative, Maxine Waters was a super-delegate to the 2008 Democratic National Convention. With only two weeks between the South Carolina and Oklahoma Primaries, we had an extremely short window to organize Oklahoma and coordinate Arkansas. Oklahoma had a small but concentrated African-American population which Freeman and I targeted in Tulsa and Oklahoma City. Meanwhile, Carol Willis ran the Arkansas efforts from Little Rock.

Saturday, February 2, 2008

I sipped hazelnut coffee and watched election coverage on the news. California Governor's wife, Maria Shriver, endorsed Senator Obama at a rally led by Michelle Obama on the UCLA campus, which was broadcast all across the country. Celebrities Oprah Winfrey, Caroline Kennedy and Stevie Wonder joined them and showed support for Barack Obama. California was a Super Tuesday state rich in delegates.

Freeman and I woke early on February 5, 2008. It was the date on which 24 states held primaries or caucuses, and 52% of all Democratic Party pledged delegates committed by the simultaneous state primary elections. We carried both Oklahoma and Arkansas, winning 30% of the African-American vote in Clinton's home state.

Senator Obama trailed in California, polling by an average of 6% before the primary and ended up losing the state by 8.3%. A large Latino turnout which voted for Hillary Clinton was the deciding factor. Clinton campaign strategists had mapped a victory scenario which envisioned the former first lady wrapping up the Democratic presidential nomination by Super Tuesday—which ended in a virtual dead heat. Barack Obama amassed 847 delegates to Hillary Clinton's 834 from the 23 states which held Democratic primaries.

Senator Clinton had overcompensated for being a female candidate. She ran on strength and experience; she was the *Inevitable* candidate. Consequently, the Clinton campaign struggled after suffering the devastating loss in Iowa. We had no strategy beyond the early primaries and caucuses. She should have run on leadership.

Louisiana, Washington, Nebraska, Hawaii, Wisconsin, U.S. Virgin Islands, the District of Columbia, Maryland, and Virginia primaries and the Maine caucus followed in February. Senator Obama won all of these contests giving him ten consecutive victories after Super Tuesday.

The Silver Cadillac turned the corner on Massachusetts Avenue as Marcel Reid drove past the SEIU Headquarters. Meanwhile upstairs, labor activists led by Stephen Lerner lined the conference table in the glass-walled room at the union's headquarters in Northwest Washington. The SEIU's private-equity team plotted new attacks on the Carlyle Group without DC ACORN's Marcel Reid. They planned demonstrations around congressional hearings looking into links between private equity and Middle East oil money, also known as sovereign wealth funds.

The union had identified friendly politicians in Washington and other state capitals to contact. Like-minded public interest groups such as ACORN, the Working Families Party and United Students Against Sweatshops were enlisted as allies. They formulated talking points and brainstormed advertising campaigns.

Lerner proposed a late-night CNN commercial labeling the Abu Dhabi government's $1.35 billion ownership of a stake in Carlyle as a potential risk to U.S. security. "We should definitely make some hay of it," Andrew McDonald, forty-nine, agreed. "Maybe do some public demonstrations around it too."

Lerner said, "We've got a long history of doing creative things to shed light on issues, which includes humor and absurdity."

The plan: Tie America's biggest buyout firms to Middle Eastern investment funds. The goal: Scare Americans into thinking their security is threatened by Middle Eastern investments in firms like the Carlyle Group, which often invested in companies which did important business for the U.S. government.

There had been private-equity hearings on Capitol Hill and new federal legislation introduced on nursing-home care, since SEIU's assault began. And new legislation had been introduced in California to stop private-equity firms from accepting new investments from countries with poor human rights records.

Thursday, March 6, 2008

I flew to Philadelphia to begin to work the Pennsylvania Primary for Hillary Clinton immediately following the Ohio Primaries. She had carried both Ohio and Rhode Island on March 4, 2008, surprise upsets, even though she had led the polls in both states.

Hillary Clinton carried the primary in Texas, but Senator Obama won the Texas caucuses held later that night. So Senators Clinton and

Obama split the *"Texas-Two-Step"* although Obama netted more delegates from the state than Clinton. Cecil McDonald, forty-six, who stood
6'2", an athletic man with a swimmer's build, traveled to Philadelphia to
set the Buffalo Soldiers up for the Pennsylvania primaries.

I picked up Cecil McDonald after church. Cecil was also from
Arkansas and had arrived fresh from the Texas Primaries. He had worked
with me during the Federal Empowerment Zones Initiative, and intro-
duced me to the Buffalo Soldiers in 1994. "I don't believe this shit man.
West Philly is a bitch. We've been doing this stuff for twenty years and
I've never, ever been booed or hissed at church before!" said Cecil.

"Yeah, that was something. We have our work cut out for us here," I
said. "But this is Philadelphia; they boo Santa Claus here."

Pennsylvania held a closed primary, which meant only registered
Democrats could vote. The established Democratic electorate was older,
whiter, more Catholic and more working-class than the earlier primaries.

Senator Obama outspent the Clinton campaign, three to one in
Pennsylvania, but his comment at a San Francisco fundraiser, "Small-
town Americans clung to guns and religion," drew sharp criticism from
Senator Clinton and nearly crippled his chances in the Keystone State.

Tuesday, March 11, 2008

Marcel Reid walked through the concave driveway in front of the
Washington Plaza Hotel for ACORN's Legislative and Policy Conference
in Washington, DC. Georgia ACORN was conspicuously absent from
this year's Legislative and Policy Conference. Unlike previous years,
ACORN had decided to skip the individual banks and mortgage brokers.
This time the Association would take on Wall Street itself—and the
entire banking and financial services industry.

Professionally dressed in a navy blue suit and business attire, Marcel
entered first. She meekly asked for Timothy Ryan, Jr., President and
CEO; Randy Snook, Executive Vice President; or Ira Hammerman,

Senior Managing Director and General Counsel, and then waited for the receptionist to respond.

The Securities Industry and Financial Markets Association had offices in New York and Washington, D.C. SIFMA was a global organization with offices in the U.S., Europe and Asia. It was an organization for all professionals in the financial services industry, and represented the shared interests of more than 650 securities firms, banks and asset managers.

Marcel waited patiently, as the receptionist went to get a Senior Manager. After waiting about 15 minutes, Marcel excused herself and walked outside. She saw the first school busses filled with protestors drive onto the parking lot across the street. Marcel propped the door open to circumvent the automatic security lock. Moments later, 800 protestors rushed in and overwhelmed the office.

The receptionist sat stunned, bewildered and confused. She never imagined Marcel was actually with the hoard of protestors who had just overtaken the building.

Scott DeFife, forty-four, the new Senior Managing Director of Governmental Affairs, seethed in anger as he walked to the lobby. DeFife handed Marcel his business card as they walked into the executive conference room to negotiate. Following the demonstration with Maude Hurd and over 600 ACORN members, DeFife agreed to a follow up meeting by March 19, 2008—in writing.

Thursday, March 13, 2008

I smelled the aroma of grilled steak and cheese wiz when we met with Blair Talmadge, a Philadelphia native and Black Politico, while Cecil, my counterpart, and I set up base camp. Philadelphia was going to be tough, because Blair was a Buffalo Solider and he was even leaning toward Barack Obama.

However, my eyebrows rose as I noticed a FOX News Clip running in heavy rotation with Sean Hannity, the conservative talk show host.

"Hey Cecil—check this out."

"Not God Bless America, but God Damn America!" thundered a tenor voice from the pulpit of Trinity United Church of Christ on Chicago's south side. It was Reverend Jeremiah Wright, sixty-six, Obama's pastor for the last 20 years. They were close. Reverend Wright had married Barack and his wife Michelle and baptized their two daughters Sasha and Malia.

The Obama campaign faced its darkest hour after the videos appeared on Fox News, where incendiary rhetoric of Reverend Wright declared that Blacks should not sing "God Bless America" but "God Damn America" instead.

Reverend Wright's sermons, made repeated denunciations of the U.S. based on his reading of the Gospels and the treatment of Black Americans. "The government gives them the drugs, builds bigger prisons, passes a three-strike law and then wants us to sing God Bless America. NO, No, No! God damn America! That's in the Bible for killing innocent people," avowed Reverend Wright in a 2003 sermon.

"God Damn America, for treating our citizens as less than human. God damn America, for as long as she acts like she is God and she is supreme," he repeated.

In addition to damning America, Reverend Wright told his congregation, on the Sunday following September 11, 2001, that the United States had brought on Al Qaeda's attacks because of its own terrorism. "We bombed Hiroshima, we bombed Nagasaki, and we nuked far more than the thousands in New York and the Pentagon—and we never batted an eye," proclaimed Reverend Wright, in a fiery sermon on September 16, 2001.

"We have supported state terrorism against the Palestinians and black South Africans, and now we are indignant because the stuff we have done overseas is now brought right back to our own front yards. America's chickens are coming home to roost," Reverend Wright told his congregation.

"I wouldn't call it radical. I call it being black in America," declared a parishioner standing outside the church.

Defensive, Senator Obama replied, "I don't think my church is particularly controversial." He described Reverend Jeremiah Wright as "like an old uncle who says things I don't always agree with."

Thinking out loud, I said. "I don't know, Cecil. This could be a game changer for the election."

Cecil agreed, "I think you're right, Michael. If we're smart, this could change everything. I'm surprised it took the media this long to discover Reverend Wright."

Obama's press spokesman, Bill Burton explained, "Senator Obama has said personal attacks such as this have no place in this campaign, or our politics, whether they're offered from a platform, at a rally, or the pulpit of a church.

"Senator Obama does not think of the pastor of his church in political terms. Like a member of his family, there are things he says with which Senator Obama deeply disagrees. But now that he is retired, that doesn't detract from Senator Obama's affection for Reverend Wright or his appreciation for the good works he has done."

Tuesday, March 18, 2008

As a result of the persistent controversy over comments pulled from the sermons given by Reverend Jeremiah Wright, Senator Obama was forced to give a seminal speech on race in Philadelphia. It was aimed, for the most part, at reassuring white voters over the Wright controversy, but it also marked the first time Senator Obama publicly addressed the generational divide his campaign had exposed among Black Americans.

"For the men and women of Reverend Wright's generation," Senator Obama said, "the memories of humiliation and doubt and fear have not gone away, nor has the anger and bitterness of those years. At times, this anger is exploited by politicians, to gin up votes along racial lines or to make up for a politician's own failings."

The speech was a rousing success, an intelligent and eloquent discussion of America's original sin, delivered in a manner which embraced and encompassed all perspectives on race and immigration. It literally saved the Obama campaign, which had reeled on the heels of implosion following the tremendous media attention driven by the Wright controversy.

Philadelphia Mayor Michael Nutter, fifty, played a central role in the presidential contest. Tough as nails, Mayor Nutter was a reformer and 14-year veteran of the Philadelphia City Council. He was also the prototype of the new generation of black political leaders.

Unlike others, Mayor Nutter sided with Hillary Clinton and enthusiastically campaigned for her. Michael Nutter emerged as the black face of the Clinton's campaign in Pennsylvania at a time when she desperately needed a solid victory.

Senator Clinton had several advantages in Pennsylvania, most importantly, former Philadelphia Mayor and Governor Ed Rendell, sixty-four, and his state-wide Democratic machine. Throughout the primary process, she relied on the support of older, white, working-class voters.

Wednesday, March 26, 2008

The follow-up meeting with Scott DeFife at SIFMA started like all the previous meetings with bank boards. Songs and chants followed by contentious discussions, but instead of predatory lending, this time ACORN negotiators began the negotiations with mortgage fraud.

Shocked, Marcel Reid listened intently as Michael Davis, a former pro basketball player for the Washington Wizards and Tonya Lombard a tax preparer with the ACORN American Institute for Social Justice (AISJ) and the Head ACORN Housing negotiator, argued the Georgia mortgage fraud issue Michael McCray had presented to the ACORN board—without him.

Marcel thought to herself. *So while ACORN portrays itself as a democratic organization whose decisions were made by its thousands of member families, history proved only one family controls ACORN—the Rathkes.*

So for all of the members ACORN claimed to represent, and for all of the organizations it supported and maintained, ACORN was the family business of Wade Rathke and run with help from his wife, his brother, and his children.

ACORN demanded $350 per initial household contact, and $150 for each subsequent referral contact for homes in danger of foreclosure. Marcel did the math in her head. *Since there are roughly 60 million households in America, if only 10% to 15% were in foreclosure, ACORN's demand exceeded $10 billion.*

DeFife was shocked at the brazenness of this demand. He exclaimed, "I came here for a haircut—not a fucking decapitation!" He stormed out of the conference room.

OBAMA Power

Tuesday, April 22, 2008

I savored sweet victory and a four-finger pour of Hennessey V.S.O.P. Senator Clinton won the Pennsylvania primary by double digits—winning 55% of the vote, a landslide statewide victory. Barack Obama had made a concerted effort to win, and nine of every ten Black voters in Philadelphia pulled the lever for Barack Obama.

Following Pennsylvania, Senator Obama was in a stronger position to win the nomination, with a higher number of delegates and popular votes. Senator Clinton had received the endorsements of more super-delegates, but with such close delegate counts, the early speculation was for the first brokered convention in decades.

Howard Dean, fifty-nine, the Democratic National Committee Chair, sought to avoid this outcome and the dispute over seating delegates from Florida and Michigan. This tension led to comparisons with the 1968 Democratic National Convention, which ended in a divided party and disaster.

Tuesday, May 6, 2008

I returned to Little Rock to provide campaign support for the Buffalo Soldiers from Arkansas with Carol Willis. We watched the Indiana and North Carolina returns together. North Carolina and Indiana held their Democratic presidential primaries. Both Senators Clinton and Obama relentlessly campaigned before the voting took place. These primaries were turning points which could make or break either campaign.

Early polling indicated Senator Obama was a few points ahead in North Carolina, with Senator Clinton leading in Indiana. Senator Obama outperformed the polls by several points in both states and won by a significant margin in North Carolina. Obama lost by only 1.1% in Indiana.

Following those contests, it became improbable, if not impossible, for Senator Clinton to win the nomination. The small win in Indiana kept her campaign alive. Although Senator Clinton managed to win the majority of the remaining primaries and delegates, it was not enough to overcome Senator Obama's substantial delegate lead.

Saturday, May 31, 2008

On the final day of primary voting, Maxine Waters switched her endorsement to Senator Obama. By then he was insurmountably ahead in the pledged delegate count. The Rules and Bylaws Committee of the Democratic Party reached a compromise on the Florida and Michigan delegate situation. The committee decided to seat delegates from Michigan and Florida at the convention in August, but only award each one half-vote.

By the end, the Buffalo Soldiers had garnered from 5% to 30% of the Black vote for Senator Clinton in various primary and caucus states. She received less than 10% of the national African-American vote.

The SEIU suffered major setbacks against the Carlyle Group. California lawmakers withdrew legislation designed to stop the state's giant public pension funds from investing new money with private-equity firms which were partly owned by countries with poor human rights records. California Governor Arnold Schwarzenegger declared, "This bill would cause a deep wound to our retirement funds and government programs when our state can least afford it." Nevertheless, the

Carlyle Group issued a bill of rights for patient care following the SEIU campaign and negative criticism from the service employees union.

Stephen Lerner told his staff, "The stakes are very high. We have stuck our hand into a beehive. Carlyle has proven us right from the start. They are the ultimate influence peddler."

Dan Cantor, Executive Director of the Working Families Party said, "We are up against the Masters of the Universe here, so we've got to be smart about what we do."

ACORN was stepping up its pressure on the Carlyle Group, when an anonymous whistleblower miraculously came forward and disclosed an eight-year-old embezzlement which involved Dale Rathke, the brother of the ACORN's co-founder, Wade Rathke. Dale Rathke had a lot of fun on credit cards and with money intended for low income and working-class families.

My cell phone rang. I answered the call, "Hello?"

"ACORN met with SIFMA today. Did you know anything about this?" Marcel Reid asked.

"How was I supposed to know, Marcel? I was supposed to be on the negotiations team, but nobody called me."

Marcel said, "Everyone on the team was there—but you."

"They never called me," I repeated. "I would have been there, if I knew."

"I know, Michael," said Marcel. "I wanted to ask to be sure."

"So, what happened?" I asked.

Marcel paused before she spoke, "Everything went fine, Michael. We presented everything—including Mortgage Fraud."

"Excuse *Me!* They did what?" I inquired.

"Jordan Ash included Mortgage Fraud as an issue at the negotiations table," Marcel said.

Stunned and hurt, I asked, "How can they present our issue without us?"

"Jordan presented Mortgage Fraud, just like you explained at the legislative policy conference."

"No way!"

"I've never seen them do anyone like that before," said Marcel. "They literally stole your issue and are using it without you."

"Damn!"

"Hold on a minute," said Marcel. "It gets worse."

"Worse than that?" I asked in stunned disbelief.

"I think they are coming after Georgia ACORN. So what are you going to do?" Marcel asked.

"I have no idea right now," I said. "But I'm going to talk to Ron and Dana and see if we can come up with something quick."

"Work fast," Marcel said. "I heard it from a reliable source. They removed the Georgia Mortgage Fraud action from the ACORN website and shut off Ron's computer access."

"They did what?" I asked.

"Yeah, I know that's cold blooded," Marcel said. "They are clearly trying to cut you guys off. I think they are going to shut Georgia ACORN down, and they will if Georgia can't pull its financial weight..."

I cut her off, "But we can, if they will let us! They stopped us from receiving local gifts and grants, and we've got Mortgage Fraud, a huge issue which ACORN could lead the nation on. They're going to take it from us?"

"I know, Michael, I've never seen them do anything like this before," she said. "You're absolutely right. There is NO reason whatsoever for Georgia to be dissolved when ACORN is rolling out your issue—as we speak."

"That's so fucked up, Marcel."

"I hope you work something out," she said. "But if you need a place to land, I think I can still bring you and Ron into D.C. ACORN."

Tuesday, June 3, 2008

I visited Carol Willis in his Little Rock home following the extended primary campaigns. I smelled fried chicken cooking in the kitchen, while

Willis was preparing to watch Senator Clinton's concession speech on television.

Senator Clinton addressed a crowd of onlookers in a post-primary speech from her home state of New York. To our surprise, she refused to concede the race for several days, although she signaled her presidential campaign was ending.

The nomination process for major political parties continues through June of an election year. But in recent cycles the candidates were chosen by the end of the March primaries. However, Senator Obama did not win enough delegates to secure the nomination until after a 17 month-long campaign against Hillary Clinton. He had a wide lead in states won, but she won majorities in several of the larger states.

Because a form of proportional representation and popular vote decided Democratic state delegate contests, the numbers were close between Hillary Clinton and Barack Obama, and the contest for the nomination continued into the summer. Senator Clinton claimed a lead in the popular vote, in May 2008.

I reflected on the historic primaries. The fatal fallacy of the Clinton campaign at the conclusion of the historic primary season was that Campaign Manager, Mark Penn, had devised a strategy to win Super Tuesday. She did, but Obama deployed a plan to win more delegates. Hillary Clinton didn't see him coming, didn't recognize the threat, and never knew what hit her.

Barack Obama conducted ACORN leadership training, and his post-law school organizing for Project Vote in 1992 was undertaken in direct partnership with ACORN. In fact, Obama taught Saul Alinsky's Power concepts to ACORN leaders and Project Vote. "To organize a community you must understand that in a highly mobile, urbanized society and the world-wide reach through telephony and the Internet, the word *community* means a community of interests, not a physical community."

Obama taught, "Change comes from power, and power comes from organization. In order to act, people must get together. Power is not to be crossed. One must respect and obey. Power is the reason for building organizations. When people agree on certain religious ideas and want the power to propagate their faith, they organize and call it a church. When people agree on certain political ideas and want the power to put them into practice, they organize and call it a political party. The same reasoning holds true across the board. Power and organization are one and the same."

Obama said, "The organizer's biggest job is to give the people the feeling they can do something. While they may accept the idea that organization means power, they have to experience this idea in action. The organizer's job is to begin to build confidence and hope in the idea of organization and thus in the people themselves: to win limited victories, each of which will build confidence and the feeling that if we can do so much with what we have now—think what we will be able to do when we get big and strong.

"The organizer simultaneously carries on many functions as he analyzes, attacks, and disrupts the prevailing power pattern. The first step in community organization is community disorganization. The disruption of the present organization is the first step toward community organization.

"This is why the organizer is immediately confronted with conflict. The organizer dedicated to changing the life of a particular community must first rub raw the resentments of the people of the community, and fan the latent hostilities of many of the people to the point of overt expression. There is no such thing as a non-controversial issue. When there is agreement there is no issue. He must search out controversy and issues, rather than avoid them, for unless there is controversy people are not concerned enough to act.

"An organizer must stir up dissatisfaction and discontent, and then provide a channel into which the people can angrily pour their frustrations. He must create a mechanism which can drain off the underlying guilt for having accepted the previous situation for such a long time. Out of this mechanism, a new community organization arises.

"The job then is getting the people to move, to act, to participate. In short, to develop and harness the necessary power to effectively conflict with the prevailing patterns and change them. When those prominent in the status quo turn and label you an *agitator*, they are completely correct, for that is, in one word, your function—to agitate to the point of conflict."

Saturday, June 7, 2008

I twisted the cork off of an amber bottle of Hennessy V.S.O.P. and relaxed with a four-finger pour of syrupy cognac. Contrary to my predictions, Senator Obama had indeed carried, not just one, but three southern states—Florida, North Carolina and Virginia on his way to victory. I thought to myself, "This has been one hell of a race," and reflected on what had transpired over the last few months.

Senator Clinton conceded the nomination to Senator Obama and pledged her full support to the presumptive nominee. Consequently, Senator Obama secured the Democratic nomination for President, after the last of the primaries had taken place, with the help of numerous super delegate endorsements. Senator Clinton vowed to do everything she could to help him get elected.

Barack Obama was the first African-American to win the nomination of a major political party in the United States. Ironically, most in the Congressional Black Caucus didn't take Senator Obama seriously as a potential nominee, and neither did the Clinton campaign.

They estimated that he would need a huge share of black votes to wrest the nomination from Hillary Clinton, which her advisers, white and black, considered a near impossibility. Clinton's strategists set a goal of receiving half the black vote in the Southern primaries, although they figured they needed as little as 30% in order to beat Obama—which seemed like a sure bet.

A feeling of impending doom flooded my mind. I realized a lot of black political operatives and incumbents who supported Clinton could find ourselves trying to explain how we ended up so disconnected from our constituents and the Black community. Many elected officials braced themselves for the strongest primary challenges in years.

Hillary Clinton underestimated the Obama campaign from the start. She failed to recognize how Senator Obama had effectively organized a statewide organization through ACORN and Project Vote's registration drives which elected Carol Mosley Braun.

That Illinois statewide organization had a tremendous impact on all neighboring states including the two make or break contests—Iowa which launched his campaign, and Indiana which effectively ended the race.

Obama became synonymous with change. He literally changed his funny-sounding name to *Change*. The Obama communications strategy inspired a mass movement—*Yes We Can*, which is what all successful community organizers do.

In contrast, her campaign was more fatalistic and used intimidation to garner support. Hillary Clinton was the inevitable candidate. She promised—*Yes She Will,* but she couldn't deliver.

Senator Clinton thought she had the advantage due to the support of former Iowa Governor Tom Vilsack, but she never realized they were actually fighting the organization which elected Carol Mosley Braun, which had amassed just across the state line. In the end, that's how a Chicago Community Organizer defeated the National Democratic Establishment.

Worse, I feared that the political careers for African-American Clinton supporters might be careening to an abrupt end if Senator Obama actually won the presidency. After all, since over 90% of African-Americans supported Barack Obama, the Buffalo Soldiers were the most visible and identifiable Black politicos who didn't. In the world of Chicago politics, payback could be fierce—Black, Democrat or not.

Suddenly, my cell phone rang. I answered the call, "Hello?"

Dana Williams called with more bad news. My day had just gone from bad to worse—the *coup de grace* was complete. Beth Butler was appointed

Southern Regional Director of ACORN and the Georgia ACORN board was removed and immediately placed in *Administratorship.*

"It may be a rumor, but I just heard ACORN is going to move Beth Butler in as Regional Director for the Southern Region."

"And get rid of Brian Kettering?"

"Well yeah," said Dana. "They'll get rid of Brian first and then they will replace the whole board!"

"Can they do that?"

"They do whatever they want to do," Dana replied.

"This is so fucked up," I said. "It's unbelievable. They're screwing Brian, our Regional Director, and us like some little weaklings."

Distraught, I said "Why are they doing this now? We've solved our financial crisis with a viable issue. Brian knows about the mortgage fraud case; he even came to one of our court dates." And I thought, *Brian might even want to take credit for that issue himself.*

"That's right. He did, but they removed Brian and replaced him with Beth Butler—a puppet for Wade Rathke." said Dana.

Instead, Wade Rathke stole Georgia ACORN's signature issue and dissolved Georgia ACORN's state board, thereby eliminating both Ronald Sykes and me.

The Mortgage Fraud Issue was huge. It was so timely and important Georgia ACORN should have become the next ACORN stronghold, like California, Texas, Illinois, New York, Louisiana and Washington, D.C.

It slowly dawned on me, how Beth Butler was both Wade's common law wife and Head Organizer of Louisiana ACORN, where the national organization resided. Wade and his family used these positions of financial power to control what was portrayed to be a democratic organization.

The reality is Wade Rathke doesn't give a damn about low and moderate income *people.* Wade only cares about low and moderate income *issues.* That's why ACORN has nation-wide campaigns to raise the minimum wage, but fought in court to pay its own workers less than the minimum, and also why ACORN/SEIU led the most successful labor organizing efforts in the country but engaged in classic union busting tactics when ACORN workers attempted to unionize themselves. ACORN uses low and moderate income people to build political power for Wade Rathke and his cronies, period.

Rathke Embezzlement

Friday, June 20, 2008

Marcel Reid held her breath in response to the carbon dioxide and engine exhaust, which emanated from a soiled yellow cab. She arrived at the entrance of Wayne State University, Michigan's only urban research university, and marveled at the flowing 203-acre campus. Her aunt had received a Master's Degree in Library Science from Wayne State and founded the first black library in Jefferson County Alabama, which she guarded from a rocking chair with a shotgun on her lap.

Marcel knew the school's history well. Wayne State University strove to develop mutually beneficial partnerships within the community as a catalyst for the region's social, cultural, economic and educational enrichment. The Walter P. Reuther Library of Labor and Urban Affairs had the largest labor archive in North America. Its mission was to collect, preserve and provide access to the documentary and visual heritage of the American labor movement, related reform movements and individual participants.

The Reuther held more than 2,000 collections related to such topics as union history and working-class organizations, African-Americans and women in the labor movement, as well as radical, social and political reform movements. Thus, Wayne State provided the perfect setting for an ACORN National Board Meeting.

ACORN President, Maude Hurd, called the National Association Board Meeting to order at 6:25 p.m. in the Faculty-Administration Building. She immediately declared, "This is an executive session. Only duly elected delegates are to remain in the room."

Fannie Brown, a former Board member from California, defiantly refused to leave the room. "Hell No! I ain't going no where, Maude!"

Maude rolled her eyes and welcomed the board and invited guests, the members of the Interim Staff Management Committee: Zach Polett, Helene O'Brien and Steve Kest, along with Attorney Elizabeth Kingsley.

Maude reviewed the agenda, read a statement from the Executive Committee and gave ground rules for this meeting. Each state delegate had one minute for questions.

Beth Kingsley, forty-six, a pudgy Brunette and attorney from the firm of Harmon, Curran Spielberg and Eisenbly, prepared a legal report. Kingsley was unassuming, but often seemed disheveled, like someone always working under a constantly missed deadline.

She began, "The national board should hear from ACORN's General Counsel on a regular basis. There are at least 100 separate corporations within ACORN and these corporate relationships should be re-examined and regularized." She passed around her summary findings -*The Kingsley Report*- to the association board, followed by a brief question and answer session.

Marcel reeled in her seat. Shocked and dumbfounded, this was the first time anyone had ever disclosed ACORN was more than a handful of related organizations. Over one hundred? That can't be right.

ACORN General Counsel Steve Bachmann entered the board room and fielded questions from the board regarding a misappropriation of funds in 1999-2000. Dale Rathke had run up $157,000 in American Express charges which he couldn't repay when the embezzlement was first discovered. Dale was Wade Rathke's brother, the co-founder and Chief Organizer of ACORN and Service Employee International Union Locals 100 and 880. Dale was the signatory to official documents for dozens of

ACORN entities, including the Elysian Fields Partnership, in which he and Wade Rathke were partners.

"We want to make you aware of some recent developments at ACORN which are connected to an event which transpired eight years ago, so you can understand the facts and the steps we have taken. Here's what happened in 1999-2001. An employee of Citizens Consulting, Inc. notified Wade Rathke, the Chief Organizer of ACORN, and then several other ACORN staff members and me, ACORN's general counsel."

An audible gasp came from the board.

Bachmann said, "Wade's brother was a big spender with money intended to support low income and working-class families, some of which came from pension funds. Dale was the Director of Citizens Consulting, Inc. at the time."

Kingsley explained, "CCI was the corporate entity which ACORN established to handle the accounting, record-keeping, and the corporate legal affairs of ACORN and other associated social justice organizations."

Zach Polett said, "Wade brought this matter to the attention of ACORN's staff management council at its regularly scheduled meeting in late 2000. The management council was an advisory body, appointed by Wade, of senior organizers and others with significant responsibilities in the organization."

"At the management council meeting, Wade proposed a plan in response to this situation," added Bachmann. "First, since his brother had no assets to immediately pay back the funds, the best course of action was to obtain an enforceable restitution agreement so the funds would be returned. Second, in order to protect the organization from political attacks from right-wing opponents, and in order to ensure restitution, the incident would not be reported to law enforcement and would be held in confidence."

Bachmann continued, "And finally Dale would be terminated from his job as director of CCI and would be removed from CCI altogether, but would be retained as an employee of another ACORN-related entity where his institutional knowledge could be utilized."

Kingsley said, "In outlining this proposed plan, Wade stated he had brought in outside counsel with significant expertise in these matters to handle the situation instead of ACORN's general counsel, and that plan had been vetted by this attorney."

Zach said, "Wade also told management council members that the Executive Committee would be fully informed of the situation, and would be asked to review and approve the proposed course of action. With these assurances, the council agreed to Wade's proposals on how to handle the situation."

"The Duplantier firm, ACORN's outside accounting firm, was asked to ascertain the scope of the losses. After several months of investigation, they determined the total loss to be *$948,607.50*," said Kingsley. "Once the theft audit was complete, Dale signed a promissory note, which included pledges from his parents and Wade for partial repayment, promising to repay the money with interest."

Bachmann said, "This promissory note included a provision signing over his anticipated inheritance to ensure full repayment. The outside auditors reviewed the potential size of the estate to ensure the amount could reasonably be said to cover the loan amount."

"After consultation with our outside auditors, the theft was consolidated on the books of CCI, and was treated as a loan from CCI to Dale," Kingsley concluded. "The Duplantier firm advised CCI it was proper to record the amount as a loan since there was a loan agreement in place with payment terms and security."

Paul Satriano and Steve Kest reported to the association board following a meeting with Dave Beckwith, Executive Director of the Needmor Fund, which was contacted by a mysterious whistleblower in May. Needmor Fund had given money to some of ACORN's charity affiliates over the last 10 years.

Satriano spoke about financial reporting and control recommendations and reported that Needmore seemed receptive. Representatives of some 30 foundations and large donors had been discussing the matter on conference calls and might establish a committee to monitor ACORN's overhaul of its management and accountability systems.

Kest was the primary contact for all foundations as Executive Director. He stated, "All ACORN grants were immediately suspended by Needmore when they heard about the embezzlement. Needmore agrees with what the Board has already done, firing Dale and removing Wade as Chief Organizer no matter what his connection with ACORN will be."

Kest had also spoken to 30 other foundations. "Some have continued to process grants for ACORN, but most are taking a wait-and-see attitude. Others have stated they are very disappointed. Catholic Charities said the board must take steps to recognize the gravity of what has happened. Catholic Charities Human Development Fund is holding off sending letters to the offices which were supposed to receive funds."

Steve Kest, Helene O'Brien and Zach Polett answered the board's questions when asked, "Exactly who knew about the embezzlement, and who was on the Staff Management Council when the theft occurred?"

Steve Kest – Executive Director
Maude Hurd – Acorn President
Jon Kest – Executive Director New York
Bertha Lewis – Head Organizer For New York
Alton Bennett – Acorn Treasurer
Mike Shea – Executive Director Acorn Housing
Zach Polett – Political Director
Helene O'brien – National Field Organizer
Amy Schur – National Campaign Director
Madeline Talbot – Head Organizer For Illinois Acorn
Keith Kelleher – Head Organizer For Seiu Local 880
Carolyn Carr – Executive Director Aisj
Mildred Brown – Chief Legislative Director
Liz Wolff – National Research Director

This was ACORN's inner circle, the Senior Staff and Executive Committee members who actually directed and controlled the behemoth ACORN universe. The senior staffers who ran the show and executive committee members lent them credibility. The national board members and the general membership were all expendable pawns.

"What about you, Maxine?" Marcel asked. "You're on the Executive Committee. When did *you* learn out about the embezzlement?"

Maxine Nelson scowled at her while sitting at a table by herself. Insulted by the question, she quipped, "How dare you accuse me."

But, her eyes dropped tellingly to the floor. "I won't dignify you with a response, Marcel."

Marcel paused and reflected, "But you didn't tell either, even after you knew."

Sheepishly Maxine nodded and agreed, "But now that this is under our watch, we are putting financial auditors, legal counsel, and a strong management team in place to make sure this organization moves forward for another 38 years."

Maude adjourned the board meeting for a much needed and overdue dinner break at 9:25 p.m. The association board members still had a lot to think about. Karen Inman retired to The Inn on Ferry Street for dinner. Located in the East Ferry Street Historic District of Midtown Detroit, the Inn was steps away from the state's finest museums, the acclaimed Detroit Medical Center and Wayne State.

Iron Ladies

Friday, June 20, 2008

Karen Inman tasted Italian herb and garlic flavored artesian crackers and smelled hot peppermint tea. She enjoyed the tranquil atmosphere of 40 unique rooms in four meticulously restored Victorian homes and two carriage houses.

The Inn on Ferry Street offered a relaxing change of pace from the standard business hotel. The Inn evoked a strong sense of history and set the standard for elegant guest quarters and dedicated service. The Old Victorians were affectionately known as *Painted Ladies,* but in the presence of Karen Inman, a lawyer, teacher and former labor organizer, *Iron Ladies* was a better term.

Karen sipped her coffee and reviewed a draft memo she had received weeks before from Brian Kettering, the former Head Organizer for the Southern Region, which was a motion to fire Wade Rathke. Wade had replaced Brian Kettering with Beth Butler as the Regional Director for Georgia and Florida ACORN. This draft memorandum was Kettering's payback to Wade for replacing him and dissolving Georgia ACORN. Turnabout is fair play.

Following the short dinner break, Karen Inman returned to the National Association Board Meeting at Wayne State University. ACORN's Executive Director, and the Head Organizer for New York had just taken the floor.

Steve Kest and Bertha Lewis notified the association board about the professional consultants the staff had retained to assist ACORN.

Kest said, "We've engaged Rubenstein for Public Relations and Mesirow Financial Consulting to review our financial systems. Sidley, Austin agreed to work as outside legal counsel—on a pro bono basis," Sidley, Austin LLP, was the Chicago based law firm where Senator Obama once worked.

"Sidley Austin has extensive criminal law experience," Bertha Lewis said, "These consultants will report to the Interim Staff Management Committee." She said, "The Interim Staff Management Committee, or ISM, will perform the day-to-day operations of this organization." They presented a completely pre-packaged deal. In one felled swoop, ACORN senior staff disclosed a $1 million embezzlement *AND* offered a prearranged solution run by the senior management who covered up the embezzlement—and their own hand-picked consultants.

The board erupted in clamor and a lengthy discussion ensued. Surprisingly, the Association Board members resisted these proposals and the ISM concept since ACORN senior staff covered up the original embezzlement. The national board angrily rejected any proposal that the ISM should be authorized to investigate the embezzlement and manage the reorganization of the association, since they were the very same senior staff members who covered up the embezzlement eight years ago.

Instead, they insisted that the national board members be in charge of the investigation and reorganization and that the senior staff assist the board members in this process. The ISM concept was flatly rejected. Consequently, the board decided to elect three board members that night to lead an *Interim Management Committee* that would report to the full board once a month. The IMC Board Members would meet with the seven supporting staff members by Saturday, June 21 2008 at 10:30 a.m. The IMC would stay in place until the next regular Board meeting in October 2008.

Toni McElroy, fifty-five, the robust Texas Chair with coal black hair with one solid gray patch, a teacher and facilitator, and Paul Satriano chaired the nominations for the election of three Board Members to direct the Interim Management Committee. The nominees from the floor covered three positions, Legal Affairs, Financial Affairs, and Organizations Structure and Governance.

Legal Affairs: Dathen Moorman, twenty-five, the Chair from Oregon, a smart-alecky, young-Turk from the mountain west; Mary Hutchins, seventy, the Chair from Missouri, a soft-spoken attorney from mid-west— she was mild-mannered and corporate; and Karen Inman, the Secretary from Minnesota ACORN.

Financial Affairs: Carol Hemingway, fifty-seven, the Chair from Pennsylvania, a gruff woman with mocha skin and short natural hair, who had mastered the art of non-speak; and Alicia Gaddis, the Chair from California ACORN.

Organizational Structure: Hugh Alleynan, forty-six, the Co-Chair form Delaware, who desperately wanted to be the sole chair, an ambitious islander, Hugh was a dark-skinned handsome man, who always looked for an angle; Marcel Reid, the Chair from Washington DC; Reverend Gloria Swieringa, the Chair from Maryland; and Stephanie Cannady, the Chair from Rhode Island.

A paper ballot vote was taken and the results were to be tabulated and announced before the close of the board meeting. John Jones, the Chair from Washington, gave the ground rules and facilitated a meeting between the association board and Wade Rathke at 11:00 p.m.

Wade Rathke greeted the board and began, "I have worked with this Board for 38 years, since 1970 when ACORN first organized back in Arkansas. I am not an optimist looking through rose-colored glasses. I'm the opposite.

"Having worked as Chief Organizer for ACORN first and stayed the longest, for nearly forty years, I have worked with all of you on hundreds of campaigns designed to empower the underclass, give voice to the voiceless and to fight for financial justice.

"It pains me to say, but eight years ago my brother Dale embezzled $1 million from ACORN and its charitable organizations between 1999 and 2000. I learned about the problem when an employee of Citizens Consulting Inc. alerted me about suspicious credit card transactions.

"An internal investigation uncovered inappropriate charges on the cards that led back to Dale. Right or wrong, we thought it best at the time to protect the organization as well as to get the funds back into the organization—to deal with it in-house. It was a judgment call at the time, and looking back, people can agree or disagree with it, but we did what we thought was right.

"We carried the full amount Dale embezzled *($948,607.50)* as a loan on the books of Citizens Consulting Inc., and we signed a restitution agreement with Dale in which our family agreed to repay the entire amount embezzled in exchange for confidentiality."

"Did he pay the money back?" asked Marcel.

Wade explained, "Dale was paid about $38,000 a year and the Rathke family has paid ACORN $30,000 a year in restitution since 2001. Clearly, this was an uncomfortable, conflicting and humiliating situation as far as my family and I are concerned. The real decisions on how to handle this had to be made by others."

He pleaded, "I never misused funds and this was not a cover-up. A small group of executives decided to keep the information from almost all of the board members and not to alert law enforcement. I'm sorry this happened, but you are not very much of a man if you won't help your own brother."

Wade clicked on a power point showing the attacks ACORN had endured. "The decision to keep the matter secret was not made to protect my brother but because word of the embezzlement would have put a weapon into the hands of enemies of ACORN.

"ACORN is a frequent target of conservatives who object to our strident and confrontational advocacy on behalf of low- and moderate-income families and workers. Together we have fought for economic justice—or at least to prevent the erosion of the financial health and well-being of our constituency of low and moderate-income families.

"These successful campaigns have been established both in the United

States and around the world. None of this work has been easy, and all of it has been met with fierce opposition at every twist and turn. But an accusation alone doesn't mean it's fact. I made the decision to step aside after someone went to our funders—after all this time."

Wade turned off the Power Point and turned to face the board. "Together, we've grown from one chapter with four members to 1,200 chapters in 105 cities with 400,000 members. I just wanted to keep the organization safe. I just want to continue our work. I would like to continue to serve in an Emeritus position."

He said, "I can still contribute to the organization as a trainer, negotiator, disaster recovery and emergency preparedness, new programs and funds development, senior professional status or advisor and resource person—anything at all. You can always look back in hindsight and see where things could have been handled differently. We thought, me and the Staff Management Council, the repayment plan was a reasonable decision at that time."

Questions and answers from the board followed Wade's presentation, which concluded at 11:55 p.m. At the stroke of midnight, Karen Inman rose, cleared her throat and read her prepared statement:

"I move that Wade Rathke shall immediately and permanently be terminated from all employment with ACORN and its affiliated organizations or corporations. Furthermore, Wade Rathke should be removed from all boards and any leadership roles within ACORN and its affiliated organizations or corporations."

Emeline Bravo-Blackwood, sixty, the Chair from Connecticut ACORN, seconded Karen's motion. A basic woman with short natural hair, Emeline was an islander, and a female entrepreneur who ran a small nursery, spoke convincingly to the board.

The vote was taken by paper ballot with 2 votes per state represented. The results were 29-YES, 14-NO, with one abstention. The motion passed, and Wade Rathke, the co-founder and Chief Organizer was *Terminated* from ACORN in a board uprising. Paradoxically, the lowly pawns had become powerful queens—iron ladies. It was the dawn of a new day, but the fact remained that the handful of people who did not disclose the fraud when they learned about it eight years ago still worked for and managed ACORN or its affiliates, which concerned many of the group's financial supporters.

The meeting adjourned following the announcement of the results of the vote on the board members to direct the Interim Management Committee: Legal—Karen Inman, Finance—Carol Hemingway, and Organizational Structure and Governance—Marcel Reid. The IMC was born.

"Free at last..."

"Free at last!"

"Thank God almighty..."

"We're free at last!"

After 38 years, the membership and board of directors had finally stood up to the Wade Rathke and the Rathke family dynasty, but much like the freed slaves after reconstruction, freedom was both exhilarating and frightening.

ACORN faced the precipice of a tremendous crossroads, either the end of an era of single family domination of the association, or the beginning of the end of ACORN itself. Only time would tell, but just like it began four decades ago, ACORN's fate laid in the hands of a cadre of strong dedicated women—Karen Inman, Marcel Reid and Carol Hemingway.

Crossroads

Ronald Sykes and I joined DC ACORN after Georgia ACORN was dissolved, and I was asked to chair the DC ACORN's Mortgage Fraud Committee.

My cell phone rang a Muddy Waters jazz/blues piano riff. I answered the call, "Hello. . . hello?"

Marcel Reid said, "I've only got a minute, but I've got to tell you the news!"

"What's wrong, Marcel? What happened?" I asked.

"Nothing's wrong, Michael. In fact things couldn't be better," she said.

"So what happened?"

"ACORN just fired Wade," said Marcel.

"ACORN did what?" I asked.

"I know, it's crazy," said Marcel. "There was embezzlement and a cover up in 1999 or 2000, and the board fired Wade and his brother Dale."

"Really?" I inquired.

"In one fell swoop both of them are gone. Can you believe this?" asked Marcel.

"Let me get this straight, Marcel. ACORN attacked the Carlyle Group late last year, and less than six months later, an eight year-old embezzlement is miraculously uncovered, and Wade Rathke, its co-founder and Chief Organizer for 38 years, was terminated in disgrace."

"Uh-hunh." I said, "And the entire ACORN family is left in shambles—right? Is that what you're telling me?"

"That's what happened," said Marcel.

Incredulously, I declared, "Okay Marcel, *you* tell me who won! Wade underestimated the level of influence a company like Carlyle wields behind the scenes, not in public but in the corridors and steak-houses of Washington."

"I didn't think of that before," said Marcel. "You could be on to something."

"We'll never know the truth for sure, but I don't believe in coincidences. With patrons like George Soros the international financier and the wealthy Saudi Bin Ladin family, Carlyle is the World Leader's Investment Fund—a real life Billionaire Boys Club."

We laughed together and then I asked, "The real question is, with Wade gone, what happens to ACORN?"

"That's why I'm calling you!" replied Marcel. "This is a once in a lifetime opportunity to finally empower the members, give them a seat at the table, and a real voice in the direction and operations of ACORN—not just Wade Rathke's friends, family and cronies."

Following the association board's meeting, the three IMC board members, Karen Inman, Marcel Reid and Carol Hemingway, met to discuss their new roles and how they planned to deal with ACORN staff. Marcel Reid beamed. "They've never respected the authority of the board before, but the association board rejected the Interim Staff Management committee bullshit flat out."

"At least they were smart enough not to let the staffers who knew about the embezzlement and covered it up, run the investigation," said Carol.

Karen agreed, "The board didn't put us on the IMC to follow the dictates of our corrupt staff. The board included the staff on the IMC in order to assist us, the board members."

"As far as I'm concerned the I-M-C means Inman, Marcel and Carol," said Marcel.

The three laughed together.

Marcel concluded, "Now there's a chance to make ACORN the type of organization it was always supposed to be—one which respects and empowers the membership, and not one that exploits them."

Wednesday, July 2, 2008

Marcel Reid sipped bitter coffee in the storefront office of DC ACORN. Belinda Ferral handed her a faxed clipping from a Rhode Island newspaper. "Stephanie is not going to like this Marcel."

Marcel read the clipping aloud. "The highest court in Rhode Island overturned the jury decision which would force three paint manufacturers to pay billions of dollars to clean up contaminated homes."

Belinda said, "I can't believe the courts are going to allow toxic paint to poison our children and neighborhoods."

The court emphasized it did not mean to minimize the severity of the harm thousands of children in Rhode Island had suffered as a result of lead poisoning. Marcel continued to read, "Our hearts go out to those children whose lives have been changed forever by the poisonous presence of lead."

The decision reversed the landmark 2006 ruling which held three companies, Sherwin-Williams, NL Industries and Millennium Holdings, liable for creating a public nuisance by making and selling lead paint more than 30 years ago, and then covering up the health risks. The cleanup costs in Rhode Island were estimated at $2.4 billion.

The Supreme Court, in its 4-to-0 decision, said the lawsuit should have been dismissed at the outset because "public nuisance law simply does not provide a remedy for this harm." The justices noted, that the paint companies did not control how their lead-based products were used. Instead, the burden of making properties safe from lead contamination should rest with landlords and property owners.

"Today's ruling is a landmark victory for common sense and for responsible companies which did the right thing," proclaimed Charles Moellenberg, Jr., a lawyer for Sherwin-Williams. "The responsibility of making sure children aren't exposed to lead paint remains squarely on property owners."

Appellate courts in Illinois, Missouri and New Jersey had already rejected similar public nuisance claims. However, the ruling in Rhode Island could affect pending court decisions in Ohio and California.

"This reversal is extremely disappointing and I disagree with it in the strongest terms," said Patrick Lynch, the Rhode Island attorney general. "Those products poisoned our infants and children, and continue to poison our infants and children, while bringing great profits to the companies which made and sold them."

John McConnell, Jr., a lawyer for the Motley Rice law firm, who represented the state, remarked, "It would cost Rhode Island homeowners billions of dollars to clean their homes and millions more for taxpayers to protect children from lead-related illnesses.

"We're clearly disappointed in the ruling," Mr. McConnell said, "Children in Rhode Island will continue to be poisoned by lead in paint, and the companies which put the poisonous paint in Rhode Island have no responsibility for cleaning up the mess they created in the first place."

The Rhode Island Supreme Court ruling effectively ended ACORN's national lead paint campaign and its international shakedown of Sherwin-Williams.

Epilogue

Over the next two years, the I-M-C led by Marcel Reid, Karen Inman and Carol Hemingway sought a forensic examination and independent audit to investigate the embezzlement and reorganize the association. New York ACORN struggled to wrest control of the association from the Rathkes and Louisiana ACORN after Bertha Lewis became the new Chief Organizer.

For the first time a Black woman was in charge of ACORN, although she was a mere figurehead for Steve Kest and Jon, his brother. Twelve board members supported the reform plans of Marcel Reid and Karen Inman. Carol Hemingway backed down, but six board members joined Marcel Reid and Karen Inman and stood up to ACORN senior management. Together they became whistleblowers known as the ACORN 8.

Anita MonCrief became an outspoken critic of ACORN and branded herself the "ACORN Whistleblower." She was often mistaken as being a member of the ACORN 8 and ultimately became a Tea Party darling because she was willing to relentlessly attack ACORN, SEIU, Project Vote and Barack Obama regardless of truth or proof.

The ACORN 8 are the national board members and community leaders who were the first to identify the nebulous Citizen's Consulting Inc. (CCI) and attempted to *"follow the money"* at ACORN; the first to seek a forensic examination and independent audit of ACORN and its related organizations; the first to seek injunctions against ACORN, the Rathkes and CCI; the first to call for a national boycott of all charitable donations, federal funding and member dues; and the first to file civil rights and criminal RICO complaints against ACORN's corrupt senior management. Unfortunately, the ACORN executive board and staff management committee thwarted their reform efforts.

To really understand the truth about ACORN, one must recall the difference between ACORN's membership and staff. There are over 400,000 low and moderate income families who paid regular dues and volunteered their toil and time to improve their local neighborhoods and communities. In contrast, ACORN staffers were low-wage workers who were often depicted as incompetent or worse in the media. ACORN staffers registered *"Mickey Mouse"* and *"Tony Romo"* to vote. ACORN staffers offered to provide tax advice and assist a *"pimp and prostitute"* in establishing an underage brothel. Anita MonCrief was a thief and a staffer.

Ironically, the most effective blows were delivered, not by ACORN workers, members or staff, but instead by a pair of aspiring journalists and filmmakers. Hannah Giles and James O'Keefe are conservative activists who exposed the lack of coverage on ACORN corruption by the traditional media while dressed outrageously as a *"pimp and prostitute."* The comical nature of the undercover video prompted the U.S. House of Representatives and Senate to withhold funding, and for the IRS and Census to cut their ties to ACORN until it ultimately dissolved and filed for bankruptcy—-*but that is a story for another day.*

By the end, various individuals and groups sounded the alarm of wrongdoing and corruption at ACORN. Most were advocates, some were activists, and others were self-promoters; all spoke truth to power. However, there were so many so-called ACORN *"whistleblowers"* that it became hard to tell the differences between real whistleblowers and mere tattle-tells.

ACORN 8, led by Marcel Reid and Karen Inman, was a group of ACORN members, leaders and national board members who were expelled for demanding a forensic examination and independent audit of ACORN and its related entities. Michael McCray joined these reform efforts, which ultimately became a separate organization with members in 15 states and the District of Columbia that engages in legislative advocacy, including federal workers' rights, participates in grassroots coalitions, and continues to advocate on behalf of low and moderate income families.

Truth To Power, led by Greg Hall, was a group of former ACORN workers and staff. Low-level ACORN workers often became scapegoats for corrupt senior management at ACORN. Greg Hall, a former ACORN organizer, supported the low-income workers who got "thrown under the bus" whenever ACORN wrongdoing was exposed. Truth To Power sought to unify and organize both current and former ACORN workers into a national service workers' union.

Anita MonCrief was a former employee of Project Vote, an ACORN affiliate, who alleged illegal coordination between the Obama Presidential Campaign and ACORN. MonCrief was fired for cause after fraudulently applying for a Project Vote credit card in her name, and then stole $1,500 on the company credit card. A darling of the far right, MonCrief was often quoted due to her incendiary and highly provocative statements. She is now a Conservative Activist and GOP operative.

Unfortunately, MonCrief and her supporters will say and do anything to harm ACORN, including making fictitious, unsupported accusations and presenting fabricated evidence. True whistleblowers pay a tremendous price for their courage, integrity and fortitude. The retaliation that targets real whistleblowers is so clearly unfair and they often discover that the corruption extends higher and further than any whistleblower ever imagines.

In an insightful article by K. R. Sawyer, *"The Test Called Whistleblowing,"* the author writes, "the true value of a whistleblower is their long-term value to society not their short-term value as individuals. Just as those who have shaped history have often not been revered and rewarded in their own lifetime so it is for the whistleblower.

"The contributions of whistleblowers occur in many dimensions and surely they are contributors to the evolution of our society. Think of

Lincoln, Mozart, Martin Luther King, Ghandi, Jesus, Mother Theresa and many others. The value to history is not measured in the balance sheet today but with benefit of hindsight. The true value of persons with integrity is inestimable." The ACORN 8—the credible ACORN whistle-blowers—-have passed these tests.

CODA

Saul Alinsky, Dr. George Wiley and Wade Rathke

Over the last 40 years, unnoticed, unequaled and unmatched, Wade Rathke, a middle-class, white guy became the *"Jim Jones"* leader of the ACORN/SEIU *"Jones Town"* family, the greatest community organizer in his generation and perhaps the biggest poverty pimp of all time.

Saul Alinsky wrote the book on community organizing in the United States but Wade Rathke mastered its lessons. Through ACORN, Rathke implemented Alinsky's vision, the creation of many local mass-power organizations which merged into a national network of popular power force, but he did so in a manner which exploited the membership in order to empower himself, his family and their cronies.

Saul Alinsky believed organizations are created, in large part, by the organizer, so he first sought to create an army of organizers. He developed a special training school for organizers with a full-time, fifteen-month program, through the Industrial Areas Foundation, which he founded in 1940.

His students ranged from middle-class women activists to Catholic priests and Protestant ministers of all denominations, from militant Indians to Chicanos, to Puerto Ricans, to blacks from all parts of the black power spectrum; from Panthers to radical philosophers, and a variety of campus activists, including Students for a Democratic Society

(S.D.S.), the Student Nonviolent Coordinating Committee (S.N.C.C.) and others.

There were also community leaders who were trained on the job to be organizers. Organizers are not only essential to start and build an organization, they are also essential to maintaining one. Building interest and activity, and keeping the group's goals strong and flexible at once is a different operation, but it is still organization.

A community organizer's goal is to create a mass movement—an army of people. Alinsky's ultimate objective was to create an army of organizers. The basic difference between local leaders and the community organizer are local leaders build power to fulfill their desires, to hold and wield power for their own purposes both social and personal. Local leaders want power for themselves, while community organizers should find their goal in the creation of power for others to wield.

Dr. George Wiley, a chemist, founded the National Welfare Rights Organization (NWRO), an organization which fought for the welfare rights of people, predominately African-American women and children.

The NWRO had four goals: adequate income, dignity, justice and democratic participation. Dr. George Wiley used aggressive strategies to overwhelm New York's welfare system and encouraged either increased benefits or social upheaval.

In 1969, Wiley hired Wade Rathke to organize welfare mothers. Wade started a Massachusetts chapter of the militant National Welfare Rights Organization. He adapted the tactics he learned as a member of the Students for a Democratic Society (S.D.S.) after being arrested for incitement to riot in Springfield, Massachusetts when the welfare recipients he led in a demonstration turned into a violent rock and bottle throwing mob.

Together, George Wiley and Wade Rathke developed a shared vision to organize the vast middle class, and not just poor welfare recipients. Together, their experiment became ACORN, founded in Little Rock in 1970, the Arkansas Community Organization for Reform Now (ACORN).

The fact is the system tolerated the civil rights movement and its leaders as long as they fought and marched for social justice, like the right to vote, the right to assemble and for public accommodations. When civil rights leaders started to talk about economic justice, that's when they went too far.

Everything was tolerated, as long as we were trying to integrate a business or neighborhood, trying to get a brother or sister a job at the post office—hire one and be done. What would have happened if civil rights leaders went to the banks and demanded fair lending and adequate financing so the same brother could start a business and then create dozens of jobs for blacks and minorities, instead of just one?

Think about it. Martin Luther King, Jr. was not assassinated until he launched the Poor People's Campaign; he was moving towards economic justice. George Wiley did not disappear until *AFTER* he started the Movement for Economic Justice in a mysterious boating accident, three years after co-founding ACORN. Wade Rathke took up where George Wiley left off.

Saul Alinsky's ultimate organizational efforts had been to achieve equal rights and equal power. The last twenty years of his life were centered on making contributions toward racial justice. Alinsky believed, "Black was the only problem that green couldn't fix," meaning racism and racial hatred ran deeper than economic self-interest.

Saul Alinsky had turned his attention for organizing the poor and minorities to organizing the middle class, but a sudden heart attack took Saul Alinsky in 1972; however, his influence continues today.

As the Chief Organizer for ACORN and SEIU, Wade Rathke achieved what Dr. George Wiley and Saul Alinsky had always dreamed. Unfortunately, Rathke did so by unlawful means and anti-democratic practices. In doing so, he violated the fundamental purpose and ideology of community organizing—which was to build a base of power for the benefit of the organization and its membership, not merely amass power in the chief organizer or management insiders.

Index

A

A. Philip Randolph
  Labor Organizing159, 160
  Martin Luther King, Jr. 161
  Organizer, March on Washington.. 160
  Pullman Porters 160
A. Philip Randolph Institute................. 162
  AFL-CIO Affiliate
    Labor Organization 159
  Bayard Rustin
    Montogmery Bus Boycott 161
Aaron Ward 94
  State Political Director,
    Clinton Re-elect 94
Abraham Funchess, Jr. 203
ACORN
  Bank Campaigns 49
  Boatman's Bank
    CRA Agreement 50
  Community Reinvestment Act 46
ACORN (Association of Community
  Organizations for Reform Now)
  Economic Justice 44
  Financial Justice Center
  Ameriquest Campaign,
    Best Practice Agreement 152
  Housing and Development
    Programs 151

Interim Management Committee
  Carol Hemingway 298, 300
  Karen Inman 298, 300
  Marcel Reid 298, 300
Interim Staff Management Committee
  288, 294, 300
Sherwin-Williams Toxic Paint Report..
  86
Social Policy Magazine 150
  Publisher/Editor-In-Chief,
    Wade Rathke 150
Staff Management Council 289, 297
ACORN 8 ....303, 304
ACORN Broadcast Radio Stations
  KABF (Little Rock) 179
  KNON (Dallas) 179
ACORN Community Labor Organizing
  Center
  Liberty Tax Services
    RAL Settlement 45
ACORN Demands
  John Hewitt 32
  Sherwin-Williams 64
  SIFMA 276
ACORN Financial Justice Center 45, 102
  Household Finance Campaign
    ACORN Settlement 152
  Predatory Lending

Money Mart Campaign.................103

Predatory Lending Campaign

Ameriquest...........................151

Household Finance 105

Wells Fargo Settlement...................151

RAL Campaign

H&R Block 40

Jackson Hewitt.....................39

Liberty Tax Services.................. 29, 39

ACORN Head Organizers

Wade Rathke, Chief Organizer........182

ACORN Housing

Mike Shea, Executive Director 45

ACORN Housing Corporation 51,
106, 107, 135, 151, 168, 182, 275

Alton Bennett, National President...151

Homebuyers Assistance Program..... 152

ACORN International..........................149

Argentina...............................149

Canada...................................149

Dharavi, Mumbai 150

Dominican Republic..........................149

India 149

Joint Projects............................ 149, 150

Kenya......................................149

La Matanza, Buenos Aires.................150

Mexico.....................................149

NEZA, Mexico City 150

Peru.......................................149

San Juan Laraguache, Lima..............150

ACORN International Partnerships

Indonesia 149

Korea 149

Philippines 149

ACORN Issue Campaigns

Paul Satriano, National Treasurer....137

ACORN Legislative and

Policy Conference....................... 100, 271

Fighting Predatory Lending and Foreclosures

Learning The Issues.........................101

Training Sessions 101

Predatory Lending/Foreclosure Fraud

Learning The Issues.........................102

SEIU Local 100...................................119

ACORN National Board Meeting

Charoltte, North Carolina.................45

Cleveland, Ohio...........................88, 91

Detroit Michigan..............................287

Detroit, Michigan.............................293

Little Rock Arkansas 134

ACORN National Convention

Ameriquest Campaign 105

Philadelphia, Pennsylvania........ 105, 152

Wells Fargo Campaign 103

ACORN National Elections.................179

ACORN Organizers.............................129

Black Organizers.............................131

Fundraising Requirements 176

Head Organizers

Local Organizers.............................182

Membership Quotas 131

ACORN People's Platform

Mike Sealy, Head Organizer (Arkansas) 163

ACORN Staff Management Council .291

ACORN's Comprehensive Immigration Reform

Learning The Issues............................101

ACORN's Financial Justice Center
Mortgage Fraud Campaign 154

ACORN's Response to Katrina
Learning The Issues 101

ACORN's Working Families Agenda 146

Learning The Issues 101

Adam Bass
SVP and General Counsel,
Ameriquest 152

Adam Clayton Powell, Jr.
U.S. Representative (D-NY) 121

Adam Miles
Government Accountability Project
Washington Whistleblower's Week 189

Adrian Fenty
Mayor, Washington DC 99

Adrianna Jones
Chair, Michicagan ACORN 101

AFL-CIO
Labor Organization 167, 177

Afsaneh Masheyekhi Beschloss
Carlyle Group 206
World Bank Treasurer 206

AISJ .... See American Institute for Social
Justice (ACORN)

Al Gore
Bill/Clinton Team Support 260
Second Tier Canidate 191
Vice President, United States
Chair, Community Empowerment Board
.... 141

Al Sharpton 175
Founder, National Action Network .. 16

Alan Wheat
U.S. Representative (D-MO) 94

Albert Wynn
U.S. Representative (D-MD) 190

Alfre Woodard
BHO African-American Surrogate .232

Alicia Gaddis
Chair, California ACORN 117, 295

Alpha Phi Alpha
Fraternal Organization 122

Alton Bennett 107
National Treasurer, ACORN 106

President, ACORN Housing
Corporation 106, 151

Ambassador's for Christ 234

America Alfaro
Delegate, National Board (ACORN).100

American Cyanamid 88

American Institute for Social Justice....135

Ameriquest 152
ACORN Campaign 103, 151

Ameriquest Campaign 152
ACORN Settlement 152

Amy Schur 87, 147
Campaign Director, ACORN National
Staff 55
Lead-based Paint Campaign 55, 56
Lead-based Paint Remediation 56
Sherwin-Williams Toxic Paint Report ..85

Ana Avendano
AFL-CIO 177

Ana Mae Weems

Civil Rights Activist 244

Andi Smith..223

    Host, Ames House Party 223

Andrew Cuomo

    Secretary, U.S. Department of Housing

    and Urban Development...................141

Andrew McDonald

    SEIU Private Equity Project 270

Andy Stern

    Carlyle Group

        David Rubenstein 207

    President, Service Employee's

    International Union.........128, 167, 206

Angela Butler

    Chair, Delelware ACORN................ 101

Anita MonCrief 60, 78, 79, 80, 81, 84,

    85, 90, 91, 195, 196, 208, 264, 303, 305

    ACORN

        Relationship with Members 75, 84

        Strategic Writing and Research

        Department....................................... 60

    Marcel Reid...75

    Marine Barracks............................ 79, 81

    Project Vote....................................60, 91

        Bad Check Restitution Program ..209

        Cash Advances 60

        Registered User, Pitney Bowes

        Postage Meter 75

        Take Back America..................... 75, 78

        Termination.....................................264

    Projet Vote

        Visa Card Application 196

    Public Assistance 79

Purchase Power Visa Card

    Project Vote, Account's Payable....196

    Visa Card..209

Antioch Baptist Church.......204, 228, 233,

                234, 247, 249, 254

Arkansas Community Organization for

    Reform Now 163, 308

Arkansas State Capitol 134

Arnold Schwarzenegger

    Governor, California 278

Arron Harris....................................221, 260

    HRC African-American Strategy Team

    Buffalo Soldiers 220

Ashley Caldwell 246

Association of Community Organizations

    for Reform Now .... 30, See ACORN

Atlanta City Council

    Dillard-Winecoff vs InterBank

    Funding Companies............................8

    Winecoff Hotel (aka the Ellis Hotel)..8

Atlanta Development Authority 8

Atlantic Richfield Co............................... 88

    World War II 78

Augustus Hawkins

    U.S. Representative, (D-CA) 120

B

Bank of America

    ACORN Partnership............................ 51

Barack Obama 191, 204, 222, 223,

    257, 260, 265, 268, 269, 274, 277, 278,

                281, 283, 284

    ACORN Leadership Training

Power Concepts 281

BHO African-American Surrogates .. 232

BHO Caucus Violations

    Iowa Press 226

Black Ministers and Politicians 260

Black Voters 219, 274

    African-American Experience 222

    Iowa Black Clergy 232

    Racial Progress 240

Buffalo Soldiers, Obama Payback ... 284

Carol Mosley Braun

    U.S. Senate Campaign 72

College Outreach 225

Community Organizing

    Iowa Caucus Turnout 258

DC ACORN

    Primary Endorsement (Democrate) .. 73

Democratic National Convention

    Keynote Speech 93

Democratic Primaries

    BHO Campaign Launch 92

    California Primary 269

    Democratic Nomination 283

    Des Monies Campaign Rally

        Black Voters 219

    DNC Proportional Representation .. 281

    February Primaries 269

    Fundraising and Media Attention 133

    Iowa Caucus

        Clear Winner 258

        Organizing The Masses 238

        Leading National Polls 255

        New Hampshire Front Runner 260

New Hampshire Returns 261

North Carolina Primary 278

Pennsylvania Primary 271

Pennsylvania Reaction 277

Philadelphia Speech on Race 274

Presumptive Nominee 283

South Carolina Primary 265

Southern (Red State) Victories 283

Super Tuesday 269

Texas Caucus 270

University of Northern Iowa 204

Grassroots Organizing Campaign .. 267

Hillary Clinton 255

Independent/Republican Outreach .. 220, 223

Jeremiah Wright 273, 274

KBBG 228

Madeline Talbott

    Keith Kelleher 72

Michael Blake 205

Michigan Ballot 267

Organizing, Iowa Caucus 205

Project Vote

    Saul Alinsky 281

    Voter Registration Drive 72

Senator Ted Kennedy Endorement ... 268

Sidley, Austin LLP 294

Stevie Wonder Campaign Theme 261

Television Ads

    Question of Experience 191

Women Outreach 220

Bayard Rustin

    A. Philip Randolph Institute 161

Montogmery Bus Boycott.................. 161

Beatriz Quinones

   Delegate, National Board (ACORN)... 110

Belinda Ferrell 78, 79, 81, 84, 85, 91, 195,
     196, 207, 208, 211, 214, 219, 264, 301

   Anita MonCrief 78, 81

   Carlyle Group...............................211, 214

   Head Organizer, DC ACORN 60

Ben Monterroso 177, 178

   SEIU Change to Win Campaign.... 177

   SEIU Position on Immigration and
     Temporary Labor 178

     We're all immigrants...................... 177

Bennie Thompson

   U.S. Representative, (D-MS) 143

Bertha Lewis 294, 303

   ACORN Organizers

     Black Organizers...............................131

   Co-chair, Working Families Party...196

   Head Organizer, New York ACORN ...196

   Rathke Embezzlement.......................294

   SEIU/ACORN Protest 197

Beth Butler 147, 180, 284, 285, 293

   Head Organizer, Louisiana ACORN.. 42

   Southern Regional Director, ACORN
     National Staff 285

   Wade Rathke, Common Law Spouse42

Beth Kingsley................................. 288, 290

   ACORN National Board Meeting

     Detroit, Michigan.......................... 288

   Rathke Embezzlement...................... 289

   Rathke Restitution Agreement........290

The Kingsley Report............................ 288

Betty Jackson

   Delegate, National Board (ACORN).. 109

Beverly Campbell.................................... 177

   Delegate, National Board (ACORN)... 118

Bianca Garza

   Delegate, National Board (ACORN)... 119

Bill Burton

   Spokesman, Obama Campaign 274

Bill Clinton 94, 234, 235, 237, 239,
                  244, 265, 266

   Al Gore...260

   Barack Obama.................................... 265

   Black America

     South Carolina Primaries 265

     Black Churches 243

     Black Ministers and Politicians ...260

     Black Politicos 133

     Carol Willis 93

     Civil Rights Community...............186

     Ernie Green...93

     First Black President 93

     Jesse Jackson

       South Carolina Primaries 265

       Rodney Slater......................................93

   Black Ministers

     Carol Willis 133

     Frantz Whitfield 232, 244, 245

   Governor, Arkansas (D-AR).............186

   HRC African-American Surrogates.....232

   HRC Rally, Waterloo 257

Bill Richardson

   Governor, New Mexico (D-NM).....223

Viability/BHO Aggressive Second
Choice 223
Billie Jo
Delegate, National Board (ACORN)... 101
Black Churches
Economic Justice................................172
Emancipation Day Services 255
Social Justice 173
Watch Night Servicc 253
Black Panther Party.............................171
J. Edgar Hoover................................ 170
Political Organizaton
Ten Point Plan............................... 170
US Organization............................. 170
Black Wall Street
Tulsa Oklahoma 268
Blair Talmadge
Barack Obama..................................... 272
Buffalo Solider..................................... 272
Boatman's Bank
ACORN
CRA Agreement 50
Bob Nash
Hillary Clinton.....................................186
Senior Advisor, Hillary Clinton
Campaign.. 244
Bonnie Mathias
Secretary, Texas ACORN.................. 101
Boys and Girls Club.........................231, 237
Brian Dunn 116
Brian Kettering 293
Georgia ACORN
Mortgage Fraud.................................285

Southern Regional Director, ACORN
National Staff
Georgia ACORN.............................285
Brook Giese
Delegate, National Board (ACORN)... 119
Bruce Braley
U.S. Representative, (D-IA).............204
Bruce Cooper
Delegate, National Board (ACORN)...102
Bruce Moore 94
Buffalo Soldiers 221, 224, 225, 228, 229,
232, 238, 257, 258, 271, 277, 278
Black Politcos.......................................185
Creed 262
Civil War
U.S. Ninth and Tenth Calvary
Divisions 185
Clergy Endorsement Forms
Hillary Clinton 248
Grassroots Organizing Campaign ..267
HRC African-American Strategy Team ...219
Iowa Caucus
Reaction...259
Rick Wade 222
Buffalo Soliders
Black Politicos 2
Bunnatine Greenhouse
Halliburton Whistleblower 190

C

C.I.O. Labor Organizing Drive
Labor Organizing................................ 125
Caitlin Harrington

BHO College Outreach 226

Cajun's Warf 139

Carlos Rodriguez
    Delegate, National Board (ACORN)... 116

Carlyle Group ...198, 206, 210, 211, 212, 214,
        215, 217, 218, 263, 269, 270, 278, 279, 299

    Carlyl Partners
        David Rubenstein 197

        Frank Carlucci...............................217

        George H.W. Bush 212

        James Baker................................212

        John Major 212

    DC ACORN 210

    George Soros...................................212

    Marcel Reid...............................209, 210

    Patient Bill of Rights......................... 279

    Private Equity Investment Firm 197

    Service Employees International Union..207

        HAZMAT Protest.........................218

Carol Hemingway 298, 303

    ACORN
        Interim Management Committee300

        Chair, Pennsylvania ACORN 295

        Interim Management Committee .. 298

Carol Moseley Braun
    Project Vote
        Obama Voter Registration Drive .. 72

Carol Mosley Braun...................... 127, 284

    SEIU Local 880.............................. 72

Carol Willis.......133, 184, 185, 186, 195, 201,
        225, 226, 227, 231, 232, 260, 268, 277, 280

    Bill Clinton.................................93

        Black Ministers 133

Black Ministers
    Kenneth Starr..............................186

    Buffalo Soldiers.................................185

    Democratic National Committee....186

    Democratic Presidential Primary
        Election Campaign Strategy 192

    Governor Bill Clinton, Arkansas.....186

    HRC African-American Strategy.... 185

    Michael McCray 185

Caroline Kennedy................................ 268

Carpenter's Restaurant 247

Carroll O'Connor
    Fair Housing Act of 1968 47

Cathedral of Faith Baptist Church 243

Catholic Charities
    Catholic Campaign for Human Development
        Rathke Embezzlement 291

Cathy Cox
    Secretary of State, Georgia................ 100

Cecil McDonald......................271, 272, 274
    Federal Empowerment Zones Initiative....271

    Jeremiah Wright 274

    Michael McCray 271

Center for Community Change............ 48

Charla Bailey...221

    HRC African-American Strategy Team
        Buffalo Soldiers 220

Charles Grassley.....................................204

    U.S. Senator, Iowa (R-IA)................. 190

Charles Moellenberg, Jr. 66

    Attorney, Sherwin-Williams......66, 302

Charles Monroe
    State Political Director, Clinton

Re-elect 94
Charles Rangel
   Alpha Phi Alpha 122
   Battle of Kunu-Ri 123
   Federal Empowerment Zone Program...122
   Hillary Clinton Campaign 133
   Low Income Housing Tax Credit 122
   Selma to Montgomery Marches........121
   U.S. Representative, (D-NY)............119
   Work Opportunity Tax Credit.........122
Charles Rangle 123
   Congressional Black Caucus 121
Charles Turner....................................84, 85
   Member, DC ACORN........................84
Cheryl Diggins
   Delegate, National Board (ACORN)...116
Cheryl Lee Ralph
   BHO African-American Surrogate....232
Chicago Title Insurance Company......183
   InterBank Funding Companies, Kelco/
   FB Winecoff......................................183
Chief Organizer 167, 182, 288, 289, 291,
                      297, 299, 309
   Wade Rathke, ACORN 158
   Wade Rathke, SEIU Local 100.........158
   Wade Rathke, SEIU Local 800 158
Chris Connors....................................70, 92
   ACORN/NPCA Board Protest.........57
   CEO and Chairman, H&R Block 39
   President and CEO, Sherwin-Williams....57
Chris Jones103, 104, 105, 106, 107, 108, 111,
               112, 113, 114, 115, 117
   ACORN Lawsuits 105

Chris Leonard...44
   Head Organizer, DC ACORN 43
Chris Ullman
   Spokesman, Carlyle Group...............207
Christian Fellowship Baptist Church..243, 254
Christie Vilsack
   First Lady, Iowa.................................244
Christopher Dodd
   Iowa Caucus
      Withdrawl From Primaries 260
   U.S. Senator, Connecticut (D-CT). 183
Citibank
   ACORN Partnership............................51
Citizen's Consulting Inc.
   ACORN
      Bookkeeping and Accounting........157
      Financial Management...................157
      Management Contract 157
   Dale Rathke, Termination...............289
   Duplantier, Hrapmann, Hogan and Maher
      Rathke Embezzlement....................290
Citizen's Consulting Inc..................45, 157
   Rathke Embezzlement
      Managers/Directors Loan 296
   Wade Rathke 296
Citizen's Consulting, Inc. 289
Claudie Harris...................105, 108, 115, 117
   Chair, Kansas City ACORN 105
   Federal Legislation 106
   Mortgage Banker's Association 117
Clean Air for Waterloo Campaign 237
CLEAR Corps...64
   Sherwin-Williams................................64

Clinton Presidential Library 134

COINTELPRO
  FBI Counter Intelligence Programs. 171, 175

Coleen Rowley
  FBI Whistleblower............................ 190

Community Development Block Grants .. 48

Community Organizing
  Labor Organizing............................... 125

Community Reinvestment Act
  ACORN..46

ConAgra.. 88

Congressional Black Caucus
  Barack Obama.......................................187
  Hillary Clinton......................................187

Corinthian Baptist Church 233, 234

Cornell West
  African-American Author, Celebrity .. 228
  BHO African-American Surrogate... 202
  East Side High School 228

Courtney Dillard............................. 7, 8, 10
  Founder, Dillard-Winecoff.......... 5, 9, 11
  Mortgage Fraud..8
  The Art of the Deal 7
    Black Donald Trump.........................8

Coya Mobley
  Chair, Dayton ACORN 100

Craig Robbins................59, 60, 130, 211, 219
  ACORN Organizers............................130
  Carlyle Group.. 211
  Deputy Field Director/Northeast
    Regional Director, ACORN 44
  Liberty Tax Services............................. 44
  SEIU/ACORN Contract 218

D

Dale Rathke 52, 279, 288, 289, 290,
                    291, 295, 296, 299
  ACORN Union Recognition Petition.. 180
  Citizen's Consulting Inc.
    Terminaton 289
  Citizen's Consulting Inc. 45
    Director, Citizen's Consulting, Inc .. 289
    Rathke Embezzlement................... 288
    Rathke Restitution Agreement....290
  Comptroller, Citizen's Consulting Inc. ...94
  Profligate Spending
    Concord, Paris France......................94
    Gucci 52
    La Cote Basque 53
    Neiman Marcus.................................. 53
    Waldorf-Astoria 52

Dan Cantor
  Executive Director, Working Families
    Party 198, 279

Dana Williams ...10, 98, 182, 280, 284, 285
  ACORN Organizers............................ 99
  Chair, Georgia ACORN...... 7, 10, 11, 98
  Community Organizing..................... 99
  Georgia ACORN Election 98
  Georgia ACORN, Campaign Reports .. 136
  Georgia ACORN, Financial Concerns.. 136
  Power... 99

Daniel Arellano
  Delegate, National Board (ACORN)... 116

Daniel D'Aniello
  Co-founder, Carlyle Group 206

Daniel Stewart

Delegate, National Board (ACORN) ... 109

Darrin Peters

    Carol Willis, Democratic Presidential

    Primary Election Campaign Strategy 192

Dathen Moorman

    Chair, Oregon ACORN 295

Dave Beckwith

    Executive Director, Needmor Fund 290

Dave's Place 163

David Axlerod 191, 221

    Hillary Clinton

        Washington, Change Agent? 191

    Obama Campign Advisor 191

David Kittle

    Vice Chair, Mortgage Banker's

    Association 116

David Patterson 255, 256

    Lieutenant Governor, New York 255

David Pluffe

    Obama Campaign Manager 221

David Rubenstein 197, 207, 263

    Carlyle Group

        Private Equity Investment Firm ... 197

    Co-founder, Carlyle Group 197, 206

    Jimmy Carter Administration

        Policy Assistant 206

    Marcel Reid, DC ACORN 209

    New York ACORN 198

    SEIU/ACORN Protest

        Halloween/Sugar Daddy 206

        University of Pennsylvania Protest 263

    Waldorf-Astoria

        SEIU/ACORN Protest 198

David Scott

    U.S. Representative, (D-GA) 119

Dawanna Dukes

    Field Director, Clinton Re-elect 94

DC ACORN 27, 30, 37, 40,

    42, 43, 73, 79, 210, 211, 214, 218, 219, 299

    ACORN Organizers

        Termination 130

    Anita MonCrief 84

    Capitol Hill 79

    Carlyle Group 214, 219

    Mayor Fenty, Protest 99

    Mortgage Fraud Committee

        Chair, Michael McCray 299

    No FEAR Legislation 144, 156

    School Modernization and Oversight

        Committee (ASMOC) 87

De Phillips

    Delegate, National Board (ACORN) ... 110

Deborah Berry 203

    Iowa Representative, (D-Waterloo) ... 202

Democratic National Committee 94, 277

    Call for the Convention 97

    Pledged Delegates 97

        Proportional Representation 265

    Super Delegates 97, 277

Democratic National Convention 268

    Brokered Convention 277

Democratic Primaries

    Al Gore

        Propective Democratic Nominee ... 93

    Barack Obama

        Front Runner 93

Bill Richardson, Governor (D-NM)
   Propective Democratic Nominee ...93

Evan Bayh, U.S. Senator (D-IN)
   Propective Democratic Nominee ...93

Hillary Clinton, Front Runner 93

John Edwards, Front Runner 93

John Kerry. U.S. Senator (D-MA)
   Propective Democratic Nominee ...93

Joseph Biden. U.S. Senator (D-DE)
   Propective Democratic Nominee ...93

Tom Vilsack, Governor, Iowa (D-IA)
   Propective Democratic Nominee ...93

Democratic Vote Builder Database..225, 257

Department of Commerce 190

Department of Transportation
   Funding 250, 253

Department of Treasury Settlement—
   Chicago Title Insurance Company 184

Derrick Richardson
   Delegate, National Board (ACORN). 101

Dexter Wimbish..............................10
   General Counsel, Southern Christian
   Leadership Conference............... 7, 9, 11
   Mortgage Fraud....................................... 9
   Non-judicial Foreclosure......................10

Diana St. Marie
   Delegate, National Board (ACORN)... 119

Dillard-Winecoff.................................... 184
   Boutique Hotel and Development
   Company 5, 7
   IBF Funding vs. Dillard-Winecoff.......8

DNC Proportional Representation
   Hillary Clinton 281

Doe's Steak House 139

Donald Coulter
   Delegate, National Board (ACORN)....115

Donald Fields
   Founder, Millicom Group 14

Donald Trump
   The Commodore Hotel........................ 7

Donna Brazile
   Field Director, Clinton Re-elect........94

Donna Rouse
   DC City Council................................. 80

Dorothy Perkins....................................... 181
   Chair, Arkansas ACORN 181
   Jim Jones Cult (ACORN) 181

Doug Wilder
   Governor, Virginia (D-VA)............... 255

Dow Jones Private Equity Analyst
   Conference...196

Dr. Ron Karenga 58, 67, 68, 170, 171
   Community Oganizing....................172
   Kwanza..170
   Marcel Reid....................................... 170

Duplantier, Hrapmann, Hogan and
Maher Citizen's Consulting Inc.
   Rathke Embezzlement.......................290

DuPont... 88
   Lead-based Paint Settlement............. 149

Duron 88

E

Earl Fortenberry
   Delegate, National Board (ACORN)... 116

Earvin "Magic" Johnson........ 234, 235, 237

Bill Clinton
Economic Development 238
Hillary Clinton
Economic Development 238
East Side High School............................257
Eastside Ministerial Alliance 245
Boardmember, Wilson Rideout 247
Community Center 253
Head start Program............................ 253
Hillary Clinton....................................246
Illinois Central Railroad Strike....... 250
President, Jay Burt 228
Religious Organization 228
Secretary, Michael Coleman 249
Stephanie Tubbs-Jones....................246
Economic Justice..19, 33, 38, 167, 172, 173, 309
Black Churches 172
Ed Loggins, Pastor, Christian Fellowship
Baptist Church....................................243
Ed Rendell, Govenor (D-PA) 275
Eddy Weatherspoon 177
Delegate, National Board (ACORN). 118
Edra Derricks... 41
Liberty Tax Services
Virginia Beach Reaction 41
Member, DC ACORN.........................38
Eileen Graham
Delegate, National Board (ACORN)... 116
El Rancho Bar and Restaurant...............133
Elena Hanggi Giddings
National President, ACORN........... 167
Eliseo Medina
Stop the Fee Increase for Citizenship ...111

Vice President, Service Employee's
International Union...........................111
Elizabeth Ratliff
Delegate, National Board (ACORN).. 100
Ella Thomas
First Lady, Mount Caramel 243
Ellis Hotel... 183
Jay Furman 183
Kelco/FB Winecoff 183
Richard Birdoff 183
Elysian Fields Partnership
Dale Rathke
Rathke Embezzlement................... 289
Wade Rathke 289
Emancipation Day Service 256
Emancipation Day Services 256
Emancipation Proclamation......................5
Abraham Lincoln 253
Emancipation Day Services 253, 255
Juneteenth Celebration 7
Emeline Bravo-Blackwood
Chair, Connecticut ACORN 297
Emile Jones..256
Empowerment Zones................... 141, 248,
See White House Empowerment
Zone Initiative,
Environmental Justice
Georgia ACORN 98
Eric Henry
Delegate, National Board (ACORN).... 110
Erica Miller
Delegate, National Board (ACORN).... 119
Erica Rambo

Delegate, National Board (ACORN).....102

Erica Young

Delegate, National Board (ACORN)... 110

Ernie Green

Bill Clinton..93

Little Rock Nine 93

Estella Willis West

Delegate, National Board (ACORN)... 109

Etharin Cousins

Field Director, Clinton Re-elect.........94

F

Fair Housing Act of 1968 47

Fannie Brown ... 100, 131, 132, 133, 169, 170, 171, 173, 174, 175, 177

ACORN National Board Meeting

Detroit, Michigan............................ 288

ACORN Organizers....................129, 131

ACORN Position on Immigration and

Temporary Labor................................178

Black Panther Party.................... 169, 170

Chair, California ACORN 129

FBI Counter Intelligence Programs

Black Panther Party.............................171

COINTELPRO 174

US Organization.................................. 171

Federal Emergency Management

Administration

ACORN Demonstration....................102

Federal Reserve Bank

Boatman's Bank CRA Hearing.........49

Hibernia National Bank CRA Hearing..50

Financial Justice Center (ACORN)

History and Introduction 102

Financial Justice Centers........................ 150

Financial Justice Centers (ACORN)...168

Mortgage Fraud....................................153

Predatory Lending................................153

Refund Anticipation Loan Campaign... 150

Flat Iron Building.. 5

Floyd Flake 247, 248

Frank Carlucci,

Chairman, Carlyle Group..................217

Frankie Robinson

Delegate, National Board (ACORN).... 101

Frantz Whitfield 231, 232, 244, 255, 256

Bill Clinton..................................244, 245

Hillary Clinton........................... 232, 245

HRC African-American Surrogates 232

Obama Faith Steering Committee .232

Pastor, Mount Carmel Missionary

Baptist Church.........................204, 231

Fred Humphries, State Political Director,

Clinton Re-elect.....................................94

Frederick Douglass Taylor....................... 9

Director of Direct Action, Southern

Christian Leadership Conference . 6, 7, 11

Fredrick Hill.. 228

Freedom Riders 32

Social Justice 33

Freeman Hendrix.......................................94

Frieda Weems...202

Democratic Activist 201, 244

Friedrich Nietzsche 18

Friendship Baptist Church 109

From the Heart—Waterloo Home

Enhancement Project, Quentin Hart,
Executive Director.............................. 235

G

Gail Scott
Delegate, National Board (ACORN)... 119
Gary Delgado......................................173, 181
Co-founder, ACORN Organizer..... 173
Gary Hart, U.S. Senator, (D-CO)....... 205
Gary Montgomery, Station Manager/
Program Director, KBOL................. 228
Gee Gee Hartman
Delegate, National Board (ACORN)... 119
George H.W. Bush 206
George W. Bush....................................... 213
George Wiley.................. 174, 307, 308, 309
ACORN
Chesapeake Bay, Dissaperance...... 175
Co-founder, ACORN..................... 173
Organizing, Middle/Working Class.. 173
Movement For Economic Justice 175
Chesapeake Bay, Dissaperance...... 173
National Welfare Rights Organization
FBI COINTELPRO 174
Founder/Director, National Welfare
Rights Organization 167
Wade Rathke, Student Organizer308
Welfare Organizing........................... 308
Georgia ACORN.... 7, 10, 98, 100, 119, 132,
135, 136, 137, 153, 154, 179, 180, 182, 183,
271, 280, 285, 299
ACORN Financial Managment....... 137
Administratorship..................... 285, 293

AT&T Bell South Merger Campaign .. 101
Federal Communications Commission. 101
Mayor, Shirley Franklin 184
Mortgage Fraud...................154, 180, 106
Predatory Lending............................ 106
Winecoff Hotel 183
Georgia ACORN Campaign Report
Dillard-Winecoff 100
Lea O'Neal... 100
Mortgage Fraud.................................. 100
Gerald Lena... 69, 70
Jury Foreman, Rhode Island 69
Gladys Conde
Delegate, National Board (ACORN)... 118
Glenn Rushing 262
Field Director, Clinton Re-elect........ 94
Political Director, South Carolina... 261
Gloria Swieringa.... 61, 62, 63, 117, 139, 140,
141, 143, 144, 148, 169, 172
Chair, Maryland ACORN.................295
National Paint and Coatings Association
Lead-based Paint Ban 63
Sherwin-Williams............................ 62
Organizing Black Churches 172
Gordon Fischer, Chair, Iowa Democratic
Party 223
Gordon Gant, State Director, Clinton
Re-elect 94
Government Accountability Project....189
Greg Hall 305
Gwendolyn Adams
Delegate, National Board (ACORN) 116

H

H&R Block 39

   ACORN Campaign...............................38

      RAL Agreement..........................39, 40

   Campaign...39

   Refund Anticipation Loans................40

Halliburton, Inc..................................... 190

Hana Sabree

   Delegate, National Board (ACORN).....115

Hannah Giles..304

Harmon, Curran Spielberg and Eisenbly

   Attorney, Beth Kingsley.................... 288

Harold Gist 201, 202, 204, 220,

           221, 222, 225, 259, 264

   Carol Willis,Democratic Presidential
Primary Election Campaign Strategy .192

   Deputy Director, HRC African-
American Strategy Team....................201

   DNC Super Delegates 259

   HRC African-American Strategy
Team, Buffalo Soldiers........................221

   Iowa Caucus Reaction 259

   Watch Night Service........................... 254

Harvey Glenn

   Member, Georgia ACORN............... 118

   The Millicom Group 118

Head Start Program 253

Helene O'Brien 61, 168, 288, 291

   ACORN Field Operations and Staffing.. 156

   ACORN Special Initiatives............... 157

   Field Director, ACORN National Staff....61

Henry Espy...143

Henry Johnson, C.I.O. Labor Organizing ..125

Herbert Morris

   Delegate, National Board (ACORN) ... 100

Heyward Bannister 262, 263

   State Director, Clinton Re-elect........ 94

Hibernia Bank

   CRA Performance Rating.................. 50

Hill Harper

   Barack Obama.....................................233

   BHO African-American Surrogate....232

Hillary Clinton 187, 191, 219, 227,

         234, 239, 275, 278, 281, 283, 284

   ABC and Facebook Debates..............261

   Barack Obama.....................................283

   Black America

      Blacks/Civil Rights Support 187

      Waning Black Support 266

   Black Churches 243

   Black Ministers and Politicians 260

   Black Voters

      Fading Black Support 260

   Bob Nash, Senior Advisor..................186

   Carol Willis, Primary Election

      Campaign Strategy............................192

   Christmas Holiday Season 245

   College Outreach.................................225

   Congressional Black Caucus 187

   Democratic Establishment 238

   Democratic Primaries

      African-American Outreach 133

      California Primary........................269

      Concession Speech 281, 283

      DNC Proportional Representation ..281

      Early Front Runner 133

Florida and Michigan Delegates.. 267

HRC African-American Outreach... 185

HRC Campaign Launch................. 92

Indiana Primary............................. 278

Iowa Post Mortem 260

John Edwards Attack Ads.............. 191

Michigan Primaries........................267

National African-American
   Vote Totals 278

New Hampshire Returns 261

Pennsylvania Reaction................... 277

Popular Vote Leader.......................281

Post Primary Speech 281

Slipping in National Polling.......... 255

South Carolina Primary................ 265

Super Delegate Support................. 277

Super Tuesday.................................269

Texas Primary.................................270

The Inevitable Canidate 284

Dr. Walter Cunningham School for
   Excellence 232

Frantz Whitfield 232

HRC African-American Strategy Team. 229

HRC African-American Surrogates 232

Iowa Caucus

   Maintained Viability.......................258

   Peace and Change........................... 245

   Third Place Finish...........................258

Maxine Waters 268

Mount Carmel Missionary Baptist
   Church 244

National Democratic Establishment ... 284

Pennsylvania Primary.........................271

Renaissance Park Senior Living Facility 246

Reverend Wilson Rideout 247

Rodney Slater 248

Tom Vilsack, Iowa Machine.............261

Women Outreach 220

Home Mortgage Disclosure Act............ 48

Hotel Winecoff 7, 8

House Ways and Means Committee ... 122

Household Finance

   ACORN Campaign
      Predatory Lending...........................103

   Leadership Council for Civil and
      Human Rights.................................153

Household Finance Campaign 103, 105

Howard Dean 223, 277

   Democratic Primaries........................223

   Governor, Vermont (D-VT)............. 205

   John Edwards 205

   John Kerry.. 205

HRC African-American Strategy Team ... 220

Hugh Alleynan

   Co-chair, Deleware ACORN 295

I

Illinois Central Railroad.............. 202, 249

   Railroad Strike 202

Ina Mason

   Delegate, National Board (ACORN) ... 100

Industrial Areas Foundation

   Founder, Saul Alinsky 307

InterBank Funding Companies....... 8, 106,
                       153, 154, 183

   InterBank/Brenner Brokerage

Company 154

Loan-To-Own Scheme 8

SEC Securities Fraud 154

Interim Management Committee
 (ACORN)...........................294, 295, 298

Interim Staff Management Committee
 (ACORN).................................294

Iowa Commission of Human Rights.. 203

Iowa State Commission

 The Status of African-Americans.... 202

 Wilson Rideout, Awardee.................247

Iowa State Initiative

 Ongoing Covenant with Black Iowa.. 202

Ira Hammerman, Managing Director/
 General Counsel, SIFMA.................271

Irene Holcomb

 City Councilwoman, Pine Bluff,
  Arkansas 110

 Member, Pine Bluff ACORN 109

J

J. Edgar Hoover 170

 Communists, Red Scare.................174

 Director, FBI..............................174

 FBI Counter Intelligence Programs 171

J.J. Moses, Pastor, Lakewood Church.. 243

J.P. Morgan Chase ACORN Partnership 51

Jack Nicholson

 Fair Housing Act of 1968 47

Jackie Young

 Delegate, National Board (ACORN).... 116

Jackson Hewitt................................40

Jacqueline Andrews, State Political

Director, Clinton Re-elect.................94

James Andrew Doyle............. 59, 62, 63, 64

 ACORN Lead-based Paint
  Negotiations 62

 Lead-based Paint Ban 63

 President, National Paint and Coatings
  Association.............................58

James Baker

 Carlyle Group...............................206

 Gore/Bush Florida Election 94

 Partner, Carlyle Group 217

 Secretary of State, United States 206

James Clyburn

 Bill Clinton

 Black America 265

 Democratic Whip, U.S. House of
  Representatives...............................133

 Hillary Clinton Campaign 133

 U.S. Representative, (D-SC) 133

James Franklin

 Field Director, Clinton Re-elect........94

James Moreland

 Delegate, National Board (ACORN)... 100

James O'Keefe................................304

James Washington 28, 29, 31, 34, 38, 39

 ACORN Organizers............................ 31

 H&R Block Campaign........................39

 Liberty Tax Service, Virginia Beach
  Protest 33

 Member, DC ACORN...................... 28

 Virginia Beach Protest........................ 28

 Virginia Beach Reaction 38

Jamie Scott................................260

HRC African-American Strategy Team. 220

Jamie Wilson

   Member, California ACORN 102

Janet Howard

   Commerce Department Whistleblower . 190

Janice Mowery 28, 32

   ACORN Demands 32

   Head Organizer, Virginia ACORN ..28, 32

   Liberty Tax Services Campaign..........32

Jasmine Guy

   BHO African-American Surrogate .232

Jay Burt..246

   President, Eastside Ministerial Alliance 228

Jay Furman

   Kelco/FB Winecoff (aka the Ellis

     Hotel) 183

Jeffrey Wigand

   Tobacco Whistleblower, The Insider... 189

Jeninah Aragon

   Delegate, National Board (ACORN)... 119

Jeremiah Wright..................... 262, 273, 274

   God Damn America 273

   Obama Faith Steering Committee . 262

   Social Gospel 262

Jesse Jackson...175

   Founder, Rainbow/Push Coalition ...16

   Presidential Campaigns......................187

Jesse Jackson, Jr..187

Jesus Salcido

   Delegate, National Board (ACORN) 116

Jim Jones Cult (ACORN)

   Dorothy Perkins.................................. 181

Jimmy Carter 205

Joanna Landreth

   Delegate, National Board (ACORN) 119

Joe Beasly 10

   Juneteenth Celebration 7

   Southern Regional Director, Rainbow/

     Push Coalition 6, 7

Joe Kennedy 120

   U.S. Representative, (D-MA) 121

Joe Lewis

   Delegate, National Board (ACORN).... 99

Joe Trippi.. 191

John Edwards

   Take Back America........................71, 75

   Democratic Primaries

     Edwards Campaign Launch 92

     Hillary Clinton, Contrast Ads 191

     Policy Proposals 134

     Presidential Campaign Suspension .. 265

     South Carolina Primary................ 265

   Hillary Clinton....................................134

   Iowa Caucus Second Place Finish 258

   Joe Trippi.. 191

   John Kerry...93

   Michigan Ballot 267

   Rural Outreach 219

   Second Tier Canidate 191

   Solicits ACORN Support....................71

   Two Americas.......................................71

John Hewitt 32

   ACORN CampaignRAL Settlement.. 45

   ACORN Demands 32

   ACORN Protest.............................31, 33

   Founder/Chief Executive Officer,

Liberty Tax Services 30

Police Complaint 34

SLAPP lawsuit 35

John Jones 169, 173, 174, 175, 177

Chair, Washington ACORN 58, 295

John Kerry

ACORN Take Back America 71, 75

Military Veterans Outreach 205

U.S. Senator, (D-MA) 236

John Lewis.U.S. Representative, (D-GA). 119

John Major 206

John McCain 73

John McConnell 302

John Robbins, Chairman, Mortgage

Banker's Association 116

John Roberts

Delegate, National Board (ACORN) 119

John Sweeney, President, AFL-CIO ... 167

Johnny Isakson, U.S. Senator, (R-GA) 119

Jon Kest 303

Jonathan Kempner, President/CEO,

Mortgage Banker's Association 116

Jordan Ash 102, 105, 107, 108,

115, 131, 150, 152, 279

Director, Financial Justice Center....102

Director, Financial Justice Centers..168

Financial Justice Center

Wells Fargo Settlement................... 150

Financial Justice Centers.................... 150

Financial Justice Team...................... 107

Jose Garcia

Delegate, National Board (ACORN) 119

Joseph Barring 235, 236

Pastor, Payne AME Church 235

Joseph Biden

Withdrawl From Primaries 260

U.S. Senator, (D-DE) 223

Viability/BHO Aggressive Second

Choice 223

Joseph Curry, Reverend 243

Joseph Sherman

Delegate, National Board (ACORN).... 101

Joyce E. Megginson

Commerce Department Whistleblower .190

Joyce Marshall

Community Leader/Radio Announcer244

Juanita's Café 139

Judy Link

Delegate, National Board (ACORN)... 119

Julie Smith 107, 108, 112, 117

Chair, Ohio APAC...............................115

Member, Cleveland ACORN 107

Mortgage Banker's Association 117

Juneteenth Celebration 5, 6, 13, 112, 182

K

KABF 150

Karen Inman.. 109, 293, 297, 298, 300, 303

ACORNInterim Management

Committee...300

Federal Legislation 107

Interim Management Committee .. 298

Rathke Embezzlment 292

Secretary, Minnesota ACORN106, 295

Karen Mendoza

Delegate, National Board (ACORN).... 110

Karen Taylor

    Delegate, National Board (ACORN) 115

Karyn Gillette 208

    Anita MonCrief 208

    Supervisor, Project Vote 91

Katrice Banks

    State Director, Clinton Re-elect 94

Katy Fitzgerald, Chair, DC ACORN,

    President, New Party 44

Kay Bisnath

    Delegate, National Board (ACORN) 115

KBBG

    Floyd Flake 248

    HRC African-American Surrogates 235

    Obama Campaign 228

    Stephanie Tubbs-Jones 246

KBOL 246

    HRC African-American Strategy Team. 228

    Stephanie Tubbs-Jones 246

Keith Kelleher 72

    ACORN Field Organizer 127

    Head Organizer, SEIU Local 880 . 127, 72

    Lead Organizer, United Labor Unions .. 127

Kelco Management and Development 8

Kelco/FB Winecoff 183

Kelly Adams

    State Director, South Carolina 261

Kelvin Simmons, Field Director, Clinton

    Re-elect 94

Kenneth Clebourne

    Delegate, National Board (ACORN) 110

Kenneth Starr 195

    Carol Willis 186

Kevin McGraw 201, 202, 204,

        221, 240, 241, 243, 260

    Carol Willis, Democratic Presidential

        Primary Election Campaign Strategy . 192

    HRC African-American Strategy Team .. 201

Kieran Quinn, Chairman-elect,

    Mortgage Banker's Association 116

Kirk Faultenheur 115, 116, 117

    Manager, Mortgage Banker's

        Association 115

Kwanza 67, 170

    Dr. Ron Karenga 170

L

Labor Organizing

    Community Organizing 125

Lanesborough Hotel 94

Larry Freeman 268, 269

    ARC African-American Strategy Team .. 268

    Buffalo Soldiers 268

Larry Hendrix

    Field Director, Clinton Re-elect 94

Larry Rodgers

    National President, ACORN 167

Lashon Campbell

    Delegate, National Board (ACORN) 101

Lawrence Daniel

    Field Director, Clinton Re-elect 94

Lead-based Paint Litigation 77

Leadership Conference for Civil and

    Human Rights 147

Learning the Issues Training Sessions 101

Ledora Gary

Delegate, National Board (ACORN)... 101

Lee Pressman, C.I.O. Labor Organizing .. 125

Legacy Hotel

Filibusters Bistro & Lounge 134

Leroy Ferrell

Delegate, National Board (ACORN) ... 100

Liberty Tax Services 30

Police Complaint 35

RAL Settlement 44

Refund Anticipation Loans 30

SLAPP lawsuit 35

Usurious Rates/Predatory Practices. 43

Linda Scamaccia

Delegate, National Board (ACORN) 115

Lisa Donner, Director, ACORN

Financial Justice Centers 168

Little Rock Central High School 134, 184

Little Rock River Market 134

Liz Bidot

Delegate, National Board (ACORN)... 118

Liz Wolff 59, 60, 70, 147, 148

Mass Demonstrations and

Negotiations 59

Reseacher, ACORN National Staff ... 59

Sherwin-Williams Campaign 59, 147

Lorita Jackson

Delegate, National Board (ACORN) 119

Louise Conway 29

Member, DC ACORN 28

Virginia Beach Protest 28

Louise Davis 123, 129

ACORN Organizers 129

Member, DC ACORN 99

Lovie Caldwell 234, 246

Lucille Puckett

Delegate, National Board (ACORN) 110

M

Madeline Talbott 72, 127, 147

ACORN Resignation 147

Carol Mosley Braun 127

Head Organizer, Illinois ACORN . 72, 127

Maduh Weisjnecki 130

Organizer, DC ACORN 129

Magic Johnson 237

Make It Safe Coalition Washington

Whistleblower's Week 189

Malcolm X 23, 159, 170

Black Nationalism 23

Direct Action 23

J. Edgar Hoover 171

Pan-Africanism 23

Spokesman, Nation of Islam 23

Manor Care 218

Carlyle Group Acquisition 207

Nursing Home Company 207

Marc Borbely 86

Marc Sidel, Organizer, DC ACORN 91

Marcel Reid 1, 27, 28, 29, 30, 31,

37, 38, 40, 41, 42, 43, 45, 50, 51, 55, 56,

57, 58, 59, 60, 61, 62, 63, 64, 66, 67, 68,

71, 72, 73, 76, 77, 78, 79, 83, 84, 85, 87,

88, 91, 99, 117, 121, 123, 124, 125, 126, 127,

128, 129, 130, 131, 132, 140, 141, 142, 143,

144, 145, 146, 147, 148, 156, 157, 158, 159,

160, 162, 165, 169, 170, 171, 172, 173, 174,

175, 177, 178, 179, 180, 181, 195, 196, 207,
209, 210, 211, 212, 213, 214, 215, 219, 264,
269, 271, 272, 275, 276, 279, 280, 287,
292, 296, 298, 299, 300, 301, 303

ACORN
By-Laws Committee 156
Interim Management Committee300
National Elections 179
Organizational Charts and Financial
    Records 155
Position on Immigration and
    Temporary Labor 177
Rathke Embezzlement 292
Take Back America 71, 75
Whistleblower Protections 156

ACORN Demands
Sherwin-Williams Campaign 58

ACORN National Board Meeting
Cleveland, Ohio 88
Detroit Michigan 287, 288
Little Rock, Arkansas 139

ACORN National Board Meeting,
Charoltte, North Carolina 45

ACORN Organizers
ACORN Membership 30
Janice Mowery 28
Termination 129

ACORN School Modernization and
Oversight Committee 86

Background
Catholic School 37
Compton, California 28
Dr. Ron Karenga 67

Faith, Hope and Charity 130
Jehova Witness 37
Kwanza 67
Miriam Reid 67
Barack Obama 72
Big Tobacco 76
Carlyle Group 209, 210, 214
Chair, DC ACORN 42, 43, 295
Charles Rangel 123
Community Organizing 126
Community Reinvestment Act 46
David Rubenstein 210

DC ACORN
Liberty Tax Services Protest 27
Membership Election 42
No FEAR Citizen's Tribunal 190
SEIU/ACORN Contract 219
Direct Action 31
Dr. Ron Karenga 58, 68, 170
Empowerment Zones 141
Home Mortgage Disclosure Act 49
HUD Lead-based Paint Report 58
Interim Management Committee .. 298
James Andrew Doyle 59
Janice Mowery 29
Labor Organizing 125
Lead Paint Lawsuit 89
Lead-based Paint Campaign 56

Liberty Tax Services
Refund Anticipation Loans 38
Virginia Beach Protest 28
Virginia Beach Reaction 37
Madeline Talbott 127

Maxine Nelson.................................292

Member, DC ACORN....................... 27

Michael McCray.................214, 215, 300

Miriam Reid.................................41, 42

Mortgage Banker's Association 118

National Board Meeting. Cleveland,
  Ohio...91

National Paint and Coatings Association
  ACORN Demands..........................64

  James Andrew Doyle.........................59

  Lead-based Paint Ban 63

  Lead-based Paint Exposure.............62

  Negotiations.....................................61

  Sherwin-Williams.............................62

No FEAR Legislation 144

NPCA Lead-based Paint Negotiations... 62

Poverty Tax 27

  Refund Anticipation Loans.......27, 38

Rhode Island Lead Paint Lawsuit 78

Secretary/Treasurer, New Party 44

Service Employees International Union ..55

Sherwin-Williams Enviornmental
  Abuse.. 88

Sherwin-Williams Campaign 59

Sherwin-Williams Toxic
  Paint Report................................. 85, 86

Stephanie Cannady 75

Stephen Lerner.....................................218

The Insider 76

USMC Sunset Parade.........................83

Wade Rathke 52

Wayne State University 287

March on Washington for Jobs and

Freedom 159

Marcia Dyson.........................233, 234, 243

  Hillary Clinton.................................233

  HRC African-American Surrogate 234

  HRC African-American Surrogates 235

  KBBG...235

Margarita Alvarez
  Delegate, National Board (ACORN)... 110

Marge Roukema, U.S. Representative
  (R-NJ) 120

Maria Bueno
  Delegate, National Board (ACORN)... 116

Maria Garcia
  Delegate, National Board (ACORN)... 119

Maria Shriver...268

Marion Barry, Member, DC ACORN. 79

Mark Baumgartner, Chief Financial
  Officer, Liberty Tax Services...............32

Mark Mays, State Political Director,
  Clinton Re-elect....................................94

Mark Penn
  Barack Obama
    Drugs and Cocaine Usage..............261

  Campaign Manager, Hillary Clinton...261

  Super Tuesday.......................................281

Marquina Wilson
  Delegate, National Board (ACORN)... 100

Marsha Coleman-Adebayo
  EPA Whistleblower...........................190

Martin Luther King, Jr.......... 160, 161, 309

  Economic Justice...............................309

Founder, Southern Christian Leadership
  Conference.. 9

J. Edgar Hoover......................................171

March on Washington 159

   I Have a Dream Speech..................160

Martin O'Malley, Mayor, Baltimore

   Maryland..61

Marvin Jenkins..254

   Pastor, Union Missionary Baptist

   Church 247, 254

Marvin Randolph, State Director,

   Clinton Re-elect....................................94

Mary Hutchins

   Chair, Missouri ACORN.................295

Mary Keith 87

   Chair, Cleveland ACORN.................92

   Chair, Ohio ACORN...........................115

   Sherwin-Williams Campaign 92

Mary McGowan..70

   Juror, Rhode Island 69

Mary Scott

   Delegate, National Board (ACORN).. 100

Mary Spencer, Vice-Chair, DC ACORN..219

Maude Hurd 92, 103, 108, 115, 116,

     117, 120, 121, 130, 144, 146, 156, 157,

     163, 166, 175, 179, 211, 272, 288, 292

   ACORN

     Organizational Charts, Financial

     Statements 155

   ACORN National Board Meeting. 288

   ACORN Three....................................120

   Financial Justice Team......................107

   National President, ACORN.....86, 167

   Wells Fargo Campaign 103

   Wells Fargo Lawsuit..........................103

Maxine Nelson 109, 110, 121

   Marcel Reid..292

   National Secretary, ACORN...........110

   Rathke Embezzlement.......................292

Maxine Waters 120

   ACORN Three....................................120

   Barack Obama Endorsement 278

   California State Assembly 120

   Chief Deputy, City Councilman David

     Cunningham, Jr. 120

   DNC Super Delegate 268

   Hillary Clinton Endorsement 268

   Maude Hurd 120

   U.S. Representative, (D-CA) 119

Maya Soetoro-Ng......................................219

Merlene Coulter

   Delegate, National Board (ACORN).....115

Mesirow Financial Consulting

   Rathke Embezzlement.......................294

Michael Blackwell

   African-American Leadership Coalition..

     203

   Director, Northern Iowa Center for

     Multicultural Education 202

Michael Blake 205

Michael Coleman............249, 250, 251, 253

   Eastside Ministerial Alliance 253

   Illinois Central Railroad Strike.......249

   Pastor, Antioch Baptist Church...204, 49

   Rodney Slater 253

   Secretary, Eastside Ministerial Alliance.. 253

   Watch Night Service...........................253

Michael Davis...275

Michael Eric Dyson 233
   BHO African-American Surrogate ... 233
Michael Frazier, Field Director, Clinton
   Re-elect 94
Michael Gronstal, Majority Leader, Iowa
   State Senate 238
Michael McCray 1, 2, 14, 15, 110, 140, 143,
   144, 160, 178, 180, 182, 274, 279, 280, 304
   USDA Whistleblower 190
A. Philip Randolph Institute Advisory
   Board Recruitment and Training
   Program 159, 161
ACORN
   Audited Financial Statements 155
   Chief Organizer 158
   Civil Rights Groups 132
   Financial Justice Team 107
   Financial Training Session 135
   Legislative and Policy Conference 98
   National Board Meeting, Little
      Rock, Arkansas 134
   National Elections 179
   New Delegate Orientation 135
   Organizational Charts and Financial
      Statements 137, 156
   Rathke Embezzlement 299
Al Gore
   Chair, Community Empowerment
      Board 141
Atlanta City Council 8
Atlanta Police Chief Richard Pennington
   Dillard-Winecoff vs InterBank
      Funding Companies 153

Bill Clinton 237
Carlyle Group 212, 214, 215
Carol Willis
   Barack Obama 185
Carol Willis, DNC Community
   Outreach Services
      Coordinator, Faith-Based Outreach..... 94
Carol Willis, Democratic Presidential
   Primary Election Campaign Strategy... 192
Cecil McDonald 271
Chair, Mortgage Fraud Committee
   (DC ACORN) 299
Dana Williams 25
Democratic National Committee
   Community Outreach Services 94
Democratic Primaries 92
Federal Empowerment Zone Initiative 93
Floyd Flake 247, 248
Fulton County District Attorney Paul
   Howard, Jr.
   Dillard-Winecoff vs InterBank
      Funding Companies 153
George Soros 300
Georgia ACORN 25
Hillary Clinton 267
HRC African-American Strategy Team
   219, 224
InterBank Funding Companies 153
KBOL 228
Larry Freeman 268
Marcel Reid 214, 215, 300
Mortgage Fraud 106, 118, 153
   Georgia Epidemic 182

NAACP................................14, 165

National Board Delegate, Georgia

   ACORN 98

National Labor Relations Board

   Office of Advice................................ 159

Neal Blakely................................25

No FEAR Legislation 144

Non-judicial Foreclosures 118

Office of Advice, National Labor

   Relations Board................................ 161

Organized Labor.................................. 125

Partner, Dillard-Winecoff................ 7, 11

Predatory Lending............................ 106

Rodney Slater 248

Saudi Bin Ladin family......................300

Saul Alinsky........................22, 132

Shirley Franklin 8

Southern Christian Leadership

   Conference................................15, 16, 165

Stacey Abrams............................8

Stephanie Tubbs-Jones....................... 245

U.S. Department of Agriculture 140

Wade Rathke........................145, 168, 300

Wellington Webb 239

Michael Muhammad.............................. 203

Michael Nutter..............................275

Michael Silverstein

   Judge, Rhode Island 208

   Special Master 149

Michelle Obama............................268, 273

Michelle Young

   Delegate, National Board (ACORN)... 116

Miguel Almaguer

Delegate, National Board (ACORN)... 119

Mike Dukakis, Governor (D-MA) 236

Mike Espy,

   Secretary, U.S. Department of

      Agriculture.. 142

      Presidential Pardon 142, 143

      Resignation 142

   U.S. Representative, (D-MS) ...142, 143

Mike German, FBI Whistleblower...... 190

Mike Sealy 166

   ACORN People's Platform 164

   Head Organizer, Arkansas ACORN ... 163

Mike Shea 46, 50

   ACORN Housing, Executive Director .. 45

   President, ACORN Housing

      Corporation 168

Mildred Brown......... 124, 126, 127, 128, 131

   ACORN Community Labor

      Organizing Centers..........................128

   ACORN Organizers...........................131

   Bertha Lewis..............................131

   Community Organizing....................126

   Healthcare Workers 127

   Labor Organizing.............................. 124

   Legislative Director, ACORN

      National Staff 124

   National President, ACORN........... 124

   United Labor Unions.........................126

Mildred Edmond

   President, SEIU Local 100................ 167

Millennium Holdings..............88, 208, 301

   Lead-based Paint Litigation Appeal...... 149

Millicom Group 14

Miriam Reid...42, 67

    Marcel Reid..42

Mitch Klein...61

    Head Organizer, Maryland ACORN 61

    Martin O'Malley 61

    National Paint and Coatings Association

    ACORN Demands...........................64

Modestine Snead...............................41, 42

    Member, DC ACORN.........................38

    Refund Anticipation Loans.................39

    Virginia Beach Reaction 41

Money Mart...103

Morg's Diner...............................246, 254

Mortgage Banker's Association......107, 111

    ACORN Millitant Action 107

Mortgage Bankers Association

    Millitant Action 115

Mortgage Fraud.............. 112, 129, 179, 180,

                    182, 279, 280, 285

    Georgia ACORN...........................98, 180

    Georgia, Texas, Florida and California..153

Motley Rice...76, 302

    Law Firm, South Carolina..................76

    Rhode Island Lead Paint Lawsuit.....77

Mount Carmel Missionary Baptist

    Church........204, 228, 231, 234, 243, 254

Movement for Economic Justice...........175

    Founder, George Wiley 309

    George Wiley, Founder 175

Muriel Handy-Jones

    Delegate, National Board (ACORN)... 116

Myron Gigger 10

    Atlanta Radio Personality 6

N

Nancy Pyle

    Delegate, National Board (ACORN)....110

National Action Network

    Civil Rights Organization 175

    Reverend, Al Sharpton 16, 175

National Association for the Advancement

    of Colored People 14, 132, 246

    Black Labor 161

    Civil Rights Organization 100

    Single Issue Organization 165

National Labor Relations Board

    ACORN Determination 181

    Labor Policy...161

National Lead Company.................See NL

                         Industries

National Paint and Coatings

    Association...........................57, 58, 62, 66

    ACORN Negotiations 61, 89

    CLEAR Corps 64

National Tenant Information Center.....48

National Welfare Rights

    Organization 173, 308

    Civil Rights Organization 308

    Founder/Director, Dr. George Wiley

        Wade Rathke, Student Organizer.. 167

NWRO Goals

    Adequate Income............................ 308

    Democratic Participation.............. 308

    Dignity... 308

    Justice 308

Wade Rathke, Student Organizer

    Adequate Income Now! 166

National Whistleblower Center
Founder, Stephen Kohn 190
Neal Blakely 13, 14, 15, 17, 18, 21, 22, 24, 25
ACORN 16
Capitalism and Democracy 19
Civil Rights
National Association for the
Advancement of Colored People .. 16
Southern Christian Leadership
Conference 16
Civil Rights Organizations 16
NAACP 16
Community Organizations
Education and Training 14
Community Organizer 13
Community Organizing 21
Building a Mass Power Base 20
Economic Justice 19
Friedrich Nietzsche 18
John Coltrane, Miles Davis 14
Martin Luther King, Jr. 18
Power 24
Rules for Radicals 19
Saul Alinsky 24
Arrests 18
Power Tactics 17
Radical's Radical 22
Social Gospel 20
Social Justice 19
Sociology 15, 19
Southern Christian Leadership
Conference 13

Needmor Fund
Rathke Embezzlement 290
New Birth Missionary Baptist Church ... 8
New Party
Working Famlies Party 44
New York ACORN 197
Nina Nunez
Delegate, National Board (ACORN) ... 110
NL Industries 88, 89, 208, 301
Dutch Boy Brand 88
Lead-based Paint Litigation 71
Appeal 149
No FEAR
Civil Rights Organization 190
Legislation 190
No FEAR Coalition 156
Civil Rights Organization 144
Washington Whistleblower's Week ... 190
No FEAR II
New Legislation 144
No FEAR Institute
Civil Rights Organization 189
Walter Fauntroy 190
Noelia Jimenez
Delegate, National Board (ACORN) 118
North Carolina ACORN
Yvonne Stafford, Chair 46
Notification of Federal Employee Anti-
discrimination and Retaliation Act
Civil Rights Legislation 189
Legislation 144
NPCA Lead Safe Training Education
and Outreach Program 63

NWRO........ See National Welfare Rights
                              Organization

O

Oak Forest Neighborhood
    Community Reinvestment Act:........ 48
Obama Faith Steering Committee
    Frantz Whitfield.................................232
    Jeremiah Wright 262
Office of the Controller of the Currency
    Hibernia Bank CRA Compliance.... 50
Opal Jones
    State Political Director, Clinton
        Re-elect 94
Oprah Winfrey.......................................268
    Barack Obama
        Women Outreach 220
Organizing the masses 259
Orson Porter
    Field Director, Clinton Re-elect........94

P

Pat Boone, President, New York ACORN 198
Pat McCoy, Organizer, DC ACORN ...91
Pat Williams, Member, DC ACORN.. 99
Patricia Hollins
    Delegate, National Board (ACORN).... 119
Patrick Lynch.. 302
    Attorney General, Rhode Island.. 70, 208
Paul Green
    ACORN Negotiations 117
    SVP Corporate Relations, Mortgage
    Banker's Association 117

Paul Howard, Jr.
    District Attorney, Fulton County
        Georgia..10
    Dillard-Winecoff vs InterBank
        Funding.. 184
Paul Satriano 136, 155, 157, 290, 294
    ACORN Financial Training
        ACORN Budget..............................135
        Georgia ACORN..............................135
    ACORN Issue Campaigns................ 137
    ACORN New Delegate Orientation
        ACORN Family 135
        National Board Composition 135
    ACORN Organizers............................ 136
        Georgia ACORN 136
    Rathke Embezzlement Needmore
        Fund: 290
    Treasurer, ACORN.............................135
Payne AME Church 233, 235, 247
Pedro Rivas
    Delegate, National Board (ACORN)....115
Peggy Morgan
    Community Activist............................ 243
Pilgrim Rest Baptist Church 234, 246
Pledged Delegates 269
Pocahontas Outlaw 29, 30, 41, 42, 43
    Chair, DC ACORN 29, 32
    DC ACORN Resignation 41
    Economic Justice.............................38, 40
    Financial Freedom Riders................... 33
    Financial Justice Centers....................40
    Liberty Tax Services............................40
        Virginia Beach Reaction 37

Refund Anticipation Loans..............38
U.S. Department of Housing and
    Urban Development.........................43
Virginia Beach Protest......................30
Virginia Beach Reaction...................41
Poor People's Campaign
Martin Luther King, Jr.....................309
Powers Hapgood
C.I.O. Labor Organizing..................125
Predatory Lending..................................112
Predatory Lending/Foreclosure Fraud
Predatory Tactics..............................104
Project Vote.........60, 78, 100, 132, 135, 196,
                208, 264, 281, 284
Anita MonCrief................................208
    Visa Card Application.....................196
    Visa Card Payments.......................196
    Visa Card Statements.....................196
Anita MonCrief, Termination.........264
Barack Obama.......................................72
    Voter Registration Drive.................72
Educational Organization.............75, 91
Executive Director, Zach Polett.........71
Purchase Power Visa Card.......209, 264
Public nuisance.......................................148
Lead-based Paint Litigation...............77
Legal Theory.............64, 69, 70, 76, 302
Pullman Sleeping Car Company.........160
A. Philip Randolph..........................160
Black Porters....................................160

City Council Election Defeat...........235
City Councilman, Waterloo.............235
From the Heart—Waterloo Home
    Enhancement Project.......................235
Wellington Webb.....................239, 240

R

Rachel Pope, Member, DC ACORN..28, 29
Rainbow/Push Coalition
Civil Rights Organization.........6, 7, 175
Reverend, Jesse Jackson...............16, 175
Randolph Dean, Deacon, Mount Carmel
    Missionary Baptist Church.............228
Randy Snook, Executive Vice President,
    SIFMA...271
Rebecca Hart, President, SEIU 100....167
Recruitment and Training Program
A. Philip Randolph Institute...........162
Advisory Board, Michael McCray...162
Refund Anticipation Loans
ACORN Issue..27
H&R Block...40
Jackson Hewitt......................................40
Liberty Tax Services............................30
Renaissance Hotel.....................................56
Rhode Island
Lead Paint Lawsuit...........44, 65, 86, 87,
                88, 148, 208
    Cleanup Costs..................................301
    Conspiracy..77
    Defendants..78
    Jury Verdict.........................68, 70, 149
    Landmark Decision..........................89

Q

Quentin Hart.....................235, 236, 243

Product Liability...............................77

Punitive Damages...........................78

Settlement 78

Sherwin-Williams...........................80

   Negotiations.................................87

Supreme Court Decision...............301

   ACORN Campaign...................302

   Ohio and California...................302

Supreme Court Reversal........301, 302

Lead Paint Lawuit

  Defendant

    Millennium Holdings..................78

    NL Industries 77

    Sherwin-Williams........................77

  Legal Theory

    Public Nuisance........77, 78, 80, 148

Lead-based Paint Litigation 70, 302

Richard Pennington............................184

  Police Chief, Atlanta Police

  Department..10

Rick Wade 221

  Candidate, Secretary of State (South Carolina)

    Buffalo Soldiers 222

  Obama Senior Advisor........................235

  Senior Advisor/Director of African-

  American Outreach..........................205

Ricky Broadway 221, 225, 227, 228, 233, 234,

235, 238, 241, 245, 247, 254, 255, 257, 258, 260

  College Outreach....................................225

  Coordinator, HRC College Outreach..224

  East Side High School

    HRS Literature Drop......................228

  University of Northern Iowa.............225

Watch Night Service...........................254

Robert Merwin, Juror, Rhode Island....69

Rodney Capel, Field Director, Clinton

  Re-elect 94

Rodney Shelton, State Political Director,

  Clinton Re-elect.....................................94

Rodney Slater.................248, 249, 253, 254,

                255, 256, 257, 258

  Bill Clinton 93

  Eastside Ministerial Alliance

    Illinois Central Railroad Strike.....249

  Hillary Clinton.....................................248

  Michael Coleman 253

  Scharron Clayton................................254

  Secretary, U.S. Department of

    Transportation 141, 248

  Transportation Oriented Economic

    Development..250

    Watch Night Service...........................254

Ron Karenga 170

Ronald Motley...76

Ronald Pughbey

  Delegate, National Board (ACORN)....118

Ronald Sykes 98, 100, 110, 117, 123, 124,

128, 129, 130, 179, 180, 182, 280, 285, 299

ACORN

  National Elections............................179

ACORN and SEIU...............................126

ACORN Organizers.............................129

  Black Organizers...............................130

Member, Georgia ACORN.........99, 118

Mildred Brown.....................................124

SEIU...124

Whipple-Bell Fellow, ACORN
National Staff 124

Rosa DeLauro,
U.S. Representative, (D-CT) 109

Rosa Lewis
Delegate, National Board (ACORN) 101

Rose Robinson
Delegate, National Board (ACORN) 101

Roslyn Dodge
Katrina Surivor, Louisiana ACORN.... 101

Rotten ACORN
Employment Policies Institute Report... 180

Rubenstein Firm
Rathke Embezzlement........................294

Rules for Radicals, Saul Alinsky.............24

Ryan O'Neal
Fair Housing Act of 1968 47

S

Saint Anselm College
Hillary Clinton....................................261

Samuel Mingo, Reverend 243

Sandra Wiekerson
Delegate, National Board (ACORN)... 116

Sanford Bishop,
U.S. Representative, (D-GA) 119

Sarah Lott-Edwards
Delegate, National Board (ACORN)....102

Saul Alinsky 17, 18, 23, 307, 309
Army of Organizers....................307, 308
Author, Rules for Radicals.............19, 22
Community Organizing....... 18, 22, 307
Founder, Industrial Arts Foundation17

Power..24
Power Tactics 132

Racial Justice.......................................309

Radical's Radical
Al Capone 23
Frank Nitti 23

Saxby Chambliss, U.S. Senator, (R-GA)... 119

SCLC Civil Rights Organization 13, 19

Scott DeFife 272, 275
ACORN Protest.........................272, 276
Managing Director of Governmental
Affairs, SIFMA 272

Sean Hannity....................................... 272

Securities Industry and Financial
Markets Association........................... 272

Sedric Crawford,
President, SEIU Local 100................ 167

SEIU ....See Service Employees
International Union

SEIU Change to Win Campaign
Labor Organizing............................... 177

SEIU Local 100
ACORN/SEIU Unionization..........127
Chief Organizer, Wade Rathke........ 158
Labor Organization 126, 167

SEIU Local 880
Chief Organizer, Wade Rathke........ 158
Contributions to ACORN
Membership Services 128
Keith Kelleher 127
Labor Organization 72, 126, 159
Labor Organizing Models
Executive Order 159

Public Authority...............................159

NLRB Representation Elections......127

SEIU Private Equity Project

    Director, Stephen Lerner...................218

SEIU Private Equity Report

    Behind the Buyouts...........................207

Service Employees International Union

    ACORN Community Labor

        Organizing Training.........................128

    Association of Community

    Organizations for Reform Now

        Carlyle Group...................................218

    Carlyle Group Protest.........................217

    Labor Organization 55, 119, 126

    Synagro, SEIU Enviornmental Protest...218

    United Labor Unions, Merger..........126

Sharon Dirocco

    Chair, Providence ACORN.............106

    Delegate, National Board (ACORN)...100

    Federal Legislation............................106

Sharon Goodson, President, NAACP....246

Sharon Patterson

    Delegate, National Board (ACORN)...100

Sheila Jackson Lee............................256, 257

    U.S. Representative, (D-TX).............190

Sheldon Whitehouse, Attorney General,

    Rhode Island...........................76

Sherman Wilburn

    Delegate, National Board (ACORN)...109

Sherri White, State Political Director,

    Clinton Re-elect....................................94

Sherridan Scwartz

    Delegate, National Board (ACORN)...110

Sherron Watkins, Enron Whistleblower...190

Sherwin-Williams...................57, 62, 66, 80,

        86, 87, 88, 89, 301

    ACORN Campaign......................88, 302

    ACORN Demands.................................58

    ACORN Negotiations..........................89

    Black Communitites..............................88

    Campaign.............80, 86, 87, 88, 89, 208

    Charles Moellenberg, Jr.....................302

    Dutch Boy Brand..................................88

    Enviornmental Abuse...........................88

    Headquarters...92

    Headquarters Protest............................88

    High-risk Neighborhoods....................58

    Industry Leader.....................................89

    Lead Detection Kits.............................58

    Lead-based Paint Litigation.........70, 71

        Appeal..149

    Public Hearings....................................88

    Toxic Paint Report...............................86

    Volatile Organic Compounds............86

    White Lead Carbonate.......................89

Sherwin-Williams Campaign.58, 59, 86, 149

Shirley Burnell

    Delegate, National Board (ACORN)...100

Shirley Franklin.....................................184

    Courtney Dillard...............................184

    Georgia ACORN

        Mortgage Fraud, Winecoff Hotel 184

    Mayor, City of Atlanta......................184

        Winecoff Hotel (aka the Ellis Hotel)....8

    Michael McCray.................................184

Sidley, Austin LLP

Rathke Embezzlement.......................294

SIFMA ....See Securities Industry and
        Financial Markets Association,

Social Gospel..273

Social Justice 19, 33, 309

    Black Churches 172

    Social Gospel 19

Social Policy Magazine

    Publisher/Editor-In-Chief,

        Wade Rathke 150

SoHo Grand Hotel................................ 9

    Mortgage Fraud...................................... 9

Sonya Merchant-Jones, Co-chair,

    Baltimore ACORN........................... 124

Sookies Restaurant 246

Sophia Tesch

    Delegate, National Board (ACORN).... 119

Southern Christian Leadership Conference 132

    Black Labor 161

    Civil Rights Organization 6, 7, 9, 13

    Poor People's Campaign.................... 309

    Single Issue Organization 165

Southern Soul Café 239

Sovereign Wealth Funds

    SEIU Private Equity Campaign 270

St. Mark's Episcopal Church................. 118

Stacey Abrams

    Assistant City Attorney, Atlanta

        Winecoff Hotel (aka the Ellis Hotel) 8

    Representative, Georgia Assembly

        (Minority Leader)..................................8

Stephanie Cannady... 71, 73, 75, 76, 77, 78, 301

    ACORN

Take Back America......................71, 75

Barack Obama.......................................73

Chair, Rhode Island ACORN...70, 295

Lead-based Paint Litigation 76

Motley Rice....................................... 76

Punitive Damages.............................. 78

The Insider 76

Stephanie Hughes

    Delegate, National Board (ACORN)... 100

Stephanie Tubbs-Jones...................246, 247

    Deborah Berry......................................246

    Hillary Clinton...........................246, 247

    Renaissance Park Senior Living Facility 246

    Scharron Clayton................................246

    U.S. Representative, (D-OH) 245

Stephen Kohn, Attorney, National

    Whistelblower Center 190

Stephen Lerner 206, 218, 269, 270, 279

    David Rubenstein 218

    DC ACORN 218, 219

    Director, SEIU Private Equity

        Project 206, 218

Steve Bachmann........................... 289, 290

    General Counsel, ACORN 45

    Rathke Embezzlement......................289

        Restitution Agreement 289

    Wade Rathke 45

Steve Bradbury

    Head Organizer, Illinois ACORN . 147

    Wade Rathke, Beth Butler............... 147

Steve Kest.......... 132, 157, 288, 291, 294, 303

    Executive Director, ACORN National

    Staff...131

Needmor Fund......................................290

Rathke Embezzlement.......................294

Steve McDonald, National President,

   ACORN... 167

Steven Simmons

   Delegate, National Board (ACORN).....115

Stevie Wonder

   BHO African-American Surragote ..269

   Obama Campaign Theme Music......261

Stormy Henry

   Delegate, National Board (ACORN)... 100

Strategic Lawsuit Against Public Participation

   Liberty Tax Services.............................. 35

Student Nonviolent Coordinating Committee

   Civil Rights Organization................ 308

Students for a Democratic Society...... 308

   Anti-War Organization.....................307

Sunday Alabi, Chair, Minnesota

   ACORN... 109

Super Delegates 259

   Hillary Clinton..................................259

Super Tuesday..................................263, 269

   Barack Obama February Primaries 269

   Hillary Clinton Reaction 269

Susan Kincaid, Radio Announcer...... 244

T

Take Back America

   Democratic Confrence.................. 71, 78

Tamecka Pierce...................................118, 178

   Chair, Florida ACORN 177

Tammie Pursley

   Delegate, National Board (ACORN).... 119

Tanya Ward Jordan

Commerce Department Whistleblower ...
190

Tawanna Baker....................................41, 42

   Liberty Tax Services

      Virginia Beach Reaction 41

      Member, DC ACORN.........................38

Ted Kennedy

   ACORN Reception 119

   U.S. Senator, (D-MA) 109

      Barack Obama Endorsement........ 268

Terrell Walker

   ACORN Organizers............................129

   Member, Cleveland ACORN 102

Theodore Carter, Deputy Campaign

   Manager, Clinton Re-elect 94

Thomas Dortch, Jr., State Political

   Director, Clinton Re-elect..................94

Thomas Graves..66

   ACORN Lead-based Paint

      Negotiations 63

   General Counsel, National Paint and

      Coatings Association 62

   NPCA State Attorneys General

      Agreement..63

Thomas Henry

   Delegate, National Board (ACORN).... 119

Timothy Ryan, Jr. President/CEO,

   SIFMA..271

Tina Martin Brown

   Delegate, National Board (ACORN)... 100

Tom Devine

   Government Accountability Project

Washington Whistleblower's Week..189

Tom Harrington

Barack Obama

Superior Organization.....................223

Howard Dean

Iowa Defeat..223

Tom Vilsack 284

Governor, Iowa....................................244

Hillary Clinton.....................................261

Tommy Vietor, Spokesman, Obama

Campaign

New Clinton Campaign Staff...........238

Toni Foulkes 71, 72

Barack Obama

Lawyer, Illinois Moter Voter Case

ACORN vs Edgar............................. 72

Toni Harp, Field Director, Clinton

Re-elect 94

Toni McElroy, Chair, Texas ACORN.. 294

Tony Augusta, General Manager, WPFW

Radio Station (Washington, DC).... 44

Member, DC ACORN....................... 44

Tonya Lombard 275

State Political Director, Clinton

Re-elect 94

Tramon Arnold.......221, 225, 227, 228, 233,

234, 235, 238, 241, 247, 254, 255, 257, 260

Coordinator, Faith Outreach...........224

Democratic Vote Builder Database .225

East Side High School HRC Liteature

Drop 228

Watch Night Service 254

Truth To Power

Greg Hall..305

U

U.S. Citizenship and Immigration Services

ACORN Demonstration................... 110

U.S. Department of Housing and Urban

Development

Settlement—Chicago Title Insurance

Company 184

U.S. Department of Justice................... 161

A. Philip Randolph 161

U.S. Securities and Exchange

Commission..8

SEC vs InterBank Funding

Companies 9, 183

ULU.................. See United Labor Unions

Union Missionary Baptist Church .247, 254

United Food and Commercial Workers

Union 207

United Labor Unions.............................126

United Students Against Sweatshops .270

University of Arkansas in Fayetteville248

University of Northern Iowa

Barack Obama Address 204

Center for Multicultural Education202

US Organization

Black Nationalist Organization 170

Black Panther Party........................... 170

Founder, Dr. Ron Karenga 170

J. Edgar Hoover.................................. 170

United Slaves (Moniker) 170

V

Vanessa Gueringer... 145, 148, 159, 160, 161, 162
  Delegate, National Board (ACORN)....102
Vermadean Griffen
  Delegate, National Board (ACORN).... 110
Vernon Bolden
  President, SEIU Local 100................ 167
Veronica Edwards
  Delegate, National Board (ACORN)....102
Victor Bernal
  Delegate, National Board (ACORN).... 110
Vino's Restaurant..................................... 139
Vivian Jones, State Political Director,
  Clinton Re-elect.................................... 94

W

Wade Henderson 152
  ACORN Partnership......................... 147
  Leadership Conference for Civil and
  Human Rights..................................... 147
Wade Rathke 45, 47, 51, 52,
    127, 133, 145, 146, 147, 149, 150, 154, 156,
    158, 163, 166, 168, 169, 173, 175, 178, 180,
    181, 182, 221, 256, 276, 279, 285, 286, 288,
    289, 290, 291, 293, 295, 296, 297, 298,
                299, 300, 307, 308, 309
ACORN
    Ameriquest Campaign 152
    Chief Organizer, ACORN National
    Staff... 42, 145
    Financial Justice Centers
      Mortgage Fraud........................... 180
    Labor Organizing............................... 158

Organizational Charts, Financial
    Statements 156
  Position on Immigration and
    Temporary Labor.......................... 177
  Rathke Embezzlement
    Restitution Agreement 290
ACORN Organizers
    ACORN/SEIU Union Busting....128
    Black Organizers.............................. 175
    Chief Organizer 128
ACORN Staff Management Council .. 289
Chief Organizer
    Rathke Embezzlement.................... 289
Chief Organizer, ACORN National
    Staff.. 60
Chief Organizer, SEIU Local 100....128
Co-founder, ACORN Organizer..... 173
Community Organizing.................. 307
Community Reinvestment Act
    Oak Forest Neighborhood.............. 47
Economic Justice................................. 166
Financial Justice Center
    Mortgage Fraud................................154
George Wiley...................................... 309
Home Mortgage Disclosure Act........ 48
Household Finance
    ACORN Settlement 152
Labor Organizing
    NLRA Collective Bargaining 159
Madeline Talbot
    Chicago ACORN.......................... 147
Marcel Reid...52
Maxine Nelson.................................... 169

Michael McCray 168

National Welfare Rights Organization . 169

   Student Organizer 166

Oak Forest Neighborhood................. 48

SEIU Local 100 / SEIU Local 880 ..128

Service Employee's International Union

   SEIU Executive Board 128

Social Justice 166

Social Policy Magazine, Publisher/

   Editor-in-chief 150

Wal-Mart Campaign 158

Waldorf-Astoria

Dow Jones Private Equity Analyst Conference

   David Rubenstein 197

   SEIU/ACORN Protest 197

Wallace Williams, Field Director,

   Clinton Re-elect.................................. 94

Wal-Mart Campaign..............................207

   Organizer, Wade Rathke 158, 167

Walter Fauntroy, Former U.S.

   Representative, Washington DC 190

   No FEAR Institute 190

Walter P. Reuther Library 287

   Labor and Urban Affairs.................. 287

Walter Reed, Jr., Director, Iowa

   Commission of Human Rights 203

Washington Plaza Hotel 100, 102, 118,

                              119, 131, 271

Washington Whistleblower's Week.....189

   Lifetime Achievement Award

      Charles Grassley, Government Waste,

      Fraud and Corrupion..................... 191

   No FEAR Citizen's Tribunal

No FEAR Coalition...................... 190

Watch Night Service 249, 254

   Black Churches 253

   Marvin Jenkins 254

   Michael Coleman 255

   Rodney Slater 255

Wayne State University 287, 293

   ACORN National Board Meeting... 287

Wellington Webb 239, 240, 244

   Bill Clinton..239

   Eastside Ministerial Alliance...........239

   Hillary Clinton........................... 239, 240

   John Kerry... 240

   Mayor, Denver Colorado 239

   Quentin Hart 239, 240

   Women's Forum at Allen College....239

Wells Fargo

   ACORN Campaign............................103

   ACORN Settlement (California) 150

   Best Practice Agreement 151

White House Empowerment Zone Initiative

   U.S. Department of Agricurure

      Michael McCray, Community

      Development Specialist 141

Will Ward..39, 40

   Economic Justice....................................38

   H&R Block Campaign..........................39

   Head Organizer, DC ACORN ... 29, 39

      Wade Rathke, Chief Organizer..... 42

   Liberty Tax Services............................. 30

   Marcel Reid, DC ACORN

      Membership Election........................ 42

   Virginia Beach Reaction 37

Wade Rathke and Beth Butler 42

William Aldinger, Chief Executive
   Officer, Household Finance 105

William Brookerd, Chair, Nevada
   ACORN 181

William Conway, Co-founder/Managing
   Director, Carlyle Group 206

William Cornelius
   Delegate, National Board (ACORN) ... 109

William Smart 262
   Director, Faith Outreach 261

Willie Campbell, Pastor, Cathedral of
   Faith Baptist Church 243

Willie Flowers 41, 42
   Member, DC ACORN 38
   Virginia Beach Reaction 41

Willie Mae Wright
   City Councilwoman, Waterloo 233
   Hillary Clinton 233

Wilson Rideout 247
   Floyd Flake 247
   Martin Luther King, Jr., Award 247
   Retired Pastor, Payne AME Church. 233, 247

Winecoff Hotel 7, 9, 10, 153, 179,
                                            182, 183, 184
   Atlanta, Georgia 5
   Juneteenth Protest 11

Woodruff Park 6
   Atlanta, Georgia 5
   Juneteenth March and Rally 6

Working Families Party 197, 198
   Co-chair, Bertha Lewis. 196
   Living Wage Legislation 197

Political Organization. 44, 196, 198, 270, 279
   SEIU/ACORN Protest 196
   Working Families Ballot Line Project
      Presidential Candidate Interviews.... 146

Y

Yolanda Pena
   Delegate, National Board (ACORN) 119

Yolanda Warden
   Delegate, National Board (ACORN) 101

Yvonne Jackson
   Delegate, National Board (ACORN) 115

Yvonne Stafford 46, 47, 110, 131, 132, 144, 177
   ACORN Organizers 129, 131
   Chair, North Carolina ACORN .. 32, 129
   CRA Agreements 50
   Whipple-Bell Fellowships 144

Yvonne Woods, Chair, Kentucky
   ACORN 101

Z

Zach Polett 45, 51, 71, 72, 78, 146,
                                    208, 209, 288, 290, 291
   Anita MonCrief 208
   Community Development Block Grants... 48
   Community Reinvestment Act 46
   Executive Director, Project Vote 71
   Hillary Clinton 73
   Political Director, ACORN National
      Staff 75
   Rathke Embezzlement 289
   Working Families Ballot Line Project ... 146

CPSIA information can be obtained at www.ICGtesting.com
Printed in the USA
LVOW042214220212

270018LV00005B/4/P